INDIANS IN EDEN
Wabanakis & Rusticators on Maine's Mount Desert Island 1840s–1920s

By Bunny McBride & Harald E.L. Prins

Library of Congress Cataloging-in-Publication Data

McBride, Bunny.

Indians in Eden : Wabanakis & rusticators on Maine's Mount Desert Island

1840-1920 / By Bunny McBride & Harald E.L. Prins.

p. cm.

Includes bibliographical references and index.

ISBN 978-0-89272-804-6 (trade pbk. : alk. paper)

1. Abenaki Indians--Maine--Mount Desert Island--History. 2. Abenaki

Indians--Maine--Mount Desert Island--Economic conditions. 3. Abenaki

Indians--Maine--Mount Desert Island--Social life and customs. 4. Indigenous

peoples--Ecology--Maine--Mount Desert Island. 5. Tourism--Maine--Mount

Desert Island--History. 6. Indian business enterprises--Maine--Mount Desert

Island. 7. Mount Desert Island (Me.)--History. 8. Mount Desert Island

(Me.)--Enviromental conditions. I. Prins, Harald E. L. II. Title.

E99.A13M42 2009

974.1'45--dc22

2009024711

Design by Chad Hughes

Printed at Versa Press, East Peoria, Illinois.

5   4   3

BOOKS·MAGAZINE·ONLINE
www.downeast.com

Distributed to the trade by National Book Network

Dedicated to our parents—in gratitude for their love and guidance,
in celebration of the seacoasts that called their names:
Robert J. McBride & Cynthia Martin McBride
Dr. A.H. J. Prins & Ita Prins-Poorter

CONTENTS

Bar Harbor brings memories to me of my grandfather George Loring Sr., my grandmother Hazel Curtis Loring, my uncle Everett Loring, and the many childhood trips my brother Adrian and I made with them from the Penobscot Reservation to Mount Desert Island. Uncle Everett drove and we always went to visit my great aunt Hattie Gordius. Hattie lived her whole life at Mount Desert, and it seemed the family was repeatedly drawn to that rocky coast with its fresh ocean breezes and the smell of salt water and clam flats.

As a child, I felt that the sole purpose of our visits was to sit and listen to adults gossip about family, etc. for hours on end—and thus to torture me. I found the entire experience boring, and what seemed to me like hours of riding in a hot, crowded car in bumper-to-bumper traffic did not produce my best memories. I saw no advantage in taking that dreaded trip every summer.

Now, as a tribal elder, I've looked back on those trips and wished I could reclaim the hours and times to ask questions that would help me understand the island's mystery, the magical "quality of place" that pulled and still pulls our people. This book has, in a way, given me back those times, helping me grasp the role Mount Desert Island has played in the life of my ancestors for generations—in particular the role that the Bar Harbor Indian encampment played in helping us survive economically and culturally.

My great- great-grandfather Frank Loring, known as Chief Big Thunder, loved Bar Harbor and spent many years traveling there seasonally and camping on the Island. In these pages I've gained some insight into why he returned year after year. Now I know that when he breathed in that salty air and smelled the pungent odor of the clam flats, his thoughts were not like those of my childhood. His mind was on finding folks to rent his canoes, sport-hunters he could guide, customers for his traditional wares, and audiences for his stories. Very often, his mind was on the show or pageant he was going to perform in or direct. He was a real showman, a very good one. I find it ironic that he shared the stage in his later years with Joseph Nicolar, a highly educated fellow Penobscot who authored the book *The Life and Traditions of the Red Man*. Nicolar "lectured" in his suit and Chief Big Thunder "entertained" in his regalia. I think my great-great-grandfather would find it amusing that his great, great granddaughter is an author, a lecturer, and a former state legislator. Well, he did become quite a politician in his old age.

As much as he enjoyed the limelight, it's clear that sometimes Frank Loring's mind was also on getting away from the summer crowds of Mount Desert Island, for he frequently headed out on his own or with fellow tribesmen to hunt seals or gulls from the shores of other islands on the Maine seacoast. Perhaps he yearned for the breath of freedom on open water, where he could feel the pulse of nature without having to explain it to anyone.

All in all, my great-great-grandfather spent his life doing what he loved—and someone once said if you do what you love you will never have to work a day in your life. It seems to me that he found a way to feel free in the changing world that surrounded him. He figured out what he could hold on to and what he could let go of. I believe that was his secret and his legacy to us.

His love of theater holds much meaning for me, as a quote from Shakespeare has guided my life decisions: "To thine own self be true." Chief Big Thunder was true to himself and his people. He did what he loved and he spoke truth to power through stories and plays.

Bunny McBride and Harald Prins have worked with the Maine tribes for many years and they are trusted and highly respected in all our communities. They have authored a number of books about our history and culture. Those books have played a role in educating the public about who we are and what our contributions were to society. Both have been honored in various ways for their work, and in 1999 I formally recognized Bunny's writing on the history of Wabanaki women by dedicating a Legislative Sentiment in her honor on the floor of the Maine House of Representatives. My deepest gratitude and thanks go to both of them for once again traveling back in time and bringing the spirit of our ancestors back to life. *Woliwoni*, Bunny and Harald.

Donna Loring

CHAPTER ONE

Manesayd'ik—At the Clam-Gathering Place

God hath planted us here. God gave us this land: and we will keep it. God decreed all things; He decreed this land to us; therefore neither shall the French or English possess it, but we will. (Penobscot Chief Espeguint to English commander, 1755)

Who Are the Wabanaki, Past and Present?

Surrounded by salt water, Mount Desert Island is a place of natural delight and seasonal abundance. Its graceful and timeless beauty has long had enormous appeal, especially for people coming from big cities. Since the mid-1800s, this peaceful wilderness has promised a quiet escape from the noisy crowds, filthy streets, and polluted air of industrialization and urban conglomerates. Not too remote and easy to reach by sailboat, steamship, or railway, this idyllic refuge was romantically imagined as a coastal paradise. That this wilderness garden, known as Eden in the 19th century, formed part of the homeland of Wabanaki Indian families since time out of mind was an inconvenient truth.

In the Algonquian languages traditionally spoken by Maine's indigenous people, the name Wabanaki is a combination of *waban* and *aki-k*. The first word translates as "white," and refers to east where the sky first turns light, and the second refers to "land-people," or inhabitants. As "People of the Dawn," Wabanakis were organized in bands of extended families, each forming part of larger ethnic groups called tribes or nations. Today, Wabanakis are divided into five distinct tribes: Penobscot, Passamaquoddy, Maliseet, Mi'kmaq, and Abenaki.

Indigenous people have lived, loved, and died at Mount Desert Island and the surrounding seacoast for more than 10,000 years. With the European invasion, beginning nearly 500 years ago, their population plummeted. Dramatically weakened by newly introduced diseases and half a dozen colonial wars, Wabanakis still surviving in what is now Maine numbered fewer than 1,200 men, women, and children when the colonial period ended in 1776. After the American Revolutionary War, an international boundary divided Wabanaki communities in New England from their Indian relatives, friends, and allies across the Canadian border.

With fewer than 200 Wabanaki warriors left to defend their large homeland against foreign intruders, the tribal communities in Maine could not avoid being dispossessed of most of their lands. From the 1780s onwards, only Penobscots and Passamaquoddies were able to hold on to tracts where they had their main villages or seasonal camping grounds. Ultimately, the first tribe secured a string of small islands in the Penobscot River, along with some shore land, above the Old Town falls. Most of the Penobscot families lived much of the year at Panawahpskek—"where the rocks spread out" (Indian Island, Old Town), where the tribe still has its seat of government. The Passamaquoddy, on the other hand, had their major village at Sipayik—"along the edge" (Pleasant Point), a small stretch of land on a saltwater bay where they caught pollock and other fish, as well as porpoises, seals, and other animals. They also secured a much larger tract of woodland and lakes in the interior, where a group of Passamaquoddies made their home at Motahkokmikuk (Peter Dana Point, Indian Township).

Beyond these three reservation villages in Maine, Wabanaki families continued to move around seasonally, camping on the shores of lakes such as Moosehead, the banks of rivers such as the Aroostook, and on the saltwater coves, promontories, and offshore islands of sea-coast bays such as Frenchman, Blue Hill, and Penobscot. While expected to keep a respectable distance from emerging and quickly growing white communities, as long as much of Maine remained a natural wilderness, they were free to camp and to hunt, fish, and gather just about anywhere they chose.

Among the scores of islands seasonally frequented by generations of Wabanaki families, Mount Desert was one of the largest and most favored. Early Wabanakis called it Pemetic, refer-ring to its range of high barren peaks—on a clear day this 100-square mile island can be seen from a few dozen miles across open water as well as from the interior highlands. Wabanaki families from different tribal communities have deep historic ties to Mount Desert Island. This is especially true for the Penobscot and Passamaquoddy because the island is positioned in the historic border region between their tribal hunting territories. So, it is not surprising that Indian families from these two Wabanaki tribes in particular have a long-standing tradition of returning to this beautiful island.

Asticou's Island Domain: Early Wabanakis at Mount Desert Island

Before European seafarers first sailed into the Gulf of Maine, Mount Desert Island was seasonally occupied by a highly mobile Wabanaki band of a few dozen families. The island formed part of a much larger domain from which this indigenous community of a few hundred people harvested natural resources. The band's total range probably included the seacoast and offshore islands from Schoodic Peninsula to the Bagaduce River, and perhaps beyond. This coastal woodland environment combined

a saltwater archipelago with a 1,000-square-mile freshwater hinterland broken by hills, swamps, lakes, and ponds, and drained by a few rivers and numerous streams. Its mosaic of tree stands included ash, elm, oak, pine, hemlock, beech, oak, and of course birch. Summers were pleasantly warm, but winters were long, sometimes blanketing the woodlands with snow for as long as five months a year.

Wabanaki family camp, 1850s, watercolor. By W.R. Herries. (Library and Archives Canada. Photo in authors' collection.)

As inhabitants of Mount Desert Island and its surroundings, Indian families developed a deep ecological understanding of a habitat blessed with an abundance of game animals, fish, birds, fruit, nuts, and roots. Adapting to the seasonal rhythms of this environment, they migrated between seacoast and hinterland. They knew precisely where to find the best encampment sites, some preferred for winter, others for summer, spring, or fall. Typically, the sites existed at well-sheltered coastal locations with good canoe-landing beaches and easy access to fresh water, food, and fuel.

One of their favorite sites was strategically located at Manchester Point (Northeast Harbor) by the entrance to Somes Sound. In the early 1600s, Wabanaki families under the leadership of Chief Asticou camped here in the summer. Other long-used coastal sites in Asticou's domain can be found at Bar Harbor and Hull's Cove, as well as on neighboring islands such as Great Cranberry, Swan's, Gotts, and Long, and also on the shores of Blue Hill Bay (such as Naskeag Point or nearby Flye Point). Included among the dozens of additional encampment sites in this domain is one by the Union River near Ellsworth Falls and another at Waukeag Neck on upper Frenchman Bay.

With stone, bone, wood, and leather, Wabanaki men and women fabricated most of their own tools and weapons, including wooden clubs, bows, arrows, and spear shafts; stone axes, knives, scrapers, arrowheads, and spear points; bone needles and fishhooks; plus bark baskets, basswood fiber nets, rawhide snares, and traps.

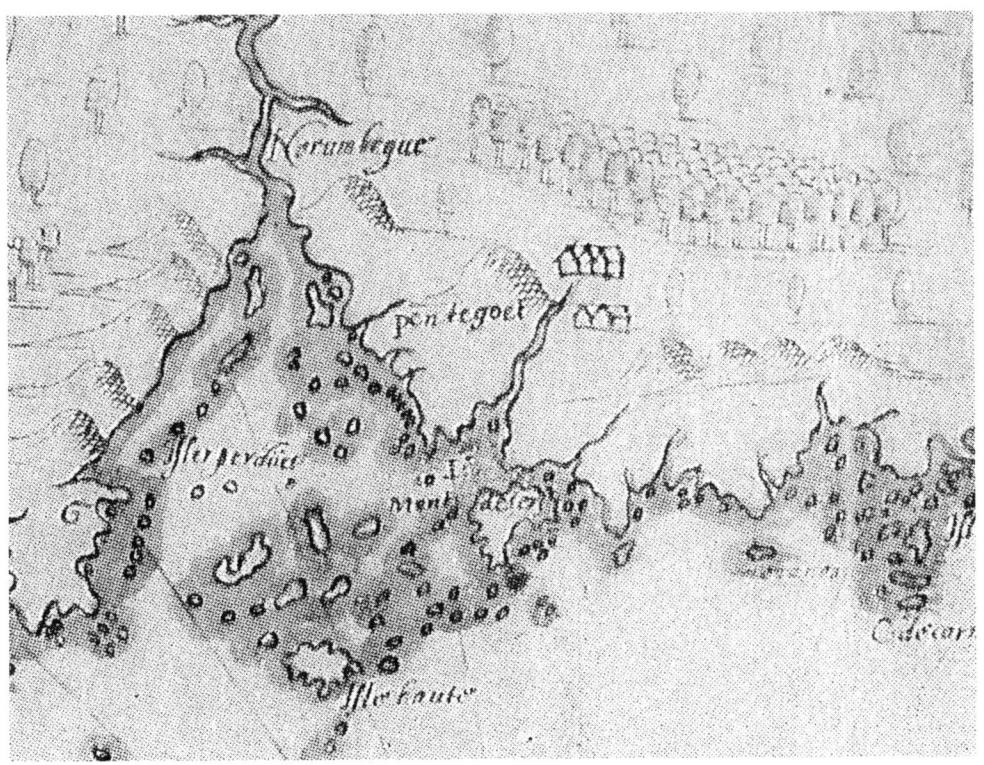

Detail of Samuel de Champlain's manuscript map of New France, 1607. (Library of Congress, Geography and Map Division, Vellum Chart Collection #15. Photo in authors' collection.)

For winter travel, Wabanakis often walked on snowshoes made of white ash or beech corded with thongs made of gut or hide. To transport goods over the snow and ice, they pulled toboggans. When their rivers became ice-free in the spring, they turned to their light-weight birchbark canoes which could seat as many as ten people. Bark of white birch also served as cover for their portable wigwam dwellings. For added warmth in winter, they lined their homes with deer skins. Hemlock twigs or balsam fir needles, topped with woven reed mats, soft seal skins, or even densely haired bear hides made the floor of their wigwams more comfortable.

Often aided by dogs, Wabanaki hunters chased their prey, especially moose and whitetail deer. They also hunted black bears, raccoons, otters, and sometimes also wolves, red foxes, lynxes, bobcats, fishers, and martens, as well as larger rodents such as beavers, porcupines, and muskrats. Especially during the summer months, they pursued geese, ducks, and other water fowl.

With a special three-pronged fish spear, Wabanakis seized sturgeon, salmon, trout, and bass. At night, they lured the fish with torches of burning birch bark. They also used nets, hooks, and lines for a variety of other fish. Moreover, they speared or caught all kinds of fish trapped behind weirs made of wooden stakes placed in a tidal bay. At such sites of seasonal abundance they gathered in large numbers for many days, sometimes even weeks. Large juicy lobsters and crabs could also be on their menu. And whatever seafood was not immediately consumed, they smoke-dried and stored in baskets for the winter.

Wabanakis also harpooned gray seal for its meat, oil, and soft pelt. Seal blubber was highly valued not only as food, but also as grease used to condition hair and protect bodies against the weather. Indians in the Mount Desert Island area may have even hunted small whales in bays, chasing them by canoe into inlets (such as the fjord now known as Somes Sound) for the kill. Certainly, many families gorged occasionally on the blubber and meat of stranded whales. When hunting or fishing was difficult or even impossible, they would move to the coast and dig mussels and clams in the mudflats. Bar Harbor was a site well-known for shellfish collecting, in particular clams, which they baked or dried by smoke. For that reason, Wabanakis referred to this bay area with its long sand bar and wide mudflats as *Manesayd'ik*—"at the clam-gathering place"—or *Ah-bais'auk*—"clambake place."

Adding to their fish and meat diet, Wabanaki families also tapped maple trees for their sweet sap and gathered wild blueberries, nuts, and young edible ferns. They supplemented their diet with cultivated crops, in particular corn, which they bartered with allied Wabanaki communities in the Kennebec and Saco valleys. Moreover, they collected medicinal roots, leaves, and bark to make teas, salves, and poultices to treat wounds and various illnesses.

The European Invasion: Violence in the Gulf of Maine

Almost 500 years ago, the first few European seafarers sailed across the Gulf of Maine and mapped a bit of the region's seacoast. But it was not until Samuel de Champlain navigated a small one-masted sailing boat to the shores of Mount Desert Island in 1604 that local Wabanakis made their first direct contact with foreigners from overseas. A cartographer who later detailed his adventures as an explorer, Champlain was guided by two

Mount Desert, from Blue Hill Bay. European fishing boats sailed the saltwater bays of Mount Desert Island beginning in the early 1600s. For the next few centuries, fishermen from New England coastal towns also frequented those waters and dried their daily catch on the island's beaches. (In Drake 1876, p. 27. Authors' collection.)

tribesmen from the Bay of Fundy. Upon seeing the island's range of barren peaks, a prominent coastal landmark for other European seafarers, he named it *Isle des Monts Deserts*.

The following summer, an English vessel sailed into the Gulf of Maine and traded with a Wabanaki band headquartered at Pemaquid and closely related to Chief Asticou's community that camped seasonally at Mount Desert Island. The expedition's objective was to find the best place to initiate English colonial settlement. In 1607, two English vessels carried colonists to the mouth of the Kennebec River, where they built a fortified settlement. Although this colonial adventure failed miserably, ever-larger numbers of English and French fishing boats began frequenting the Maine coast. Crews salted or dried their catch on the islands and bartered with Wabanakis, who eagerly exchanged beaver and other furs for a variety of trade goods, such as copper kettles, iron knives, woolen blankets, and colored beads. The region's indigenous people also purchased firearms and alcoholic drinks, not only beer, rough cider, and wine, but also distilled liquors such as gin and rum.

In 1613, a French sailing vessel anchored at Mount Desert Island, with colonists on board looking for a place to build a new settlement. They recognized the advantages of building a stronghold on the west bank of Mount Desert's great fjord (Somes Sound), at a sheltered place now known as Fernald Point. Three Jesuits accompanied them. These "black robes," as the Indians called them, were responsible for the spiritual needs of the Roman Catholic settlers and of the French fishermen who labored along the coast in the summer. Situated across the water from Chief Asticou's encampment, the Jesuits also expected to convert the island's Wabanaki community. Dedicating their mission to the Holy Savior himself, they named it Saint-Sauveur. With that divine protection at such a wonderful location, plus friendly heathens almost within shouting distance, what could go wrong?

Lured by the beauty of early summer days on the fjord's peaceful shores and relishing an abundance of wild food, the French may well have imagined they had landed in a new Eden. This illusion was shattered, however, when a well-armed English privateer from Virginia sailed into Penobscot Bay. Unaware that these foreigners were from a rival nation, local Wabanakis told them about their new neighbors settling down at Mount Desert Island. Seeing the French as interlopers in the Gulf of Maine, the English commander launched an assault on the French, taking them completely by surprise. The attackers killed a few Frenchmen and captured most of the others. Taking the ship as their prize, the English loaded it with loot and destroyed what could not be carried away.

This June 1613 sacking of Saint-Sauveur marked the beginning of a long string of violent clashes between the English and French, competing for colonial power in the Gulf of Maine. Throughout much of the 1600s and 1700s, Wabanakis found themselves engulfed in the ebb and flow of colonial warfare. Sometimes, Dutch privateers also joined the violent scramble. In addition to many documented conflicts, countless unrecorded clashes occurred between rival fishing captains, fur traders, tribal chieftains, bounty hunters, and many others.

European seafarers also introduced killer diseases, including smallpox, cholera, and influenza. These scourges, added to the lethal combination of firewater and firearms, almost wiped Maine's indigenous coastal people from the face of the earth. Within a few decades, up to 90 percent of the Wabanaki had perished in this American-Indian holocaust. With epidemics and warfare nearly annihilating the indigenous communities occupying the seacoast from Mount Desert Island to Cape Cod, much of this land was cleared for European settlement. Confronted with fast-growing numbers of English settlers in quickly expanding colonies south of Penobscot Bay, Wabanakis resorted to forging alliances with the French colonists.

Wabanaki shoreside encampment, mid–1800's. Long holding on to their traditional way of life as migratory hunters, fishers, and gatherers, Wabanaki families often set up wigwam encampments in places accessible only by canoe. Difficult to spot by those unfamiliar with the wilderness, they could be almost invisible to strangers entering their seacoast domain. (In Brown, p. 237. Authors' collection.)

French missionaries played a crucial role in building and maintaining strong relations with the region's Wabanakis, converting almost all of them to the Catholic faith. One of the many colorful French adventurers on the Maine seacoast was Antoine de la Mothe de Cadillac. In 1688, the French colonial government granted him the rights to Mount Desert Island as well as a stretch of coastal land at the head of Frenchman Bay. Together with his French-Canadian wife, Cadillac lived briefly on the island, probably at Otter Creek. French fur traders were also important and some of them adapted well to the coastal woodlands, even marrying into indigenous families. Their *métis* offspring played a significant role as French-Wabanaki cultural brokers and often mediated in times of stress and violence.

Dangerously situated on the Anglo-French colonial frontier, Mount Desert Island was always exposed to surprise attacks by enemies who might come at any time and from any direction. Peril continued even during the peace between the colonial wars, as pirates from as far away as the Caribbean added to the threatening uncertainties of the region.

Mi'kmaq encampment near Halifax, Nova Scotia, ca. 1791, watercolor. By Hibbert N. Binney. (Nova Scotia Museum, Halifax. Photo in authors' collection.)

For the next three generations, any plans for establishing a permanent residence on Mount Desert Island were bound to be squashed, but this doesn't mean it remained completely uninhabited for more than seventy years. In fact, small Wabanaki hunting groups continued to camp there periodically to hunt, trap, fish, and gather. In times of peace, white fishermen occasionally came ashore to dry their daily catch on beaches. And last but not least, the island sometimes served as an inter-tribal rendezvous for canoe-faring Wabanaki warriors who assembled there in times of war to launch raiding expeditions against New England coastal settlements.

In the mid-1700s, Wabanakis realized that their French allies lacked the strength and determination needed to help them in their struggle to remain free and independent in their own homeland. In 1761, the British army defeated the French conclusively in Canada. Completely outnumbered and outgunned, Wabanaki chiefs were forced to accept the imposed terms of peace agreed upon by the European rivals and told their warriors to lay down their weapons.

White Settlers at Mount Desert Island

Having lost so many friends and relatives to colonial warfare and disease, the ravaged Wabanakis feared for their future—and with good reason. As soon as possible, Massachusetts Province (already controlling southern Maine) expanded its political reach from Penobscot Bay to the St. Croix River. Swarms of land-hungry colonists and wealthy investors scrambled to get large grants of "free" land in Indian country.

Mount Desert Island was viewed as an especially great prize. No wonder the British royal governor residing in Boston obtained it as his personal property in 1762. To check out his private domain, Sir Francis Bernard boarded the government sloop *Massachusetts* and told its captain to sail to Penobscot Bay. After inspecting new military fortifications, he arrived at Mount Desert Island. Sir Francis went ashore at Southwest Harbor, where he heard news that four white squatters (including Abraham Somes and Eben Sutton) had already settled their families at the head of the fjord (later named Somes Sound).

Alarmed by the influx of white settlers encroaching on their ancestral lands, Wabanaki tribal leaders felt desperate. Abowadwonit, the old chieftain of the Passamaquoddy, complained to Sir Francis: "We think it hard that you settle the lands that God gave us without making us sum consideration." Ignoring his plea for justice, colonial authorities in Boston claimed that Indians had long ago abandoned Mount Desert Island and the neighboring seacoast. Accordingly, they ordered these "uninhabited" lands to be surveyed and granted or sold off. Thousands of white settlers from New England towns migrated up to the central and east coasts of Maine, where they cut down the trees, built new houses, barns, and sheds, and fenced off cropland and pastures for their animals. They relied on farming, but many also fished, clammed, trapped, and hunted for food.

Confronted with the destruction of their wildlife habitats, Wabanakis understood that their way of life was in serious jeopardy. Indigenous families who traditionally hunted and fished in the Mount Desert Island area joined friends and relatives in the Penobscot River Valley who had their head village at Indian Island. Others were taken in by the Passamaquoddy, or moved to Abenaki villages in the St. Lawrence Valley. A few

Maliseet family traveling upriver by canoe, 1791, probably in the St. John River. By author-traveler Patrick Campbell. (Library and Archives Canada. Photo in authors' collection.)

joined Maliseet bands in the St. John Valley or relocated among the Mi'kmaq. These adoptions were made possible, in part, because Wabanakis all spoke related Algonquian languages and dialects, had a long tradition of intermarriage, and were allied as "brothers" in the Wabanaki Confederacy.

Wabanakis in the American Revolution and Its Aftermath

During the American Revolution, Chief Joseph Orono of the Penobscot tribe emerged as a prominent tribal leader in the Wabanaki Confederacy. His famous forefather Chief Madock-awando and other relatives had long camped along the Eggemoggin Reach between Penobscot Bay and Blue Hill Bay, where they hunted, trapped, fished, and clammed for generations. As such, the Orono family had deep ties to Mount Desert Island just a few miles across Blue Hill Bay.

Soon after the outbreak of the American Revolution, Chief Orono and other Wabanaki chiefs pledged their support and warriors took up arms in the American struggle for independence. When the war ended in 1783, the British agreed on the St. Croix River—running into Passamaquoddy Bay—as its new border with the United States. After withdrawing its troops from Penobscot Bay, Britain also left Mount Desert Island in American possession. The new border, however, divided the Wabanaki homeland between the two international powers. As soon as peace returned, white immigrants flocked by the tens of thousands to Maine, its population leaping from 54,000 to 300,000 in just three decades. With fewer than 1,200 of their own people remaining in Maine, the Wabanaki now faced extinction as indigenous people.

Among the thousands of newcomers was Cadillac's granddaughter, Marie-Thérèse de Grégoire. Born and raised in France, she successfully petitioned the Massachusetts government in 1786 to recognize her hereditary title to Mount Desert Island. Because the island's western half was already claimed and settled, she had to be content with the half that faced Frenchman Bay. Establishing a residence at Hull's Cove, the French madam and her aristocrat husband could be considered the island's first "rusticators."

The Wabanakis, of course, had a much older and better claim, but had to accept much less. In the late 1700s, the Penobscots secured a mere 100,000 acres of their vast ancestral territory from the Massachusetts government. Protected as reservation land, it included Indian Island and about 200 small islands above the first falls in the Penobscot River, plus several woodland tracts on both sides of the river. In exchange for giving up their rights to the rest of their ancestral territories, Penobscot households were entitled to a yearly distribution of corn, pork, salt, tobacco, cloth, blankets, silver dollars, and ammunition. Three decades later, almost all of the tribe's hunting lands were sold off, leaving the Penobscots with fewer than 5,000 acres.

The Passamaquoddy were also forced to accept a meager deal, retaining just 23,000 acres of woodland on the upper Schoodic River and fewer than 100 acres at Pleasant Point (Sipayik) on Passamaquoddy Bay. Other Wabanaki groups were left with no reservations at all in Maine (until the late 20th century). They did, however, manage to secure a few dozen small reserves on the Canadian side of the new border drawn through their homelands by white foreigners.

During the next few decades, Wabanakis kept their migratory lifestyle, spending weeks or months hunting, trapping, fishing, clamming, fowling, and gathering eggs and berries in the saltwater bays and at offshore islands from Penobscot Bay to the Gulf of St. Lawrence, including the Mount Desert Island area. Among those who frequented Chief Asticou's old domain were Chief Orono, his wife (addressed as Madam Orono), and several other Penobscot families, who often camped on White Island and Black Island (now called Conary) located between Blue Hill Bay and Eggemoggin Reach. Speaking both Penobscot and French, the old *métis* leader may well have paddled his bark canoe to Mount Desert Island for a visit with the de Grégoires at Hull's Cove.

However, the kind of friendly welcome Orono may have enjoyed at Hull's Cove was not to be expected everywhere. Wabanakis knew that many white settlers feared and even loathed them. Some settlers, including a few who had been "Indian fighters" in previous decades, actually chased them away. And on occasion there was violence—even murder.

Wabanakis in the Industrial Revolution: Where Is Eden?

In 1820, Maine became a state, inheriting Massachusetts' treaty obligations to the Penobscot and Passamaquoddy. To manage its "Indian problem," the state's governors appointed special "Indian agents." Seeking an end to the migratory traditions of these "restless, savage people," the agents tried to make them settle down as farmers. Yet, acculturation efforts by reservation agents showed only limited success, as most Wabanakis preferred to hold on to their traditions and continued moving with the seasons through their ancestral territories, including the Mount Desert Island area.

Soon, Wabanakis journeyed not only by canoe or sailing vessel, but also aboard paddlewheel steamships and by about 1840 on railways. Increasingly dependent on the cash economy, some canoe-faring tribesmen hunted

Sabyk Alnambay Udenek, Pleasant Point Indian Village, 1866. (In Vetromile. Author's collection.)

SAW-MILLS ON THE PENOBSCOT RIVER, AT OLDTOWN, MAINE.

"Saw-mills on the Penobscot River, at Oldtown, Maine," 1854. In the mid-1830s, a milldam was constructed at the falls just a few hundred yards downriver from Panawahpskek, the Penobscot tribal village on Indian Island. Water passing through the dam's spillway powered these large sawmills processing boards, staves, and other wood products. This industry, however, created an environmental disaster for the local Penobscot Indians: huge numbers of logs obstructed their river travel and sawdust polluted the water. (*Gleason's Pictorial Drawing-Room Companion,* 20 May 1854. Authors' collection.)

porpoises, primarily for the high-quality oil, which was in growing demand as fuel for newly built lighthouses all along the Atlantic coast. Others turned to part-time wage labor, hiring themselves out at farms, fisheries, and lumber camps. Indian families also supplemented their incomes by making and selling utility baskets, broomsticks, and barrel staves, as well as moccasins (used by loggers in lumber camps). In addition, they found an emerging market for specialty baskets, porcupine quillwork, birchbark toys, and other luxury crafts. Some, having knowledge of traditional Wabanaki healing methods, became traveling Indian "doctors" (or medicine men and women), peddling medicinal herbs throughout the Northeast. However they earned it, cash was used to purchase flour, lard, molasses, tobacco, tea, chocolate, candles, beads, silver, textiles, blankets, canvas, kettles, knives, axes, and a host of other products the Wabanakis had long ago come to appreciate.

Traveling by steamboat or train, Wabanakis enjoyed some of the pleasures of the Industrial Revolution. But, modernization also added to their problems. The enormous demand for wood, not only for construction, but also for fuel, led to the destruction of their forest domain. To cut and haul the timber, thousands of loggers, not only New Englanders, but also French-Canadians, Irishmen, and other cheap laborers recently immigrated from Europe, traveled upriver in the fall and spent the winter months deep in the Maine woods, cutting timber and hunting for the pot. By the mid-1800s, Penobscot tribesmen were outnumbered 1,000 to 1 by non-Indian loggers in

their ancestral forests. As soon as the ice thawed, massive flows of logs came crashing down the rivers. Businessmen invested in building dams near waterfalls, thus capitalizing on this endless supply of "free" energy to power their big sawmills. Nowhere was this more evident than on the Penobscot River, where, as early as 1840, half of Maine's 200 million feet of lumber production was sawed (most of it within a 12-mile stretch of river above Bangor). Penobscots, living on Indian Island just above the falls at Old Town, found themselves in the middle of this riverine highway. With several double sawmills at the falls, they could not avoid the noise of millions of cubic feet of timber being transformed into boards, staves, posts, and shingles. These products were transported on rafts to the wharves in Bangor, where they were loaded on lumber schooners and shipped to coastal cities such as Portland, Boston, and from there far beyond.

Witnessing this environmental catastrophe unfolding before their eyes, the indigenous families must have been anxious to leave the crowds of laborers and the log jams, human filth, and thick sawdust polluting

"View of Oldtown on the Penobscot River, Maine." By the mid-1850s, Panawahpskek found itself in the middle of a busy riverine highway. From 1847 onward, steamboats transported passengers and goods between Old Town and upriver settlements as far as the Piscataquis Falls. The first steamer in the area, under the ownership of the Penobscot River Navigation Company, was the *Governor Neptune*, named after the famous old tribal leader John Neptune (ca.1767–1865). The most prominent building on the island is the Roman Catholic church dedicated to Saint Anne. Built in 1836, this whitewashed wooden building replaced a more humble structure. Just thirty years earlier, Wabanaki homes at Indian Island were invariably wigwams built of logs and bark. Since then, all had been replaced by framed and shingled "white man's houses." (*Gleason's Pictorial Drawing-Room Companion*, 20 May 1854. Authors' collection.)

their river, not to mention the screaming saws that destroyed the serenity of their island home. To escape from this mess, Indian families periodically left for the seacoast, not only to sell

baskets or herbal medicines, but also to seek solace in nature. The open water and vast vistas of saltwater coves and offshore islands offered some relief from the pressures of industrialization surrounding them at Indian Island and, to a lesser extent, Pleasant Point.

But even the old-time pleasures of fishing, clamming, fowling, and hunting along open coastal waters offered no lasting escape from the harsh reality that expanding white communities were quickly eclipsing Wabanakis—and cooking up tales about the Indians' demise. Replacing history with folklore, storytellers omitted or twisted the facts, or simply made things up about drunk, dumb, or sadly unfortunate Indians getting their just desserts. One legendary story tells of a settler killing a drunken Indian named Swunkus at Black Island, west of Mount Desert Island. Another features two tough Indians who tried unsuccessfully to hold their ground against a white settler who intruded on their hunting camp near the head of Frenchman Bay. They were both robbed and killed.

Probably the most popular legend in 19th-century settler folklore at Mount Desert Island is the one told by one of its first white squatters, Abraham Somes. This old farmer-fisherman later claimed that he had first "discovered" the island in 1755, then moved his family there seven years later. Somes built his family homestead on the northwest flank of the fjord that carries his name, as does the village that grew up around him. In 1816, he wrote his story:

> I [Abraham Somes] mean now to give you a history of my discovering the Island of Mount Desert
> which took place a short time previous to the war with Great Britain and France in this Country
> which took place in the year 1755 at which time the Indians were the only owners of the soil. I

was in a Jebacco boat and one Eben Sutton of Ipswich [Mass.] in another, were in company, and in making discovery of the best places to carry on the fishing business steered our course to the Eastward we went into several harbours by sounding, at length we arrive off Mount Desert we concluded to make an attempt to see if there was any suitable harbour in said Island and by sounding we run in and anchored in the South West harbour now called, soon after we had anchored our boats, we were boarded by a number of Savages in their Canoes and among them was the Governor of the Island who informed us that that land looking and pointing all around was his. We conceived them to be friendly and very peaceable began to talk with them about purchasing land of the Governor. I asked the Governor how much Occopy [rum] I must give him for that Island [Greenings Island] which is a small island which lay between said Harbour and the sound, he answered Oh! A great deal, one whole Gallon. Then the said Sutton asked the Chief how much for that Island [Sutton Island] pointing to an island laying to the Eastward of the former island that I had bargained for [and] the Governor said two quarts. We paid them the Rum. He took a piece of birch bark and described the same to us but we not understanding neither the description nor the worth of the Island never attended to the subject nor took care of the birch bark and left them to drink their Occopy and to take the good of their bargain.[1]

Swindling the indigenous peoples out of their ancestral lands was a long-standing, albeit illegal, tradition. Given the common practice of aiming to get the better of Wabanakis, whether by making them drunk, forging documents, or using some other less obvious trick such as boldly interpreting an exchange in one's own favor, Somes knew that his story, as popular "history," was acceptable and even welcome entertainment for fellow settlers on the Maine seacoast in his day. In due time, all such legends—false, invented or somewhat true—became part of Mount Desert Island's folklore and found audience with a fresh wave of newcomers—the "rusticators" who ventured to Mount Desert Island in the latter half of the 1800s to escape city life and experience the wonders of nature.

CHAPTER TWO

Still in Eden:
Wabanakis, Settlers, and Artists

The Indians of our State are in a transition from the hunters' life. Their forest game is so far exhausted as to afford them but partial employment, and a scanty and precarious reward for their toil and supply for their necessities. A part of them, at some seasons of the year, eke out a miserable existence by leading a wandering gipsy-like life amongst our white population, supplying them with baskets and other articles of Indian ingenuity. (Maine Indian Agent Report, 1847–1851)

First Came the Settlers

After the Wabanakis, that is. During the four years covered by the Maine Indian Agent Report quoted here, Adelma Somes was gathering her own childhood memories about Wabanaki Indians. Later, she wrote them down in a collection of reminiscences about growing up in Somesville at the head of Mount Desert Island's fjord. Adelma, or Dell as she was called, was the great-granddaughter of Somesville founder Abraham Somes, a white fisherman who claimed he first visited Mount Desert Island in 1755 and bought land from the Indians for a gallon of rum—a transaction he said was verified on a "piece of birch bark" that he promptly mislaid. Six years later, Somes returned to put down stakes between the freshwater pond and the great saltwater inlet or fjord, and in 1762 he settled his family there to stay.

From early on, the Somes family associated with Wabanakis who came to the area seasonally to hunt, trap, and fish as they always had, but also to trade with the newcomers. Dell recalled her grandfather John Somes saying that during his boyhood in the 1770s one of the Indians who camped nearby taught him how to make a scoop net for fishing, another tribesman made him a pair of snowshoes, and an Indian woman showed him how to make woodsplint baskets.[1] Who were these nameless Natives? As with so many settler narratives about Mount Desert Island (and countless other North American places), a history of complex cross-cultural encounters simply folds into a series of short nostalgic tales about generic Indians who come and go from nowhere in particular.

By 1789, just six years after the Revolutionary War, the entire island was officially incorporated as the township of Mount Desert. Several years later, it was divided into two: The area northeast of Somes Sound took the name Eden,[2] while the rest of the island fell within Mount Desert Township (which split again in 1848 when Tremont was incorporated as a town). The population of hard-scrabble fishers, loggers, farmers, shipbuilders, artisans, and maritime traders lived modestly in scattered homesteads and emerging villages—including Hull's Cove and Bar Harbor on the Frenchman Bay side, and Southwest Harbor, McKinley (now Bass Harbor), Northeast Harbor, and Long Pond (now Seal Harbor) on the Blue Hill Bay side.

Camden in the Old Days, 1842, oil on canvas. By Robert McFarland. This painting of a Wabanaki family encamped at nearby Penobscot Bay gives an idea of how some of the Somes Pond encampments must have looked in the mid-19th century. (Photo in authors' collection.)

Industrious and determined, settlers on both sides of the island busied themselves "taming" the seacoast wilderness. They set up fish weirs and fences. They felled trees to clear the thickly forested land for farming and grazing. They built sawmills to make boards, staves, and shingles for building wooden boats, dwellings, barns, fences, and barrels. They cut hay in the salt marshes and turned ancient forest trails into paths and dirt roads. Bit by bit, they altered the environment so familiar and so vital to countless generations of Wabanakis who had relied on the abundant natural resources offered there.

Bark Canoe, Maine Indians, 1830, watercolor and pencil. By Titian Ramsey Peale. The Wabanaki who camped near the Somes' homestead in the 1830s no doubt traveled there in well-packed canoes by way of age-old routes. An accomplished artist, naturalist, and explorer, Peale participated in the Stephen Harriman Long Expedition to the American west, 1819–1820, and the worldwide U.S. Exploring Expedition under the command of Charles Wilkes, 1838–1842. He spent most of the interlude between these journeys on the east coast, investigating and drawing insects and animals. He made this particular drawing while moose hunting in Maine. (American Philosophical Society.)

A Frenchman who visited the northeastern part of the island in 1792, offered this description of settler life:

These inhabitants cultivate enough land to provide themselves with potatoes, corn, barley and vegetables, but they spend most of their time cutting wood into shooks [sets of pieces used in assembling packing boxes] and barrel staves which they sell at good profit to merchants. Each family has a small boat from which they catch cod, and cure it, and exchange it with the merchants for flour, sugar, soap, molasses, oil and other articles that they want. All have cows and farmyards, poultry of every kind and fine pigs. They make cheese which they sell at wholesale. On the day of my arrival there were five ships in Frenchmans Bay, one of which sailed for London, one for Santo Domingo, and three for Boston, loaded with plank, timber, shooks, bark, and even cordwood, which the people cut on the edge of the bays of the forest.[3]

In 1820, Dell's uncle Daniel Somes established the island's first public house in the middle of the village that also bears the family name—Somesville. Named Mount Desert Tavern, it was commonly referred to as Somes Tavern, and most likely Daniel's family lived on the premises. Daniel had

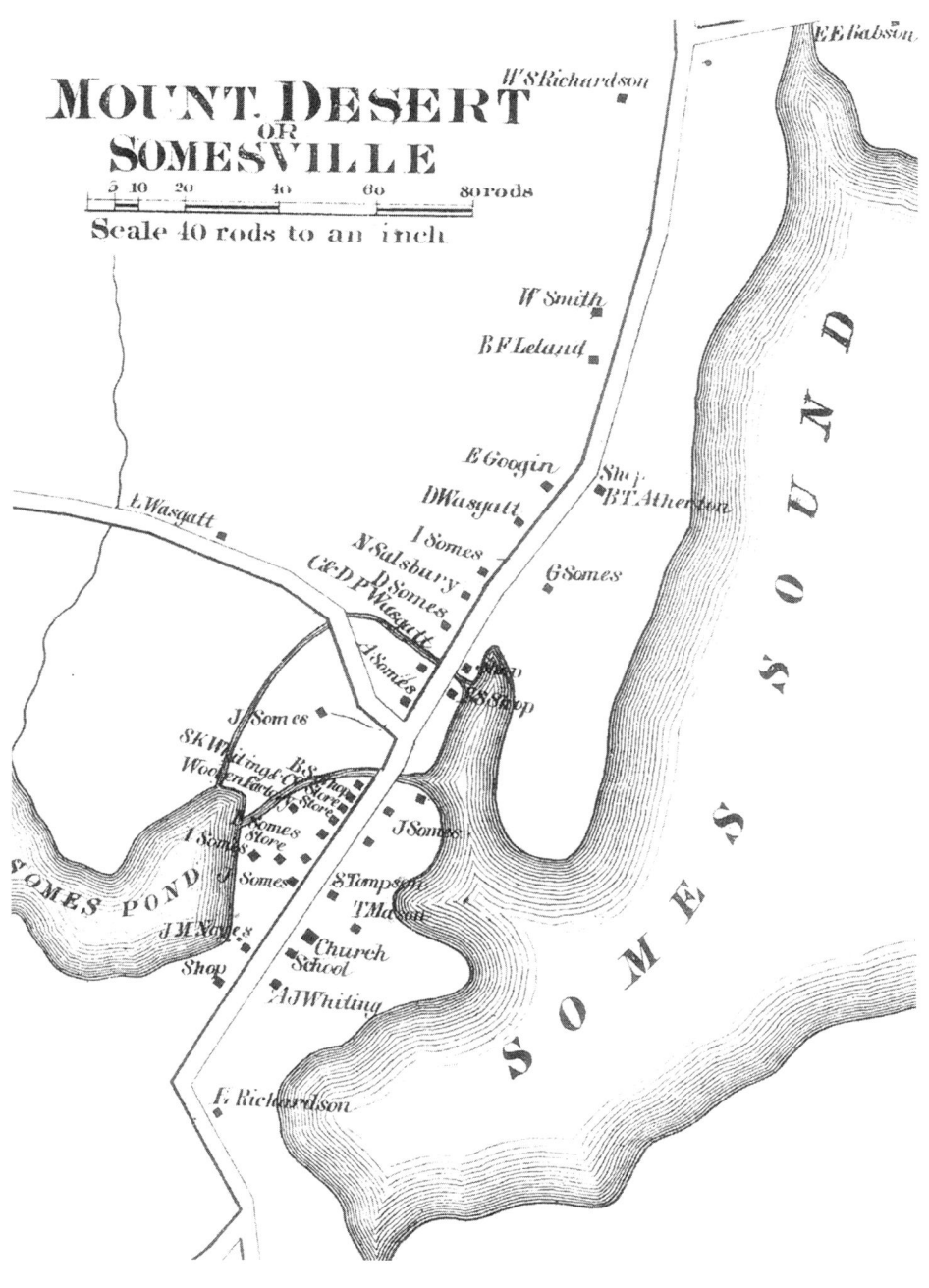

Mount Desert Village (Somesville), 1860s. The north-south road is Main Street and the east-west road is Oak Hill. One of the Indian wigwam camps Dell Somes referred to was located just off the west edge of this map, where Oak Hill Road passes by the northeast edge of Somes Pond. (Collection of the Maine Historic Preservation Commission.)

The earliest known photo of Daniel Somes's house (early 1860s), site of the tavern he established in 1820. Expanded into Mount Desert House by his son and namesake in 1831, it gained fame as the island's first hotel "celebrated for its homely good cheer and its quaint rooms and furniture." From this photo's angle, the sign on the pole can't be read. Photo by Heywood. (Collection of the Maine Historic Preservation Commission.)

no qualms about selling liquor, even though some family members disagreed. In 1831, following Daniel's death, his son Daniel, Jr (with wife Sally Trask) took over the business and changed the name to Mount Desert House, indicating that boarding was now available to visitors.[4] Before long, stagecoaches pulled by teams of horses stopped here to deliver mail, packages, and passengers, including many of the island's earliest summer visitors. By 1837, the year of Dell's birth, Somesville had become the hub of Mount Desert Island, with nine families, a small store, blacksmith and shoemaker shops, a tan-yard, bark mill, saw mill, lath mill, shingle mill, and grist mill, plus two shipyards and a schoolhouse.[5] By the time Dell reached her teenage years, the island's population had topped 3,000—not counting the Wabanaki families who still came there seasonally to hunt, fish, and gather berries, and, increasingly, to market their wares to the growing population. As described by Dell, penning her first-hand recollections from the 1840s:

> The Indians of the Penobscot Tribe, since I can remember, were always camping around the
> fresh water ponds, I suppose for the purpose of trapping mink and muskrats. . . . They made
> beautiful baskets and did beautiful bead work. I remember, it must have been around 1847,
> of several camps in my grandfather's pasture. They were on the edge of the pond (then called
> Lily Pond now called Somes Pond). I can remember so well of going with my mother and
> several other women to their camps made of boughs; one Mary Ann the fortune teller, Mrs.
> Glassene [Classian] in another, and there were some others that they did not seem well enough

acquainted to visit. The Glassene boy went to school with us. . . . One party of Indians camped on the Oak Hill Road by the Pond and I remember of riding over one winter day in a sleigh with my father, my sister and my brother.[6]

A later photo of Mount Desert House (late 1880s), the boarding-house-turned-inn established by Daniel Somes in 1820 and expanded by his son, Daniel, Jr. after his father's death in 1831. Among other improvements not evident in the earlier photo, shutters and a sign board have been added to the house, along with a new sign on the pole that reads "Mount Desert House 1888." (Collection of the Maine State Preservation Commission.)

The Indian camp near the Somes homestead was not unusual. Wabanakis, dispossessed of almost all territories where their ancestors had ranged freely for hundreds of generations, gravitated periodically to white settlements all across Maine. They did so for several reasons, not the least of which was that these newly emerging settlements were often located on strategic or ecologically advantageous sites long frequented by their ancestors. Moreover, these indigenous families could no longer survive solely on a traditional subsistence strategy that combined hunting, fishing, gathering, and trapping furs, for they were thwarted by the state's shifting fish and game laws and loss of hunting territories due to white private ownership and environmental destruction.

Facing poverty and hunger, Wabanakis increasingly depended on cash, which they earned as hunting and fishing guides to white sport-hunters, as day laborers on wharves loading or unloading ships, and as loggers or river drivers in the lumber industry. Some also earned their keep as seasonal farm workers. Many, however, relied on making woodsplint baskets and other handcrafted goods for sale to locals. In addition, some Wabanaki specialized in canoe building and women made great quantities of moosehide moccasins used by thousands of lumberjacks in forest camps. A few Wabanaki men and women survived, in part, as traveling "Indian doctors," capitalizing on indigenous healing practices based on traditional herbal medicines.

Patching together such mixed livelihoods, Wabanakis avoided the dark and noisy confines and exploitative low wages of sawmills, textile mills, and other factories, and held on to a tradition of moving freely with the seasons. Tribal reservations may have been the home base for Wabanakis, but most spent nearly as much time in temporary encampments—far from the overseeing eyes of church-appointed clergy and state-appointed Indian agents.

Newspapers and magazines of the day frequently featured news about small Indian bands camping temporarily on a riverbank at the edge of a New England town in order to peddle baskets, medicinal herbs, and other goods or services. This 1863 excerpt about Penobscot Indians from Old Town comes from the "Editor's Easy Chair," a regular feature in *Harper's Magazine*:

> In the course of his summer wanderings the Easy Chair came upon an Indian encampment by moonlight upon the sea-shore. There were but a dozen tents pitched upon the grass between the road and the beach, and all the tents were different in form. The Indians . . . sat during the day weaving baskets or making bows and arrows and little canoes, and in the evening they sat around the tents or were closely shut up within them. On this evening the moon was in the first quarter and shed a watery light upon the camp, which at a little distance, was weird with the faint illumination of the canvas from the dips [candles] inside. As the Easy Chair came still nearer he heard the music of a hand-organ grinding a polka, and saw a group sitting and standing under a tree silently looking upon two or three couples who were dancing the polka upon the grass, while two or three small children rolled and turned head over heels upon the ground as lightly and smoothly as balls of wool. The music changed to a slow and melancholy waltz, and the mysterious couples wheeled duskily about, the moonlight glistening upon the sea and the surf languidly plunging behind them. There was no chattering, there was no sound at all, in fact, but the melancholy organ and the sea. . . .
>
> One of the older men, with whom I afterward talked, told me that there were about eight hundred of them in Old Town, some sixty miles from the mouth of the Penobscot. They talk English imperfectly, but speak chiefly old Penobscot mingled with English words. . . . The Indians live peaceably with their white neighbors, he said; and in the winter, when field-work is over, many of them make the baskets and pretty wares which they bring southward to sell. They encamp somewhere upon the shore . . . and stay until they have sold out, or until September comes and visitors go home. Long, long ago, the old man said, he had camped at Nahant [Massachusetts], but since then, until this year, he had not been away from Old Town except in the winter to catch muskrats and minks. "For musk-rats we get forty cents. . . . For mink fi' dollars." He took me to the side of his tent and showed the trunk of a small ash-tree. By beating the outside vigorously the pith is made more pliable, so that it can be more readily worked [into strips for making baskets]. . . .
>
> I asked him if his people dwindled or increased. "We are going," he said, musingly, and the sea plashed between his words. . . . Afterward I saw one of the Indian women seated upon a rock between the beach and the road, steadfastly watching the gay procession of equipages that

flashed by in the afternoon sun. Whatever her thoughts were, her silent figure was as touching and tragical as a Sybil. By the side of the sea she sat, the lone mother of dead empires as much as Rome; sylvan empires that have disappeared more wholly than the glories of the seven hills.[7]

Echoed by countless other similar descriptions in books and newspapers, this passage reflects mainstream American society's conflicted feelings of celebration and concern about the rapid industrialization transforming their lives. With technological advancements came a romantic nostalgia for a disappearing world associated with primitive people in a wilderness governed by natural law. Viewing the continent's surviving indigenous peoples as "vanishing Indians" about to be destroyed like the primeval environment that was their home, society at large idealized an invented "Indian" stereotype. At the same time, it denied natives their human rights, repressed their authentic traditions, and seized or destroyed their natural resources. Simultaneously romanticized and discriminated against,

TOP: Penobscot Indian Woman, ca. 1875, watercolor by Mary Ann Hardy (painted from a childhood memory). (Abbe Museum.) MIDDLE: Molly Molasses (Mary Pelagie Nicola), 1865, photographed by S.W. Sawyer, Bangor. (Authors' collection.) BOTTOM: Molly's daughter, Sarah Polasses, ca. 1827, oil on canvas, by Jeremiah Pearson Hardy. (Tarratine Club, Bangor.) In the early 19th century, Wabanaki women commonly wore loose belted dresses, traditional peaked caps (usually beaded), and a blanket or shawl over their shoulders. During the 19th century, it became fashionable among Wabanakis for women to wear black top hats, sometimes adorned with a wide silver band and ostrich or rhea feathers.

Wabanakis had good reason to be puzzled by such displays of ambivalent racism.

A poem in Dell's reminiscences reflects the romantic nostalgia of the age while providing more details about the Penobscots who camped near her girlhood home:

> I loved the Indian, when he built his wigwam by the pond
> And hunted, unmolested. No canvas wigwam had he,
> But one of boughs, I've sat and watched the [women]
> Doing their beadwork, and wished I were an Indian.
>
> They were our friends, and we were theirs;
> They came and we welcomed them; they lived upon our land,
> No rent was paid or asked, our children played with theirs
> And loved the Indian.
>
> They often made us visits, wearing their bright plaid shawls
> And shining beaver hats. They sat at table with them on;
> It was their custom. We treated them like honored guests,
> And they looked it. Why should we not?
> Were they not here before us?[8]

Clearly, like most others in her generation, this great-granddaughter of pioneer settler Abraham Somes, who dubiously claimed he had bought his precious real estate from an Indian chief for nothing more than a gallon of rum, was unaware of the ambivalent racism she expressed. Reading Dell's words today, how can anyone miss the irony of her wishing to be "an Indian" while painting the indigenous Wabanaki as friendly strangers who "lived upon our land" as "guests" from whom "no rent was paid or asked"?

Dell's reminiscences of old-time Somesville also mention wintertime Indian performances presented in the local woolen mill around 1847. The shows featured "the chief" and "a tribe of Indians from Old Town, some fifteen or twenty," who were "camped down on the salt water shore opposite Parkers" at Clark Point in Southwest Harbor. "Crowds flocked to those Indian shows. . . . They stayed all winter, hunting, fishing, and giving shows."[9] Frank "Chief Big Thunder" Loring may have participated in, and perhaps helped organize, these events. About twenty at the time, he was already on his way to becoming a well-known showman. In the years that followed, Loring became one of the most familiar Wabanakis on and around Mount Desert Island—known as a provider of "Indian entertainments," as well as hunting guide services, canoe lessons in Bar Harbor, and medicinal treatments wherever he happened to be.

All Wabanakis knew the basic traditional herbal treatments of their ancestors, such as flagroot (*Acorus calamus*), a panacea used for general health and to treat a host of particular problems. And the specialists among them—Indian medicine men and women—knew how

to prepare a great variety of treatments from nature's vast pharmacopeia—infusions, decoctions, poultices, ointments, and plasters. According to another descendent of Abraham Somes, when the village's first white doctor, Kendall Kittredge, arrived in 1799, he learned many of his "formulas and mixtures" from the Indians. His great grandson relayed that Dr. Kittredge was convinced—probably not without reason—that some of the Indian panaceas were more effective than treatments he'd learned in medical school. [10]

View across Frenchman's Bay from Mount Desert Island after a Squall, **1845, oil on canvas. By Thomas Cole (1801–1848). This view of Frenchman Bay was highly familiar to Wabanakis who for many decades camped seasonally on the Bar Harbor shore, a site of natural abundance also frequented by their ancestors since time immemorial. (Cincinnati Art Museum, gift of Alice Scarborough. Accession #1925.569.)**

By the 1850s, Penobscots had stopped camping in Somesville. Beyond facing diminished game in the area, they (along with other Wabanakis) were lured by opportunity to other parts of the island, in particular Southwest Harbor and Bar Harbor. Pressed by the growing need for money in the cash economy that engulfed them, Indians were drawn to locations that offered the best possible prospects for marketing their traditional skills (craftmaking, canoeing, hunting/guiding, and cultural performances). Ideal among these places were the waterside resorts springing up on the shores of Maine's ponds, lakes, and ocean bays in response to the growing romantic primitivist ideal. The saltwater shores of Mount Desert Island soon topped the list of destinations

Next Came the Artists

The 1844 visit of New York painter Thomas Cole (1801–1848) marked the start of Mount Desert Island's influx of summer tourists and cottagers. Cole was the founder of the Hudson River School, a mid-19th-century American art movement in which landscape and seascape painters

Fog off Mount Desert, 1850, oil on academy board. By Frederic Edwin Church (1826-1900). In the summer of 1850, Church traveled to Mount Desert, the first of many visits he would make to Maine over the course of his life. As he described in a letter: "It was a stirring sight to see the immense rollers come toppling in, changing their forms and gathering in bulk, then dashing into sparkling foam.... We tried painting them, and drawing and taking notes of them, but cannot suppress a doubt that we shall neither be able to give the actual motion nor roar to any we may place upon canvas." (John Wilmderding Collection. Image courtesy of the Board of Trustees, National Gallery of Art, Washington, D.C.)

shared an aesthetic vision influenced by romanticism. Their naturalistic, if dramatically idealized, renderings aimed to draw viewers into the beauty and grandeur of the pristine and still unspoiled American continent. Traveling to Maine with fellow artist Henry Cheever Pratt, Cole stopped at Somesville for several days and then ventured to the island's eastern shore, staying at the Lynam farm by Schooner Head. His diary entries exude wonderment over the scenes he encountered on this trip. In his words, the vistas were "delightful," "magnificent," "romantic," "the grandest." They featured "threatening crags, and dark caverns in which the sea thunders," along with "truly fine" views of islands "belted with crags which glitter in the setting sun" and "a range of mountains of beautiful aerial hues." [11]

Other artists had ventured to Mount Desert before Cole, including his teacher Thomas Doughty in the 1830s. However, it was Cole's vociferous enthusiasm for the island's rugged maritime scenery, combined with the compelling drawings and paintings born of his visit, that prompted other New York artists go there—most famously, his dear pupils Frederic Edwin Church and Fitz Henry Lane. Each of them made his first trip to the island in 1850 and lodged with Albert Higgins in Bar

Harbor. In the years that followed, they and numerous other artists inspired by Cole frequented the island.

Because Cole's fame and influence as a painter of "unposed" landscapes was already enormous when he turned his gaze on Mount Desert, his paintings of the island had a far-reaching impact, influencing both the aesthetic leanings of fellow artists and the vacation plans of the general public. For Americans, especially those of means, his paintings (as well as those of Church, Lane, and others whose brush-strokes followed his) were elegant calls of the wild. They aroused curiosity about the island's dramatic geography and ignited imaginations about how such a naturally grand setting might invigorate bodies and souls worn down by the noisy masses, industrialization, and pollution of urban life. After all, beyond painting the glories of the natural world, Cole had penned a famous essay about this in the popular *American Monthly Magazine.* He concluded his "Essay on American Scenery" with these words:

Bar Island and Mount Desert Mountains from Somes Settlement, 1850, oil on canvas. By Fitz Henry Lane (1804–1865). This view was a familiar one to Wabanakis who camped by the Somes settlement—as it would have been to their ancestors, including Chief Asticou who resided nearby in the early 1600s. (Collection of Erving and Joyce Wolf.)

> Nature has spread for us a rich and delightful banquet. Shall we turn from it? We are still in Eden; the wall that shuts us out of the garden is our own ignorance and folly. . . . May we at times turn from the ordinary pursuits of life to the pure enjoyment of rural nature; which is in the soul like a fountain of cool waters to the way-worn traveler. [12]

Then Came the Rusticators

Seeking those "cool waters" in an edenic habitat long enjoyed by Wabanaki families exclusively, white urbanites from Boston, Providence, New York, Baltimore, and other cities on the Atlantic seaboard began flocking to Mount Desert Island, eager to spend some days "rusticating," or tramping about in nature—while, ideally, spending their nights in the comforts of a real bed. At first, hotels were few, but on both sides of the island paying guests were welcomed into the homes of numerous enterprising locals eager to supplement their livelihoods.

Among early tourists to the island was Charles Tracy, a noted New York lawyer. Inspired by Frederick Church's painted and spoken descriptions of the place, Tracy brought his family to Somesville for the month of August 1855. Traveling with friends, including Church and his sister, their party numbered twenty-six, plus one piano. Arriving by steamboat at Southwest Harbor, the group dined at Henry "Deacon" Clark's Island House Inn and then continued on to

> Some's Tavern at Somesville, part by wagon, part by sailboat. They spent their days driving in a buckboard or walking. Everything they saw they raved over. The people were hospitable, and not unduly inquisitive like most Yankees. . . . The food – fresh milk and cream, berries, hot biscuits, fresh fish and meat, new peas and potatoes, pies and puddings – were excellent. Before leaving, the Tracys gave at the Somes Tavern a party of eighty people, all but a few of them permanent residents. . . . A local fiddler and a flautist made a three-piece orchestra with the piano; they danced until 2 a.m. . . . The Tracy children were enraptured with the Island life, and one of them, who later became Mrs. J. Pierpont Morgan [marrying the millionaire banker and art collector], was instrumental in bringing that eminent financier to Bar Harbor. [13]

Members of the Tracy group also rode over to Bar Harbor, continuing on to Schooner Head, where they spent a night at the old Lynam farmhouse. They even climbed Newport Mountain (now Champlain Mountain). Astounded by the view of the "wide, wide blue Ocean" from the 1,058-foot summit, Charles Tracy described it in his trip logbook as "the most grand, most impressive, most beautiful and yet most fearful of all the things in the complete prospect."

Shortly before the Tracy family visit, Bar Harbor storekeeper Tobias Roberts opened Agamont House, the village's earliest hotel. (The first entries in the register were made 5 July 1855 by Frederic Church and fellow New York artist John F. Kensett—so apparently, Church's time with the Tracys was part of a longer island sojourn for him that summer.)

Two years after establishing Agamont House, Roberts built a crude wooden wharf at the end of Main Street in Bar Harbor, making steamboat landing possible in Bar Harbor and increasing the potential for hotels there. By 1872, Mount Desert Island boasted some two dozen hotels, more than half of them in Bar Harbor. The island's more moneyed "rusticators" (city-dwellers retreating to the country for comfortable relaxation) had begun separating themselves from a growing number of middle-class tourists by building their own summer "cottages." The first to do so was Alpheus Hardy, a well-to-do Boston merchant who bought a piece of

northeast Bar Harbor known as Birch Point and had a cottage of the same name built there in 1869. It is said that Hardy's inspiration for summering on the island came from an old (Wabanaki?) woman who approached him in Boston selling medicinal herbs: "Hardy chatted with her and was enchanted by her description of the mountains, woodland paths, and rocky shores of the island where she had grown them. Hardy determined to visit the island. . . . He came, saw, and was conquered." [14] Then, on land purchased from Stephen Higgins, he built his cottage. He encouraged friends to follow his lead and some did, including his business partner, Charles J. Morrill, as well as J. Montgomery Sears. [15]

Newport Mountain, Mount Desert, 1850, oil on canvas. By Frederic Edwin Church (1826–1900). In 1855, inspired by Church's Mount Desert Island paintings, his lawyer friend Charles Tracy came to the island for the month of August with a party of twenty-six, including his entire family and numerous friends. Many in the group climbed Newport Mountain (now Champlain Mountain). Tracy described the view of the "wide, wide blue Ocean" as the "most beautiful and yet most fearful" scene of the entire trip. (John Wilmerding Collection, promised gift. Image courtesy of the Board of Trustees, National Gallery of Art, Washington, D.C.)

By 1880, a veritable cottage construction boom was underway, especially in Eden (on the Frenchman Bay side of the island), where each rusticator's new summer home seemed more extravagant than the last. Transportation and lodging options continued to multiply, and by 1887 the island's total summer visitor count reached 20,000. [16]

Of course, all of these visitors, as well as the local farmers, fishermen, and boat builders who welcomed them, were latecomers compared to the region's Wabanaki Indians, in particular the Penobscots and Passamaquoddies, who continued coming to the island. Gradually, their seasonal presence at Mount Desert Island grew to pre-contact proportions as they pursued

In 1855, Bar Harbor storekeeper Tobias Roberts opened Agamont House, the village's earliest hotel, pictured here. Two years later, he built a crude wooden wharf at the end of Main Street, making steamboat landing possible in Bar Harbor and increasing the potential for hotels there. (Collection of the Bar Harbor Historical Society.)

summer tourists and cottagers as buyers for the goods and services they had to offer. In B.F. DeCosta's 1871 book, *Rambles in Mount Desert*, the author noted that Penobscots "are frequently seen in the vicinity of Mount Desert." That same year a chronicle by a group of excursionists who made a rare visit to the Penobscot reservation at Old Town noted, "In the summer months nearly all the young and able-bodied residents are away at the seaside, scattered all along the New England shore, at the noted summer resorts, where they pitch their tents on the beach and drive a thriving trade in small products of their skillful handiwork. Hence, at the time of our visit, we saw only the old patriarchs and a few children." [17]

Wabanakis Resort to Resorts

With each passing year, Wabanaki numbers at Mount Desert rose in concert with the rise of summer tourism on the island. Fancy woodsplint and sweetgrass baskets catering to the Victorian taste of the time proved to be the most marketable items, but seal skins, mounted antlers, moccasins, snowshoes, seagull breasts, carved paddles, and birchbark items such as toy canoes, picture frames, and boxes embroidered with dyed porcupine quills remained popular. Some tribesmen made rustic furniture, but full-size birchbark canoes, typically about eighteen feet long and fit for crossing saltwater bays and travel to offshore islands, were the prized, big-tag item. In addition, skilled Wabanaki hunters paddled their canoes to open water where they shot and harpooned porpoises, extracting and selling the oil—used to fuel lighthouses and lubricate clockworks. During the Wabanaki's most prosperous years of summer sales at Mount Desert Island and other seaside resorts (1875–1905), Indian agent reports featured such comments as:

About 20 [Indian] families are at Bar Harbor, selling their wares and catching porpoises. [18]

The year as a whole has been one of more than usual prosperity to the tribe. The revival of business has brought them constant and remunerative employment. The basket trade has been active, and all, except the persistently indolent, have reaped substantial benefits. [19]

The summer season was profitable to those who went abroad to vend their manufactured articles. [20]

The growing resort trade [on MDI] has discouraged farming by encouraging Indians to sell baskets, sea gull breasts, canoes, etc. [21]

The summer at the seaside generously added to their supply of cash, and basket-making has been fairly profitable throughout the year. [22]

The one thing, perhaps, which militates most against the highest success in farming is the yearly departure from home in the month of July of nearly if not quite three-fourths of the entire tribe, who go to the seaside and other summer resorts, for the purpose of selling their baskets and various other articles of manufacture. [23]

Sunset, Bar Harbor, 1854, oil on paper. By Frederic Edwin Church (1826–1900). Here, in the right-hand corner, we see a fish weir at the edge of the bar that runs between Mount Desert and Bar Island. During much of the 1870s and 1880s, the Indian encampment in Bar Harbor was situated along the town's north shore near the bar. (Olana State Historic Site, New York State Office of Parks, Recreation and Historic Preservation.)

Ironically, while heralding nature and the ideal of humankind living in harmony with it, the notable artists who frequented Mount Desert Island in the 19th century paid little heed to Maine's

Encampment of Passamaquoddy Indians, Bar Harbor, Aug. 17, 1877, pencil on paper. By Xanthus Smith (1839–1929). This drawing is the earliest known rendering of the Bar Harbor encampment, made by the Pennsylvania artist during his first visit to Mount Desert. The title is misleading, since other Wabanaki groups in addition to the Passamaquoddy also camped there at the time. Many lived in the makeshift shacks pictured here and had separate sale tents, visible in the background on the left side of the drawing. (Clark Point Gallery, Southwest Harbor.)

first inhabitants, most of whom continued to live their lives in pulse with the natural world. There is no evidence that it occurred to the Hudson River painters to immortalize Wabanakis on paper, canvas, or board. One explanation for this may be that unlike Comanche, Pawnee, or other Western Indians who still dressed in feathers and leathers, Indians in Maine increasingly wore clothes quite similar to those of most rural folk at the time—except when participating in tribal ceremonial events or public performances. Also, while drama surrounded tribes in the "Wild West" who were still engaged in a desperate fight for their freedom, indeed, their very lives, Indians on the Atlantic seaboard practiced a seasoned subtle and savvy accommodation and resistance strategy born of almost three centuries of painful experience dealing with Europeans and Americans.

A rare exception among these artists is Xanthus Smith from Pennsylvania, who sketched the Bar Harbor Indian encampment during his first summer sojourn on Mount Desert Island in 1877. For the next two decades, Smith made the island his "field of study," fascinated by its "beautiful mountains, lakes, rocky coasts, islands, and bays." [24] Initially, he based himself in Bar Harbor, but its rapid development as a fashionable resort made the place less appealing for his artistic endeavors. By the mid-1880s, he had gravitated to the quiet corners of Southwest Harbor. Most often he stayed at the Claremont Hotel, established in 1884. In 1885 he painted a lovely oil of the inn—an oceanside view of the place that captures its broad veranda and the long walkway that leads down a sloping sweep of lawn to the hotel's famous dock. Beginning in the 1870s, photographers paid a bit more attention to Mount Desert Island's original inhabitants, photographing Indian encampments on the island for posterity and souvenirs. Many of their images were printed and reprinted as stereocards.

A dark, rather haunting image of the Bar Harbor Indian encampment at the foot of Bar/ Bridge Street was made by Charles S. Reinhart, the one other 19th-century artist known to have given some attention to Wabanakis while on the island. Reinhart, an illustrator, was a frequent contributor to *Harpers* and other well distributed 19th-century magazines. He created many drawings for Charles Dudley Warner's 1886 serial story about American resorts for *Harpers New Monthly Magazine.* Chapter 8 in the series included his drawing of a lone Indian in silhouette paddling along the encampment shore. It stands in striking contrast to Reinhart's other illustrations for that story—drawings described by Henry James as "a rich *bourgeois* epic, . . . an incomparable collection of pictorial notes on the manners and customs, the aspects and habitats, in July and August, of the great American democracy; of which, certainly, taking one thing with another, they give a very comfortable and cheerful account." Although Reinhart's depiction of the encampment appeared in a story that ran in 1886, he must have made it earlier, for Wabanakis were forced to relocate from their Bridge Street shore location in 1884—a move that the artist's somber rendering seems to foreshadow.

Indian Village, Bar Harbor. Original drawing by Charles S. Reinhart. Engraved for *Harper's New Monthly Magazine*, August 1886, p.423. The drawing must have been made in 1883 or earlier, since Indians were forbidden to camp at the foot of Bridge Street after that year. (Courtesy of *Harper's* Magazine.

CHAPTER THREE

By Canoe, Sail, or Steam:
Getting to Mount Desert Island

The steamer **Electa** *recently took home the Indians with their wives and families belonging to the Passamaquoddy tribe who have been at Bar Harbor for the season. There were twelve families on board with all their baggage, canoes. They paid $60 for the steamer to take them to Pleasant Point near Eastport where they live.*
(Mount Desert Herald, 10/11/1883)

When it came to getting to Mount Desert Island, Wabanakis showed great creativity and flexibility. Initially, they paddled and portaged their canoes, taking various traditional lake, riverine, and inner coastal passages and avoiding long stretches of difficult open sea travel. Passamaquoddies coming from Indian Township, for instance, could canoe west across Big Lake and West Grand Lake, travel south into Third Machias Lake, then follow the Machias River to the coast, and from there paddle via a coastal route to Mount Desert, with portages along the way. From Pleasant Point, one could go via Cobscook Bay to Machias Bay and then on to the island, with periodic portages. [1]

Penobscots, canoeing from Indian Island and other locations along the Penobscot River, could travel inland water routes east to the Union River leading to Blue Hill Bay. Or they could follow the *Minnewokun* ("many directions route"), paddling from the Castine peninsula at Penobscot Bay, up to the head of the Bagaduce River, and then carrying a half-mile down to Eggemoggin Reach. From there they could travel the length of the Reach to Naskeag Point and on to Mount Desert. (Or, more safely, they could avoid rounding Naskeag Point by paddling just 4–5 miles along the Reach, turning up the Benjamin River, making a short carry to Salt Pond and continuing on to Blue Hill Bay and Mount Desert—entering the island at Squid Cove or Pretty Marsh.) The Bagaduce canoe route to Eggemoggin Reach is half the distance of going around Cape Rosier. Plus, by traveling the Bagaduce, entirely protected from the sea and wind, canoeists avoided the dangerous tides and strong currents of Cape Rosier.

And this route also allowed Wabanakis to travel without being seen by potentially dangerous strangers. Finally, by choosing the right time, one got a significant boost from the strong tidal currents in the Bagaduce. This would have been especially helpful when returning to Old Town on a going tide. To canoe past Cape Rosier, going against the strong river and tidal currents is hard work; by contrast, one would paddle *with* the currents down the Bagaduce. Similarly a coming tide would help carry one upstream. [2]

Bar Harbor Steamboat Landing, ca. 1880. At the end of the pier is the steamer *City of Richmond* and to the right is the *Lewiston*—two of the early boats that brought passengers and freight to Mount Desert Island. Steamboats were essential factors in the island's growth as a summer resort. (Collection of the Maine Historic Preservation Commission.)

Easy Going by Steamboat and Train

After steamboat service to Mount Desert Island became available via Rockland and Machiasport in the 1850s and 60s respectively, many Wabanakis used it, typically paying a fee to have their canoes transported with them. Those coming from Old Town could travel by train to Bangor, take the Boston-bound steamship as far as Rockland, and there catch another steamer to the island. Until steamer service from Eastport became available, those coming from the Passamaquoddy villages had to first get to Machiasport either by canoe or by land to catch a steamer to Mount Desert. [3]

Prior to 1857, steamboat service to Mount Desert Island had just one port of call: Southwest Harbor. [4] Anyone wishing to visit Bar Harbor had to make the rest of the journey by land—unless they had a canoe or sailing boat of their own. That changed when store- and innkeeper Tobias Roberts built a simple wooden wharf at the end of Main Street in Bar Harbor, making it possible for the steamboat *Rockland* to add the town to its run—and increasing bookings for the hotel Roberts had established in 1855. A decade later, the steamer *Lewiston* began making regular stops in Bar Harbor:

> Capt. Deering of the steamer *Lewiston*, perceiving the importance of Bar Harbor as a future place of resort, induced the Eastern Railroad Co. to purchase several acres of land for the building of a wharf to accommodate the steamers which might visit this harbor, little dreaming that in a very few years the hum of thousands of voices would echo and re-echo along these mountain vastnesses, and the whole landscape be dotted with splendid places and innumerable cottages to accommodate the moving and bustling throngs. [5]

The *Lewiston* ran between Portland, Mount Desert, and Machias. In 1872, the *Eastport Sentinel* noted that those who wished to visit Bar Harbor from Eastport could take the circuitous route of traveling first to Portland on the International Steamship Company's *City of Portland*, then turning back northeast on the *Lewiston* to land in Bar Harbor. The other option was to go

> by land to Machiasport then by steamer to Bar Harbor. The drive from Eastport to Machiasport was delightful, the only drawback being the innumerable mosquitoes and in the woods between Dennysville and East Machias, horseflies. The view along the road from Dennysville to Machiasport has changed very little for the last thirty years. At Machiasport we board the steamer *Lewiston*, stopping a short time at Jonesport and Milbridge and reaching our [Bar Harbor] destination at half past ten. [6]

Passamaquoddies commonly preferred to catch the ferry at Machiasport, but they typically made their way to Machiasport via traditional canoe routes rather than over land.

Over the next decade, steamboat service to Mount Desert expanded, tourism grew mightily, and in 1881 the *Mount Desert Herald* reported: "Thirteen years ago the little steamer *Rockland* made one trip a week between Rockland and Milbridge, touching at Bar Harbor. Now we have steamers *City of Richmond, Lewiston, Mt. Desert, Little Buttercup, Acadia*, and *Queen City of Bangor* all running to and from this port." [7]

Whether coming to the island from west, east, north, or south, Wabanakis appear to have welcomed the expanded transportation options just like everyone else. Sometimes the *Herald* mentioned their use of steamship travel. In 1881 the paper reported: "Our Indian population is increasing rapidly. Every steamer brings additions to the colony." [8] Three years later it noted: "Over fifty Indians from the Passamaquoddy Tribe arrived at Bar Harbor on the steamship *Frances*." [9]

Steamer *Mount Desert* leaving Southwest Harbor, circa 1900. Built by Goss & Sawyer Co. at Bath, Maine, 1879, for the Rockland, Mount Desert, & Sullivan Steamboat Co. Known as "Old Mounty," it traveled between Rockland and Bar Harbor, stopping at Bass Harbor, Southwest Harbor, and Sullivan. It was 163 feet long, with a capacity of about 150 passengers. In 1904 the J.T. Morse took over Old Mounty's Rockland–Bar Harbor run. (See Short & Sears, p.159.) (Photo by G.A. Neal. The Southwest Harbor Public Library Photographic Collection.)

1881 advertisement for steamboat service to Mount Desert Island. (Authors' collection.)

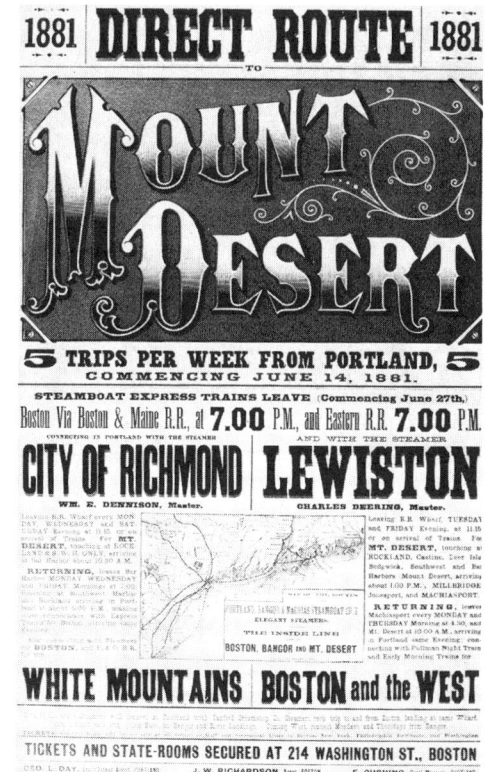

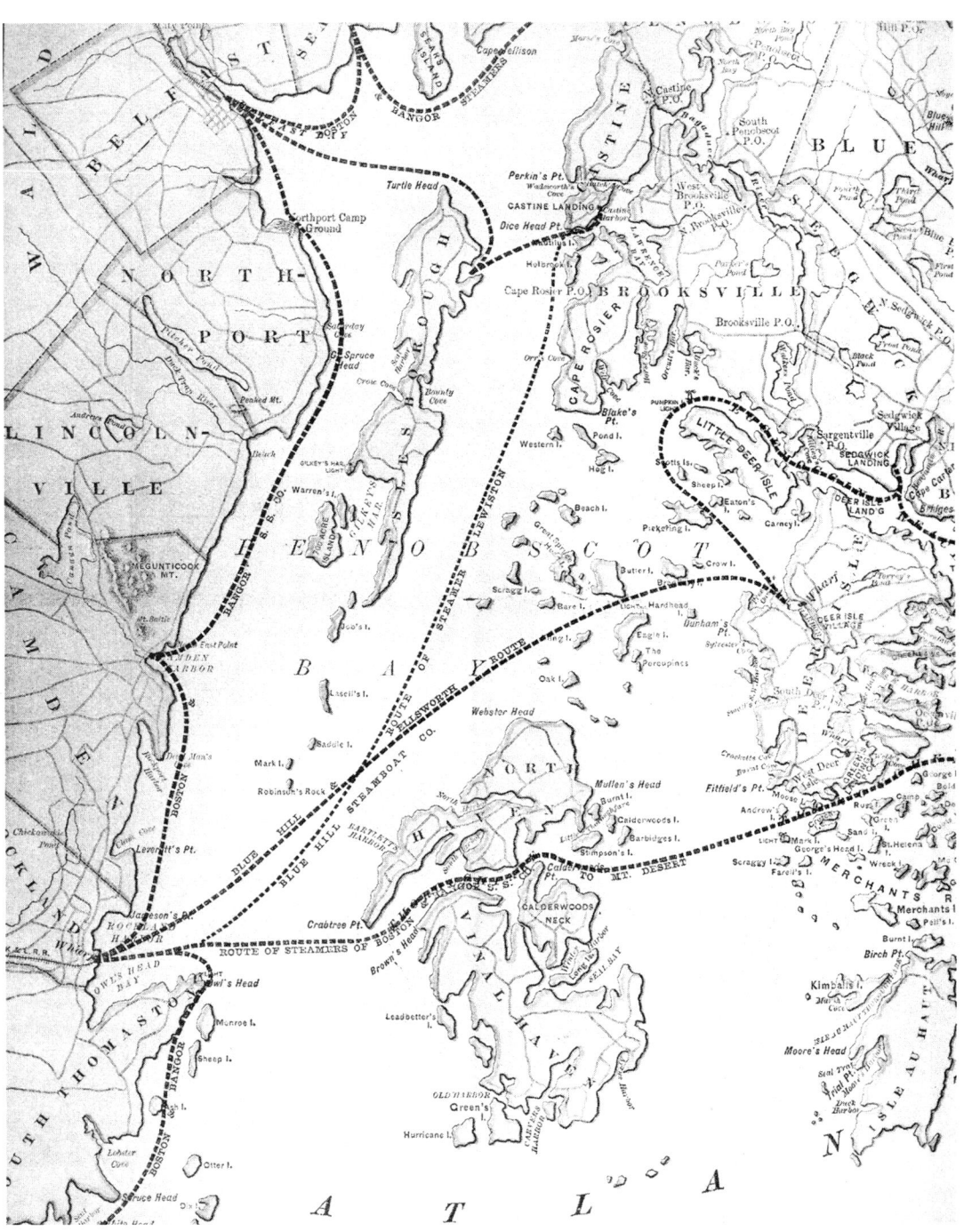

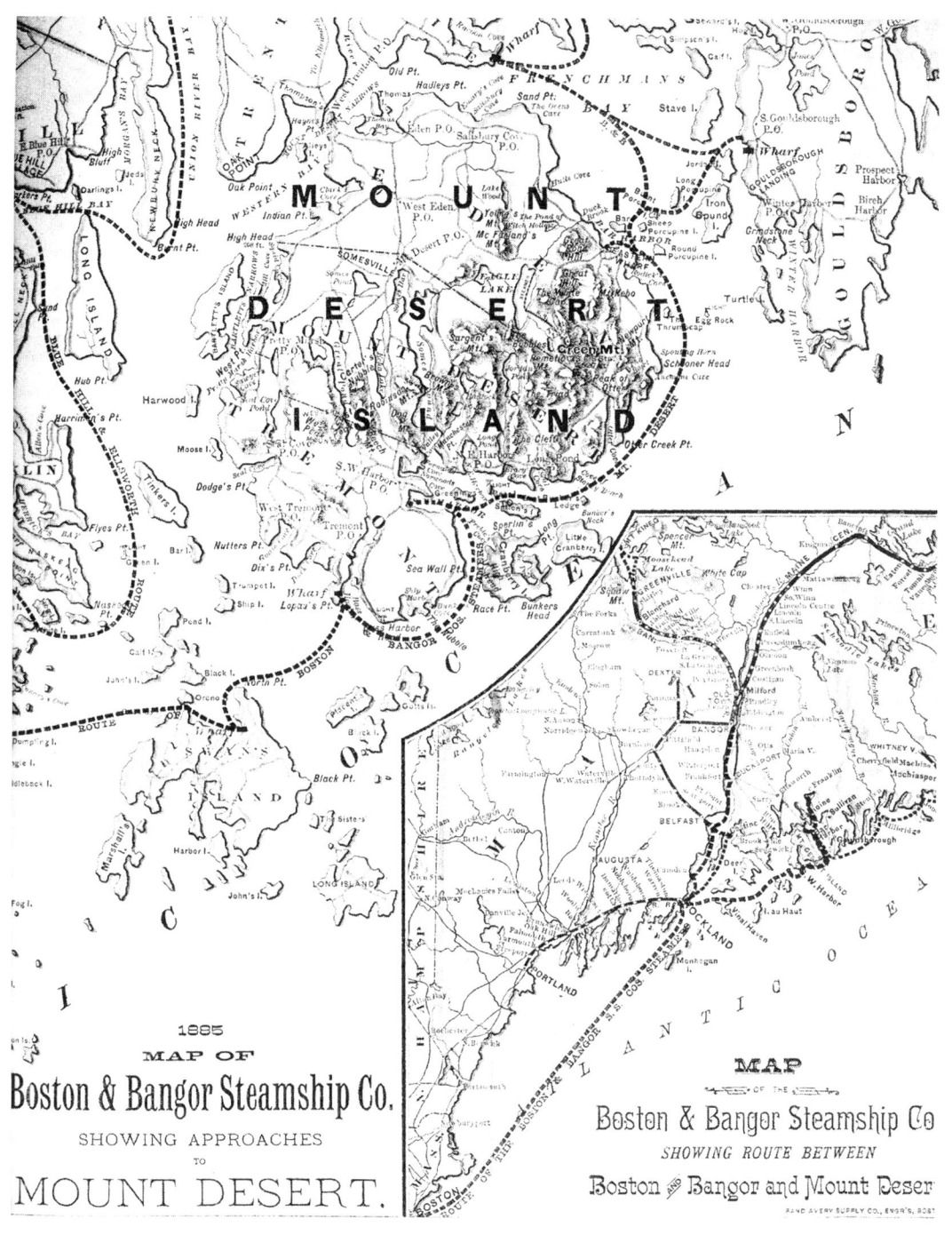

1885
MAP OF
Boston & Bangor Steamship Co.
SHOWING APPROACHES
TO
MOUNT DESERT.

MAP
OF THE
Boston & Bangor Steamship Co
SHOWING ROUTE BETWEEN
Boston and Bangor and Mount Deser
RAND AVERY SUPPLY CO., ENGR'S, BOST

Boston & Bangor Steamship Co.
Showing route between Boston and
Bangor and Mount Desert Island.
(Rand Avery Supply Co., Engravers,
Boston. 1885. Photo of map in
authors' collection.)

It was in 1881 that the railway from Boston was extended to Bangor, joining the more than forty-year-old tracks that already connected Bangor to Old Town. Two generations of Penobscots were already accustomed to traveling by rail to Bangor. Back in 1857 when Henry David Thoreau went to Indian Island and contracted Joseph Polis as his guide, he noted "Wishing to know when the [railway] cars left Oldtown, Polis's son brought one of the last Bangor papers, which I saw was directed to 'Joseph Polis.'" [10]

For Wabanakis living on Indian Island at Old Town or other reservation islands farther up the Penobscot River, getting to Bar Harbor became especially easy after 1884. That year a railroad extension was completed from Bangor through Ellsworth to the Mount Desert ferry terminal on Hancock Point. From there it was just a short ride to Bar Harbor on the steamer *Sebenoa* (purchased that year by Maine Central Railroad) or one of her successors. [11]

From the 1890s onward, the newly established rail line of the Sunrise Route carried passengers, including tourists, to Eastport and from Calais to Princeton. This railway passed through the small Passamaquoddy Indian village at Pleasant Point, providing Indian families with the opportunity to sell colored baskets, sealskin moccasins, and miniature bark canoes, as well as wooden bows and arrows for children. Of course, Passamaquoddies planning on spending part of their summer at Mount Desert Island could also now take the train, bringing with them their canvas tents, loads of baskets, and, not infrequently, their canoes as freight. Soon afterward, the same was true for Passamaquoddies at Peter Dana Point, who paddled their canoes to nearby Princeton, where they caught the train to Calais and continued on to Mount Desert Island.

A Canoe Will Do

Even after the introduction of train and steamboat transportation, some Wabanakis continued to travel all or part of the journey to Mount Desert Island by canoe, as evident in this 1893 excerpt from the Bangor *Industrial Journal*:

> Francis Dana, a well-known Indian hunter and guide whose home is at East Machias, having built a 16-foot birch canoe, started out last week to find a customer for it. He put to sea Friday in his frail craft, and having no sail paddled to Bar Harbor, where he disposed of the canoe, and returned home by Saturday's steamer. The distance is sixty miles, and the water was rough. [12]

Long-distance canoe travel did have its ups and downs, as revealed in this 1885 news bit about the Passamaquoddy tribe's resident priest who sometimes transported baskets from the reservation to the Mount Desert Island encampments:

> Rev. Mr. O'Dowd, Catholic priest at the Indian settlement at Pleasant Point, whose visit to Bar Harbor we noticed recently, had a rough passage while returning. At Machiasport he met an Indian from Pleasant Point who was going to Eastport in a canoe. The Indian was afraid to go so far in a canoe alone, and Mr. O'Dowd, who has become accustomed to that mode of travel

Wabanaki family summer camp at Bar Harbor, perhaps Birch Point, circa 1879. The same "Providence Line" sign posted on the tree appears in a later photo of the big Indian encampment at the foot of Bridge Street. The sign suggests that the person who possessed it had traveled that line between Providence, Rhode Island, and Boston—and also that s/he traveled between Maine and Boston by one of many steamboat and rail combinations then available at numerous points in Maine. It was not at all unusual for Wabanakis to travel such distances to market their wares. Among many examples is Frank "Chief Big Thunder" Loring, who camped all over New England, including in Rhode Island, where he stopped over "for several weeks" according to the Warren Telegraph of 2 June 1860 . (Photo by Bryant Bradley. Collection of the Maine Historic Preservation Commission.)

Wabanakis in well-packed seagoing canoes, Isle au Haut Thoroughfare, 1890s. By John C. Turner. (Collections of the Revere Memorial Library, Isle au Haut. Photo courtesy of Bill Bunting.)

and can wield a paddle as well as some Indians . . . readily consented to go with him. Soon after they started, a heavy fog shut out the sight of land, and when night came on a storm arose, and the priest and Indian found themselves on the ocean fifteen miles from any land, a high sea running, thick fog all around, the wind blowing, and nothing between them and the waves but a bark. They paddled through the darkness till 11 o'clock, the Indian much frightened and the priest nearly tired out, when they landed on a small island by chance, wet and tired. They were cared for by a fisherman.[13]

Former Passamaquoddy governor John Stevens of Indian Township, born in 1933, offered more recent memories of family travels to Mount Desert Island. He noted that his mother, Maria Lewy Stevens, was born at the Bar Harbor Ledgelawn Indian encampment in the summer of 1909 while her parents Eleanor and Wallace Lewy were there selling crafts. And he recalled how his grandparents and parents continued the tradition of going to Mount Desert for the summer season well into his boyhood during the 1930s—still traveling part of the distance by canoe. In Stevens' words:

[They left from the] big landing place at [Peter] Dana Point in front of our house. I remember them all getting ready to go. Usually early spring, around May. . . . They went by canoe [to catch the train at Princeton to Calais or Eastport]. A lot of kids went with their parents. But we didn't. I think my mother and my father and my grandmother and grandfather, they had so much junk—I mean stuff they'd sell—and they had only one canoe, and it was long, I remember. It might have been 15 feet. But to me it was longer than that, and wide. It was a sea-going one. To me it was a very nice looking canoe, and I would have loved to go with them. . . . They had huge tents. [I remember them] packin' 'em right in their boat, and other wares that they had. A lot of stuff that they use, I guess, that they make baskets out of. They take it with 'em. They used to have a tea [kettle] and they said, "That has to go with us." My father [always] said, "If you have tea, you'll survive.". . . There'd be about five, six families goin'. They'd all go together. [14]

More than bidding his family farewell, Stevens remembers greeting them when they returned to Peter Dana Point from a successful summer of marketing their wares on Mount Desert Island: "I used to love to see 'em come back [because] they had sweet stuff. They had candy, they had cookies, you know? Stuff that we didn't have here. And *soda*—I always remember Moxie. It tastes like hell, but it was something different than tea!" [15]

Among other recollections of Wabanakis canoeing to the Mount Desert Island area is one from Robert Fifield, a lifelong Deer Isle resident born in Green Head in 1923. Speaking of his boyhood years, he said:

Passamaquoddies Tom Joe Lola (front) and Louis Mitchell, ca. 1905. Mitchell, a tribal representative in the Maine state legislature, played an important role in the preservation of native rights and traditions. Also an expert hunter, guide, and canoeist, he gained notoriety for paddling his canoe all the way around Mount Desert Island in just 12 hours. (Courtesy of Donald Soctomah.)

Passamaquoddy tribal leader Wallace Lewy, ca. 1930. Lewy and his family traveled part of the distance from Peter Dana Point on the Indian Township reservation to Mount Desert by canoe for many summers from the 1800s through the early 1900s. Born about 1869, Lewy was the maternal grandfather of former Passamaquoddy governor John Stevens, a central figure in the 1980 Maine Indian Claims Settlement. (Courtesy of Donald Soctomah.)

I remember every summer, Indians coming here [to Deer Isle]. There were several groups . . . [and] they'd come down and set up their tents, and they would go fishing off the islands. They'd sell baskets as well. There were several paths to our area that they would take. Typically, they would come across the [Eggemoggin] Reach and go past the western part of the island and go down to Deer Isle village [Northwest Harbor] to the salt water pond. They'd go along the pond for a ways and take canoes across it to the other side of the road, to the Sunshine area [Long Cove], carrying their canoes over land on the eastern part of that island. They'd canoe down to Isle au Haut and any of the other islands. Most of the Indian activity, though, was before my time. I do remember that they had a little village in Deer Isle, near Sunset. I can remember the wigwams being out in the field there. [16]

Travel Aid

Also noteworthy are references reaching back to the 1820s telling of Wabanakis traveling by stagecoach.[17] Although no specific mention has been found of Indians using this mode of travel to Mount Desert Island in particular, horse-drawn stagecoach service between Bangor and the island was available by 1872 and it is highly likely that quite a few took advantage of this. As mentioned in one popular article that year,

There are many persons who are made unhappy, not to say ill, even, by going on board of a steamboat, and who can not endure so much of motion, which at times is serious in passage from Portland to Rockland. To these there is the pleasant resource of a stage ride from Bangor all the way by land to any part of Mount Desert; for although this is an island, there is one point where the mainland is reached by means of a bridge. This gives you a drive of some fifty miles over superb roads through a picturesque country, and behind such handsome horses as I have never elsewhere seen coupled to a stagecoach. . . . During two summers I passed at Bar Harbor there was a gentleman who every week drove down from Bangor to Bar Harbor. He would start about nine in the morning of Saturday, and arrive just before sunset. [18]

For Wabanakis, traveling the distance by train in combination with stagecoach, walking, and canoeing was also common. For Penobscots, the train connection between Old Town and Bangor, available since the late 1830s, made it easy to catch the Bangor—Mount Desert Island stage. When traveling with goods to sell, Wabanakis packed their bundled baskets and other crafts on top of the stage (or train or ship deck), covering them with canvas.

Wabanakis quite frequently requested and received money for travel fares from Indian agents who managed the state-controlled Indian funds. This was especially true when individuals were stranded or needed to travel for emergency purposes. Among many examples: accounting records in the Penobscot Indian agent's report for 1867 show that he gave the well-known

Among the most notorious Penobscots of her day, Molly Molasses (ca. 1775–1867) had a reputation for hard bargaining among Indians and non-Indians alike. She came from a family known to have *m'teoulin* (magic or spirit power), prompting some white folks to think of her as a "witch." While living primarily at Indian Island or a dozen miles downriver at a Penobscot encampment in Brewer, she often traveled about the state hawking her wares. Sometimes she stopped in the vicinity of Mount Desert Island and Ellsworth—just south of where she was born in a canoe on Green Lake. Situated in the Union River Valley, Green Lake formed part of an old travel route between Indian Island and Mount Desert. Copy of photo in authors' collection. Collection of Maine State Museum)

Penobscot Mary Nicola, better known as Molly Molasses (born ca.1775) "1 ticket of 50 cents to go to Ellsworth to stop with her son" (Piel Molly Nicola, born ca.1791). Like so many other Wabanakis of the day, Molly survived largely on the basis of trading and selling crafts.[19] It is likely that her son (fathered by Lt. Gov. John Neptune) was doing the same in Ellsworth. Perhaps he was residing there for a season. Or he may have stopped over en route back to the Penobscot after fishing, clamming, or seal- or bird-hunting in the Mount Desert Island area.

Surely this was familiar territory for Molly. After all, according to her own account, she was born in a canoe on Green Lake.[20] This long sweep of water located in the Union River Valley about six miles northwest of Ellsworth, is on an old Wabanaki canoe route between Mount Desert and Indian Island. Over the centuries, countless other Wabanaki families plied these waters en route to and from Mount Desert Island. Who knows how many besides Molly took their first breath here—or their last.

CHAPTER FOUR

Boating, Tramping, Rocking, and Tea: Rusticators On the Rise

Everyone has his own idea of pleasure, and it must be a scene of many and varied attractions that will please all. Bar Harbor comes as near affording universal satisfaction to humanity's craving for happiness as any place in this terrestrial sphere possibly can. Nowhere is there a better field for enjoyment than in this little Eden.

(Sherman's Bar Harbor Guide, 1890)

Climate and Scenery Are Enough

By 1872, Bar Harbor boasted its own steamboat wharf and fifteen hotels—more than twice as many inns as Somesville, Northeast Harbor, and Southwest Harbor combined. Despite the increase in lodgings, the town remained quite small and rustic in comparison to Newport, Rhode Island, New England's most fashionable watering hole. The visitors who came to Mount Desert Island in ever-growing numbers still arrived with high expectations for nature's offerings and modest ones concerning food, bedding, and entertainment. After all, the purpose of coming to this unspoiled part of seacoast Maine was to immerse oneself in nature—to purify mind and body with cool ocean breezes and to experience the inspiration of scenic vistas and the exhilaration of vigorous mountain hikes. As the *Eastport Sentinel* reported that year:

> The crowds that flock to Bar Harbor every year are willing to overlook the food, while it is not a fashionable resort but frequented more than any other. . . . The people who pass the summer on the rough, rocky island leave their big trunks at home. During the day, parties of several persons start off on a walking expedition of five, ten and fifteen miles to one or another of the many objects of interest on the sea shore or up the mountains. There is a vigorous sensible, healthy feeling in all they do.[1]

Throughout the 1870s, noted one observer, Mount Desert Island was a place where "rusticators" existed "largely on climate and scenery," experiencing life that was "altogether of an out-of-door character, easy going as to costume, and informal as to manners and customs." An 1872 *Harper's Magazine* article offered details about that "costume" [2]—garb geared for people who intended to "pass all day in the open air, either in lengthened pedestrian expeditions, in sailing or rowing upon the waters of the beautiful day.":

> The ladies wear wide-brimmed hats and picturesque costumes of red and blue flannel, cut short
> above the feet and ankles, which, in turn, are incased in stout walking shoes. The gentlemen
> appear in warm, rough clothing, which will stand the wear and tear of a tramp over the rocks and
> through the bushes and which will offer some resistance to the fogs, which penetrate like the rain. [3]

Rusticators with truly modest expectations continued to rent rooms in the homes of locals, while taking their meals in hotels. [4] No matter where one stayed, for most visitors the Mount Desert Island experience began on a steamboat wharf—most often at Southwest Harbor or Bar Harbor. Those disembarking at Southwest Harbor in the 1870s found themselves surrounded by a view of the mountains unequalled elsewhere on the island "in breadth and scope, in grace of outline and varied forms and color." But the image of an edenic island yet untouched by industry was spoiled by the big lobster cannery situated right at the pier:

> Now most of the visitors to Mount Desert, even the prosaic folk, go prepared to enjoy the pictur-
> esque, the beautiful, the sublime. Just as they are about to be ushered into this new world of romance
> and delight, to be met upon the threshold by thousands of lobsters, raw, boiled, cooked, and canned,
> is discouraging to say the least. But one may remain a while with quiet interest at Southwest Harbor
> and have nothing to do with lobsters. Very fair hotels and boarding-houses are to be found at the
> landing and for a mile or more up the main road which follows the shore of the harbor. [5]

A medley of posted and hand-held hotel signs awaited visitors when they stepped off the boat at either Southwest Harbor or Bar Harbor. Would-be rusticators quickly learned that anyone wishing for the more comfortable lodgings needed to make arrangements well in advance of arrival. From the piers, guests and their luggage were picked up and driven to their vacation quarters on rough roads in open horse-drawn buckboards—a rollicking ride that, depending upon the passenger, either confirmed or refuted the joys of "rusticating."

Once unpacked and settled in, vacationers faced an array of options: Clamber up a mountain? Hike a woodland trail? Tramp across the mudflats? Rock about on the seaside ledges? Investigate tide pools or coastal caverns? Boat around the bays or lakes (powered by oar, paddle, sail, or steam)? Brave an island tour in a buckboard? Tip a glass and discuss books at the Oasis Club? Visit the Indian encampment? Some combination of these? Most visitors took advantage of sailing opportunities. As noted by one journalist in 1872: "Sailing-parties form a marked feature of a sojourn at Bar Harbor, for the neighborhood abounds in pretty, picturesque places to visit." [6] Continuing with romantic enthusiasm, the writer jumped back and forth between sea and land:

There are as many attractive expeditions on the land as the curiosity, the limit of time or the power of endurance of the seeker may permit; for besides the places of special interest, there are the mountain roads, with every-varying glimpses of wide-extended views; the by-paths through the woods, fragrant with the perfume of the pine; the fields, with the search after wild weeds and flowers, the cran-

Sailing yachts and the steamer *Mount Desert* by the Bar Harbor wharf, 1900. Built in 1879, it ran between Rockland and Bar Harbor for twenty-five years, stopping at Bass Harbor, Southwest Harbor, and Sullivan. (Collection of the Bar Harbor Historical Society.)

berry, ground-pine, and cedar, the ferns and mosses; the line of broken rocky shore, with its wealth of the foliage of the sea in every pool left by the retiring tide; and that nameless delight in watching the restless waves as they surge and foam over the sunken ledges and up the pebbly beach. . . .

Eagle Lake, a body of fresh-water some mile in width and two or three miles long, is . . . . is situated between Green and Dog mountains, some fifteen hundred feet above the ocean. . . . Every rod of its shore is a study for the artist, while the sportsman may catch all the trout he desires. . . .

From Bar Harbor to the top of Green [Cadillac] Mountain is a walk or ride of about four miles. Any person of ordinary leg-power, after he has respired the electrical atmosphere of Mount Desert a few days, will insist upon walking to the summit, and he will find the road good and the ascent easy and gradual, with no very rough climbing any part of the way. Those who wish to drive will have earnestly pressed upon their consideration a great many small wagons and carry-alls, but I would advise them to choose the so-called "mountain wagons," such as are in general use all about the White Mountains [of New Hampshire]. These are made very strong; the body of the wagon is hung on leather straps, instead of resting upon springs, and although it is a rough way of traveling, yet it is altogether safer. Whether you ride or walk, after you have passed over half the way you will gaze upon the most beautiful views you have ever seen. . . . The singular charm of the panorama to be seen from the summit of Green Mountain may be attributed to the fact that it embraces both the sea and the land. [7]

An Agreeable Luxury

By the mid-1880s, there were dozens of hotels to choose from on Mount Desert Island, including Rodick House at the corner of Main and Cottage streets in Bar Harbor. Twice expanded, it had become Maine's largest and most famous hotel, with 400 guest rooms accommodating up to 1,000 people, a broad wraparound veranda, and a sweeping lawn where visitors strolled and competed in playful sporting events with locals, cottagers, and encamped tribesmen. One visitor of the day described arriving at the Bar Harbor wharf, "alive with vehicles and tooters for the hotels," and being swept up and taken to the Rodick: "Our party, holding on to their seats in a buckboard, were whirled at a gallop up to Rodick's and ushered into a spacious office swarming with people. . . . The first confused impression was of a bewildering number of slim, pretty girls, nonchalant young fellows in lawn-tennis suits, and indefinite opportunities in the halls and parlors and wide

The landmark Bar Harbor Reading Room grew out of the town's first club, the Oasis (founded in 1874,) where men gathered to drink and talk. (Maine Historic Preservation Commission.)

Mt. Desert Reading Rooms, Bar Harbor, Me.

piazzas for promenades and flirtations." [8] Perhaps the best-known room in the Rodick was the so-called fish-pond, a large hall where young people "assemble after breakfast and the early dinner, and in which the girls [are] supposed to angle for their escorts." [9] Bar Harbor was becoming such a social scene that it was said, "If you cannot find friends here, you are a subject for an orphans' asylum." [10]

Clearly, the joys and solace of nature were no longer reason enough to venture to Mount Desert Island. People still came to the island in answer to the call of the wild, but hotels now offered many amenities, and activities were on the rise that had little or nothing to do with nature. A travel writer of the day summed up the situation like this: "An agreeable luxury, for the most part refined, though occasionally ostentatious, has replaced the earlier rudeness of board and lodging, and 'the season' is a matter of dinner dances, musicales, yachting parties, and balls, in the place of the 'hops,' buckboard rides, and picnics." [11] The *Mount Desert Herald* put it this way:

Rodick House, Bar Harbor, 1885. Built by David Rodick in 1866, and greatly expanded in 1875 and 1881, the Rodick became Maine's largest and most famous hotel in the 1880s, boasting 400 guest rooms accommodating up to 1,000 people. On its sprawling lawns, visitors strolled daily during the summer season and on special occasions competed in playful sporting events with locals, cottagers, and Wabanakis. (Authors' Collection.)

> The spirit of change which pervades all mundane things, has wrought a great transformation at Mount Desert. The pioneer pleasure seeker of two decades ago would be at a loss to find the little tavern which then sheltered the handful of summer visitors, if he should look for it among the score or more of modern hotels which now flaunt their walls of serried windows in the face of the fashionable tourist. The primitive amusements of the elder days, have been supplanted by 'hops' 'club-houses' and 'tea at four o'clock:' the picnic, that foe to digestion, has given place to tennis, and the rough simplicity of the buckboard is fast fading out of existence between the

incoming of spring-wagons, dog-carts and liveries, and the dashing four-in-hand. It needs no prophet's eye to discern that in a few years the island will be utterly given over to the luxuries, frivolities and follies of a modern watering place.[12]

These changes prompted one island watcher to advise people to avoid Bar Harbor altogether because, "It has lost half its charms by becoming so fashionable."[13] Yet, noted a journalist for *Harper's*, the *principal* occupation at Bar Harbor in the 1880s was still "outdoor exercise, incessant activity in driving, walking, boating—rowing and sailing—bowling, tennis, and flirtation." All this activity, he explained, sprang from the "peculiar and delicious" quality of the air, "which stimulates to unwonted exertion. . . . In this latitude, and by reason of the hills, the atmosphere is pure and elastic and stimulating, and it is softened by the presence of the sea."[14]

According to an 1883 article in the *New York Times,* for the Bar Harbor visitor "who cares not for the fashionable life, there are many pleasant ways of spending the day." One could go out painting, take a walk up to the "brawling stream" of Duck Brook, or stroll the fields and woodland paths to gather some of the island's "sixty varieties of wildflowers." The *Times* also suggested driving to Somes Sound (in the island's quieter western region), stopping for dinner at the still cozy Somes House and then returning to Bar Harbor by moonlight.[15]

CLIMBING UP NEWPORT.

Climbing Newport [Champlain] Mountain, 1886. Original drawing by Charles S. Reinhart. Engraved for *Harper's New Monthly Magazine,* **Vol. 73, No.435, p.421 (Courtesy of** *Harper's Magazine.***)**

Mountain hikes, sometimes along old Wabanaki Indian trails, remained popular, especially trekking up Newport [Champlain] Mountain. This "very agreeable" climb, wrote the *Harper's* journalist, was not difficult—although, "if the sun is out, one feels, after scrambling over the rocks and walking home by the dusty road, like taking a long pull at a cup of shandygaff (ale or beer mixed with ginger ale, ginger beer or lemonade.)" Also, "because it is some two or three hundred feet lower than Green [Cadillac] Mountain and includes that scarred eminence in its view, it is the most picturesque and pleasing elevation on the island." [16]

Postcard promoting Mount Desert Island's Green Mountain Railway, ca. 1890. A small steamboat shuttled visitors across Eagle Lake to the base of Green (Cadillac) Mountain. From there, they took the cog-train railway to the summit, where they could dine and sleep at the Green Mountain Hotel (Summit House), then roll out of bed to see the sun rise from the ocean. The mountain's summit is the vantage point from which one can have the earliest peek at dawn in the United States. (Jesup Library Collection.)

It took longer to scramble up to the 1,532-foot summit of Green Mountain (renamed Cadillac in 1918). The highest point along the North Atlantic seaboard, this mountaintop offers climbers a uniquely wondrous view of the sun rising from the ocean; for it is sometimes the vantage point for the earliest peek at dawn in the United States. For some visitors, the appeal of ascending the mountain grew in 1880, when a tea house was erected atop its pink-granite head. (Perhaps they served shandygaff!) Soon thereafter, the tea house was expanded into the Green Mountain Hotel (or Summit House), and a cog train (toothed-rack) railway was laid from the base of the mountain to its top. This made it possible for those who were unable or disinclined to hike to instead enjoy a leisurely ride to the summit, overnight at the hotel, and wake up to the magical sunrise. Special stagecoaches servicing the Green Mountain Railway left from Bar Harbor's West End Hotel four times a day. They picked up passengers at other hotels en route, then took them to Eagle Lake to board the small steamer *Wauwinet,* which carried them to the train station at the foot of the mountain.

FORTUNE TELLING

THE "BELLE" OF THE CAMP

THE CAMP

Visiting the Indian Encampment

Some visitors were aware that some of the trails they followed up the mountains and through the forests of Mount Desert Island had been blazed by Maine Indians centuries ago. Those who knew this—along with those who did not—were curious about the Passamaquoddy and Penobscot families who encamped every summer on the island to market their traditional wares and their skills as canoeists and hunting guides. The location of the Indian encampment in Bar Harbor shifted over the decades, but remained a favorite destination for the island's tourists and summer residents. The local paper commonly announced the comings and goings of Wabanakis, just as it did that of cottagers. The 1881 *Bar Harbor Blue Book & Mount Desert Guide,* which featured a map and listed "by streets" the locations of the town's businesses and cottages, included the Indian encampment. It provided profiles of hotels, attractions, and drives, along with rules and rental rates concerning vehicles "with one horse" or "two horses," "per hour" or "per day." The *Blue Book's* section on Indians noted:

> Of the small remnant of [Wabanaki] now left, the Penobscot Indians live at Oldtown, the Passamaquoddy at Eastport, and a few are scattered through the State. Visitors at Bar Harbor are

familiar with them, as they make an encampment there for the season, finding a ready sale for their baskets and other wares, and many a passenger for their birch-bark canoes. [17]

Many Mount Desert Island tourists and summer residents visited the Indian encampment in search of a guide to take them out in canoes to sightsee, fish, or hunt. Some came in response to the ads Indians had posted in local papers. For example, Passamaquoddy Louis Mitchell's recurring notice in the *Mount Desert Herald* offered birchbark canoes in which he and other "experienced" Indian paddlers would "take parties to the several Islands in the bay and around Mount Desert Island" or carry "sporting parties to places where porpoise and seal may be shot." [18]

In the 1880s, hunting guides could be hired for $1.50–2.50 a day.[19] Among the many Indian guides rusticators found at Mount Desert Island were Penobscots Frank "Chief Big Thunder" Loring, Joe Francis, Mitchell Francis, and Newell Mitchell, along with Passamaquoddies Wallace Lewey and Joe Mell (Mitchell) Pierpole.[20] Joe Mell's 1883 *Mount Desert Herald* ad read: "Fall hunting in Maine. Parties wishing to Hunt or Camp in Maine can secure an Excellent Guide by addressing Joe Pierpole, Princeton, Maine, the best Indian guide in the Schoodic waters. Two nice canoes and good accommodations for six persons. Will warrant that good deer hunting be found." [21]

Wabanaki guides awaiting sport-hunters on Bar Harbor's shore between the wharf and the Indian encampment, ca. 1881. Note rifles in men's hands and animal skins draped on boats. (Photo by Kilburn Brothers. Collection of the Maine Historic Preservation Commission.)

One of the people who answered Joe's ad was William Lyman Underwood, grandson of William Underwood, who established the Underwood Canning Company in Boston around 1825. In 1880 young William set up a fish cannery in Southwest Harbor and oversaw the operation for two decades. Beginning in 1883, he and Joe ventured into the woods together every spring and fall for forty years. In his book *Wilderness Adventures,* William's extensive narrative about Joe included this comment: "There is no better guide for the woods than a man who has lived and been brought up there, as has Joe. . . . Nothing escapes Joe's keen eyes. His power of sight, especially the knack of finding things, is nothing short of marvelous." [22]

On Your Mark, Get Set, Go!

Amateur athletic tournaments, including running and canoe races, were a big part of summer life in Bar Harbor during the late 1800s and early 1900s—commonly sponsored by hotels and other businesses for promotional purposes. Wabanakis often played a significant role in these and other local celebrations. For athletic events, competitions were sometimes racially segregated—Indians against Indians and whites against whites. This was clearly the case in the 1883 athletic tournament in Bar Harbor, described as follows in the *Mount Desert Herald*:

> The proceedings of the athletic tournament proved a great attraction and thousands of gaily dressed people were in attendance. The athletic and funny sports . . . took place on the great lawn on the north side of The Rodick [hotel]. . . . For the 100 yards run there were eight entries. . . . The other races and games took place in the following order:
>
> 100 Yards Run (Indian) Entries: Johnny Magie, Lola T. Lola, Frank Stanley. Lola T. Lola came in first; Frank Stanley second.
>
> 1-Mile Run (Indian) Entries: Joseph Lola, Sebatis Lola [2nd place], Mitchel Francis, Lola T. Lola [1st place]. . . .
>
> Three-legged race (Indian.) Entries: Joseph Lola, Sebatis Lola, Mitchel Francis, Johnny Magie, Sopi[el] Mitchel, Charles Mitchel. Won by Joseph Lola and Sebatis Lola. . . . Nobody succeeded in climbing the Greased Pole, and only two Indians attempted it. . . .
>
> [Afternoon] Double Canoe Race (Indian) Won by the Lola Brothers. 1st prize, $10, 2nd prize, $5. [23]

During Bar Harbor's athletic tournaments three years later, a dispatch from the town reported:

> The rocks were covered with spectators to witness the races today, the yachts and boats in the harbor were also crowded. The sailing races began at 1 A.M. with a light breeze. The course was triangular, within the Porcupines, and the sloops and cat boats were required to go over the course three times. After several attempts the wind died away and the race declared off. . . . The boat and canoe races began at 4 P.M. The first race was a tub race between three Indians, which created much merriment. . . . There were two entries in the single canoe race and F. Lyman won it. . . . The Indian canoe race was the most beautiful and graceful event of the day. [24]

Buckboarding: A Rollicking Good Time

Touring about in buckboards was the fallback activity for just about everyone. According to one 19th-century tourist, riding in a buckboard was like being in a see-saw and a baby jumper at the same time. Buckboards, she elaborated, "are composed of four long boards laid side by side, supported only at the extreme ends where they are hung over the axles [with] seats in the middle. They are neither elegant nor graceful, but easy, 'springy' vehicles, which having neither sides nor top covers, give unimpeded views and are excellent for sight-seeing, though not precisely the thing for rainy weather." [25]

Despite an increase in more comfortable vehicles, buckboarding remained one of the most relished activities at Mount Desert Island throughout the 19th century—perhaps because it was such a bonding experience. As one journalist noted, "The exhilaration of the long spring-board, the necessity of holding on to something or somebody to prevent being tossed overboard, puts occupants in a larkish mood that they might never attain in an ordinary vehicle." [26] So it was that summer visitors gathered many blurry views of the island's varied and glorious scenery while bumping along in these open carriages. [27]

Buckboarding on Mount Desert Island, 1884. This illustration features Bar Harbor cottager, the Hon. James G. Blaine (second seat, right) and friends. One-time editor/owner of *The Kennebec Journal*, Blaine was elected several times to the Maine legislature and U.S. Congress (serving as Speaker of the House in both), had three serious runs for U.S. President, and served as Secretary of State under Presidents Garfield, Arthur and Benjamin Harrison. (*Frank Leslie's Illustrated Newspaper*, 23 August. Authors' collection.)

Chatwold, the summer home of Joseph Pulitzer, Schooner Head Road, ca. 1890s. The extravagantly wealthy publisher of New York *World* leased this cottage estate from Louise Bowler Livingston in 1893. The following year he purchased it and commenced making extensive renovations and additions, including building a tower and expanding the stables to hold his 26 horses. (Jesup Library Collection.)

Natural Life, Artificial Conditions

By the end of the 1880s, a cottage-building boom had transformed Bar Harbor. The "Cottage Era" was in full bloom. New roads made buckboard riding less adventurous and the town's high-society social scene sapped much of the energy previously devoted to nature. This was true for wealthy visitors staying in the high-end hotels and all the more so for the "cottagers," whose sumptuous summer homes resembled cottages about as much as a moose resembles a mouse. The well-born or self-made millionaire owners of these summer homes included prominent names like Astor, Pendleton, Procter, Pulitzer, Sears, and Vanderbilt—capitalist barons of the so-called Gilded Age.

A peek at Mount Desert Island's conspicuous wealth can be found by picking up the local paper from just about any summer day in the late 1880s and 1890s. In fact, dispatches from Bar Harbor reached far beyond the island, picked up by newspapers across the state and the rest of New England. Here are excerpts drawn from three typical samples:

> Mr. Frederick W. Vanderbilt will arrive at Bar Harbor directly in his yacht 'Vidette.' He will remain some time.
>
> Last evening Mrs. Burton Harrison, the distinguished cottager from the South, gave a grand party in honor of her guest, Matthew Arnold. Everybody went who could get an invitation and many self-invited people were there.
>
> The dance at the West End [Hotel], last evening, was crowded with spectators. Dance at the Marlboro [Hotel] tonight.

Col. Shepard, son-in-law of the late W. H. Vanderbilt, has given much in aid of the Methodist church here.

There was one of the finest masquerade balls ever given at Bar Harbor at Mrs. P. Walley's summer villa, on Eden Street, last Tuesday night. The first of the place were there. There were the cottage aristocracy, the rich and distinguished hotel guests and every one almost who was of more than ordinary note. . . .

The lawn tennis tournament at Mrs. Howard's has been seriously interrupted by the wet weather. The great excitement today will be the equestrian tournament at half-past three. . . .

Mrs. T.B. Musgrave gave a Monday party and invited a large number of Generals and Judges. . . . .

Mrs. George Place gives a musicale every Monday morning, as she does in New York. . . .

We hear that the Bangor Opera Company is likely to come here next week.

The Vanderbilts live very much by themselves and they can well afford to. In wealth they are the first in this country, their social position is assured, and in culture and literary attainments they are sufficient. They take great pains to merit the good opinion of the world, but as to what opinion the world entertains toward them they appear to be entirely unconcerned.

Col. Eliot F. Shepard and Mrs. Shepard, who was Miss Vanderbilt, will close their visit at "Devil-stone" with the end of this week.

The coachmen's ball at the Casino was a point of attendance and a great success. . . .

Bishop Doan, of Albany, lectured to women on woman's part in Christian work, at the St. Saviour Episcopal church, last Monday, and so affected them that many shed tears. The Bishop is very popular with the church people at Mount Desert.[28]

The private [railway] car of Mr. Stewart, of New York, was attached to the train from the west which arrived last evening. It was formerly the Vanderbilt private car and is on the way to Bar Harbor. [29]

Mr. Henry F. Sears of Boston, gave a dinner to 26 guests at the Malvern [Hotel] Tuesday evening, having a special orchestra from Boston for the occasion. The veranda was enclosed, beautifully furnished, banked at the sides and corners with fir trees and lighted with Japanese lanterns. Among the guests were the Marquis Imperial of the Italian legation.

Mrs. Charles Ewing Green has given several pretty entertainments in honor of her niece, Miss Carter, daughter of Oliver S. Carter, the millionaire.

The Pulitzers have taken many companies of friends for trips about the bay in the Creedmore and have entertained much at Chatwold their beautiful home at Cromwell's Harbor. [30]

A *Scribner's Magazine* journalist, intrigued by Bar Harbor's nature/culture contrast, made this comment: "Wandering through the streets of the little village one is struck again and again by the sharp contrast between what may be called the natural life of the place and the artificial conditions which fashion has imposed upon it." [31] The local paper described the scene like this:

The hotels hold hops and dances almost nightly in the height of the season, and yachting, canoe-ing and boating about the interesting points of Mount Desert Island are within the reach of all. The wealthy summer dwellers have a common meeting place, where gayety and sport reigns supreme throughout the season—the Kebo Valley Club —which is situated but a short distance from the village, at the foot of Kebo Mountain on the Eagle Lake road. The Kebo club house and attractive grounds are scenes of brilliant assemblies. There is a pretty little theatre there, where plays are given in which the participants are members of the social set. A restaurant is connected, and most of the dinners which were formally given in the private houses are now held there. Last August [U.S. Navy] Secretary [Hilary A.] Herbert and the officers of the North Atlantic fleet were royally entertained there with a grand naval ball, and there many of the debutantes of the season are given their 'coming out' reception. Frequently gymkhana races, horse races and field sports are held on the trim grounds. [32]

During the 1890s, Kebo Valley grounds were developed to include tennis courts, croquet lawns, a ball field and a golf course, as well as a race track where horses from the Pulitzer family competed for the coveted "cottager's cup" with those from the Sears and Van Nest families, among others.[33] In 1900, another cottager, Colonel Edward Morrell of Philadelphia, made a large sweep of his land available to the Horse Show and Fair Association. Catering to wealthy patrons, including so-called "robber barons" and their ilk, it was named (ironically) Robin Hood Park. For a dozen years it was the site of Bar Harbor's annual August horse show. (The park was situated about two miles due south of Bar Harbor's pier—where The Jackson Laboratory is today.)

The town continued to have horse shows for many years, long enough for John D. Rockefeller's youngest son David to ride his pony Sunset in the 1925 "fancy dress"

Kebo Valley Club, described in an 1890 guidebook as "the center of amusement for the fashionables." Established in 1889 at the foot of Kebo Mountain on the Eagle Lake road, Kebo featured a small theater and restaurant, along with croquet lawns, tennis courts, a ball field, and racetrack—plus a golf course (from 1892 onward). (Jesup Library Collection.)

competition. Dressed in Plains Indian regalia from head to toe, ten-year-old David won the event. The war bonnet that topped his outfit was given to his father during a visit to the Taos Pueblo Indian Reservation the previous summer. Having first visited Mount Desert as a college student in 1893 and renting the Sears' cottage in Bar Harbor after marrying and starting a family with Abby Aldrich, J.D.R. bought Eyrie Cottage in Seal Harbor and expanded it into a 100-room summer mansion. The family spent considerable time on the island in the summer season—but the children saw little of Bar Harbor. David recalled that as a teenager, he wasn't allowed to go to dances in Bar Harbor because his mother thought they were a bit too racy. [34]

It seems that from early on, it was apparent that Mount Desert Island's western and south shore villages— including Somesville, Southwest Harbor, Northeast Harbor, and Seal Harbor—would follow a different course of development than Bar Harbor. Generally speaking, these places drew a greater proportion of the cottagers

David Rockefeller, son of Seal Harbor "cottagers" Abby and J.D. Rockefeller, atop his pony Sunset in the fancy dress competition at the Bar Harbor horse show, 1925. Wearing Plains Indian regalia, including a headdress his father acquired out West, young David won first prize. (Photo by Laurance Rockefeller. Courtesy of the Rockefeller Archive Center.)

and visitors inclined toward nature and artistic or intellectual pursuits. A cottager in Northeast Harbor described it like this in 1905: "There were certain difficulties and disadvantages to the remoteness of the place, but on the whole the life of constant contact with nature, untouched and unspoiled, in this marvelous atmosphere and the relations established with the people who lived here, more than compensated for whatever privations one had to bear." Continuing, he quoted another summer resident, Johns Hopkins University president Daniel Gilman, who said that three things always came to mind when he thought about Northeast Harbor: "the air that he breathed, the views that he looked at, and the people that he met", and, he added, in his gracious way, "whichever way I put them they make an ascending climax." [35]

Canoe Club

One of the most cherished clubs at Mount Desert Island was the Canoe Club based in Bar Harbor, at one point boasting more than 300 members. While newspapers wrote about "cooing, wooing, and canoeing" and guidebooks described the sport as a "favorite amusement," club members were

Rusticators canoeing in Frenchman Bay, 1886. Original drawing by Charles S. Reinhart. Engraved for *Harper's New Monthly Magazine,* Vol. 73, No.435, p.419 (Courtesy of *Harper's Magazine.*)

serious about mastering the "fine art of paddling." Most aspired to having their own Indian-made paddle and birchbark canoe, and many turned to proven experts from the Indian encampment for instruction. Frank "Chief Big Thunder" Loring and his tall and handsome son Mitchell were especially in demand. After all, in addition to being terrific canoeists, they also spoke fluent English and Loring Sr., in particular, could make any canoeing adventure fun. Members socialized regularly at the canoe clubhouse on Bar Island and made every effort to be present for the club's two major events—the annual canoe parade and races. Both occasions were always chronicled in the local paper, and news about the parade was often reprinted in other papers, such as this excerpt from the *New York Times,* 27 August 1883:

> Friday afternoon the annual flower parade of the Canoe Club took place, and, though the skies were lowering, the rain held off. Every invitation was accepted, and at least 300 persons sailed over to Bar Island to watch the gay flotilla round the points. Each of the fifteen or twenty birch-bark boats was trimmed with flowers—some in green, pink, yellow, blue . . . and as they glided over the water and then moored in front of the clubhouse, the sight was an exceedingly pretty one. Philip Livingston [prominent from New York's old wealth], as Commodore of the club, accompanied by his wife, led off in a canoe decked with ferns and sweet peas. There were the usual dancing and light refreshments in the clubhouse, and just before the dinner hour of Bar Harbor, 6 p.m., the show was over.

The Canoe Club was so popular with the upper crust that one of Bar Harbor's more artful summer people included it in the first act of his humorous opera, "The Professor's Daughter," intended for the 1898 World's Fair in Omaha:

Dr. O. Preston Sweet, of Boston, the author and composer, has been in Bar Harbor this week. The object of his visit was the location of certain scenes for an opera which he has written, which is entitled "Bar Harbor, or the Professor's Daughter." Dr. Sweet has been engaged in writing the opera for a long time and it has been lately finished with the exception of a few minor things as to scenery, etc., which he is now at work on. The opera is a work of American art. It is purely American. The first and third scenes are laid at Bar Harbor and the second at Bowdoin College at Brunswick.

The first act will open with a regatta between the Mount Desert Canoe Club and a club from abroad. The scenery will allow a general outline of the village and will be recognized by all who have ever visited this beautiful spot. . . . It will take some 60 people to produce the opera. The libretto is exceedingly funny and the music is said to be entrancing. [36]

Playing Indian: Improving on the Red Man

Plays, lectures, concerts, and exhibitions were part of the entertainment fare all across Mount Desert Island—and much of this could be provided by the numerous poets, authors, scholars, and musicians counted among the cottagers and their guests. Also, Bar Harbor's local amateur theater group gave plays at Kebo Valley Club and some of the Wabanakis at the Indian encampment were experienced performers and musicians. Among those who presented plays, lectures, concerts and exhibitions at Kebo Valley and other Bar Harbor venues was Frank "Chief Big Thunder" Loring, well-known all across New England for his "Indian entertainments," which included 'primitive' dancing and storytelling as part of an "exemplification of Indian customs and relics." [37]

Beyond stage performances, Loring and other Indians from the Bar Harbor encampment were commonly called upon to enhance events and celebrations in the town. For example, the *Bar Harbor Record* announced on 24 June 1896, "A week from tomorrow begins the most important event in the life of Eden and Bar Harbor—the centennial. . . . Mr. Fennelly, the chairman, is rapidly completing the make-up of the procession. One of the features will be Queen Francis of the Passamaquoddy tribe and several Indians in their original costumes."

By the turn of the century, the American public expected spectacular "Wild West Shows" with recently captured tribal horsemen from the Great Plains. For regional Indian entertainers like Loring and his troupe, it became more challenging to attract a paying public. Having become quite famous as Chief Big Thunder, Loring was now in his early seventies and was ready to pack it in as a traveling showman. How could he possibly match the untrammeled fantasies of American popular culture and put up with seeing white patriots seriously playing red warriors?

Looking historically at Indian-white relations, we see a turn toward the bizarre at Mount Desert Island in 1900. Although all across the United States it had become quite common for white children and even adults to "play Indian," this was the year when Bar Harbor saw its social life enriched with the founding of its own "tribe" (chapter) of the "Improved Order of Red Men Society." (No doubt, some of its members had been active in the Bar Harbor Improvement Society.) A national patriotic organization, which restricted membership to white Protestant males in good social standing, the "Red Men Society" had been founded in the 1830s. As the oldest

"Playing Indian." Cousins Peggy Hoe, Susan Herter, and Theodora Dunham hold Edward Dunham Jr. hostage by their play tent, set up shoreside at Seal Harbor, ca. 1905. Theodora and Edward were the children of New York University professor of pathology Edward Kellogg Dunham and his wife Mary Dows, a wealthy heiress to one of the largest grain dealers in the country. They built their cottage, Keewaydin, overlooking the Seal Harbor steamboat landing in 1898. (Courtesy of Lydia Vandenberg.)

of various patriotic societies in the country, it was also the most widespread, especially in the eastern states. The Bar Harbor chapter, number 86 among the 116 groups ultimately established in Maine, took its name from one of the five so-called "civilized" tribes—the Cherokee. One cannot help wondering what the Penobscot and Passamaquoddy Indians, almost all of whom were Roman Catholics in addition to belonging to authentic tribes, actually thought when they found out that their esteemed white Protestant "brothers" had become "Cherokee." Surely, Big Thunder and his "unimproved" Wabanaki Indian friends must have thought it was a big joke. A commentary about the organization, written in 1928 when "tribes" were still active, offers a window on the nationalism at the heart of it:

One of the largest fraternal societies and the oldest and largest strictly American fraternity is the Improved Order of Red Men. . . . The earlier patriots, who founded the Old Sons of Liberty in Colonial times, never knew what real American liberty was, they having lived under kings all their lives, and having no vote or voice in some of the most important matters pertaining to their own government. Their first vision of real freedom was caught from the wild [Indians], who roamed the forests at will rejoicing in the unrestrained occupation of this great new world; who selected their own sachems and forms of religious worship; and who made their own laws and tribal regulations, which were few and simple . . . while the white men, who came here, were continually followed up and hampered by unreasonable laws and regulations, imposed by a distant king and his local appointees . . . and were burdened by unjust taxes. They began to chafe under their thralldom, which finally resulted in the "Boston Tea Party," the Declaration of Independence, and the War of the Revolution.

The order was first introduced into the State of Maine by the institution of Squando Tribe, No. 1, at Biddeford, November 6, 1875. This tribe and others instituted prior to 1888 were placed under the jurisdiction of the Great Council of New Hampshire. On October 25, 1888, the Great Council of Maine was instituted in the city of Bath. . . . At that time there were nine tribes in the Reservation of Maine: Rockmego, No. 2, Auburn; Machigonne, No. 3, Portland; Nahanda, No. 4, Rockland; Cogawesco, No. 5, Portland; Abenakis, No. 6, Bangor; Mecadecut, No. 7, Rockport; Segochet, No. 8, Warren; Pokumkeswawaumokesis, No. 9, Lewiston; Mavooshan, No. 10, Pemaquid. These tribes had a combined membership of 698.

The cardinal principles of the order are Freedom, Friendship, and Charity. One of the greatest works of charity done by the order is the care of indigent orphan children in private homes. The order is now caring for some 3143 orphans annually. . . .

The word 'Redmanship' means

"Red Men" patriot poster, ca. 1890. In 1900 Bar Harbor established its chapter of the nationwide Improved Order of Red Men Society—a patriotic organization open only to white, Protestant American males in good social standing. (Authors' collection.)

Americanism. The history of the Improved Order of Red Men is coincident with that of the United States of America. It is a purely pure American organization. *To become a member of the Improved Order of Red Men, one must be a white American citizen.* [38]

So it was that white Protestant patriots, seeking to express their American nationalism through a largely imaginary "Native" cultural repertoire, invented traditions they considered representative of "the sublimity and grandeur of the unsullied characteristics of the primitive race." Conforming to the "Indian" character of their clubs, called "tribes," they ranked their officers as sachems, sagamores, and braves, and gathered around a "council fire" kindled in the center of their "wigwam." They also donned quasi (Plains) Indian costumes and used Indian calumets (pipes) and other "paraphernalia" in their meetings. Notably, all documents of the Order were dated from the year of the "discovery" of America by Columbus (G.S.D. = Grand Sun of the Discovery). [39] Thus, the founding date of Bar Harbor's Cherokee Tribe was G.S.D.408. It was all indicative of a profound ambivalent racism of which they themselves were hardly aware, if at all.

Ultimately, membership in Bar Harbor's "Cherokee tribe" grew to 131. Among other branches in the Mount Desert Island area was the "Eggemoggin Tribe, No. 11, Imperial Order of the Red Men." The *Mount Desert Herald* reported on the latter's inaugural meeting, held November 15, 1888 at Green's Landing (Stonington, Deer Isle). According to the paper, members of the new group—"composed of the most prominent businessmen of the place"—had elected a grand sachem (along with senior and junior sagamores, a prophet, chief of records, keeper of wampum, first sanup, guard of wigwam, guard of forest and warriors) and ordered "first-class paraphernalia." Also, noted the paper, "A Council of Pocahontas [for white women] will be organized in about three weeks." [40]

While America's indigenous peoples were expected to disappear, if not biologically then at least culturally, the invented Indian of the white man's imagination was becoming an omnipresent fetish of American popular culture, appearing in a growing array of forms—from "improved" Red Men societies to postcards to advertising logos. In time, the list would grow to include everything from sports-team mascots to the names of fighter planes. As noted in the *Portland Tribune* in 1844: "We are more in love with Indian names in this country than we are with the Indians themselves, and often having despoiled them of their lands, their lakes and territories, the sentimentalists are very desirous of complimenting them by restoring aboriginal titles." [41]

From Terrestial to Eternal Paradise

With all the laughter, leisure, and luxury on Mount Desert Island, we can easily forget the suffering and sweat of its working poor—cooks, carpenters, masons, chimneysweeps, gardeners, stable boys, deckhands, machinists, laundrymen and women, and, last but not least, maids. Bar Harbor's construction boom attracted thousands of skilled and unskilled day laborers, both men and women, many of whom had worked since childhood. Among the multitude of largely undocumented workers were Irish, Italian, German, and French-Canadian immigrants who, unlike most of their wealthy employers, were Roman Catholics.

During the colonial period, New England's Protestant authorities forbade the practice of Catholicism
within their jurisdictions. That posed a problem for the
Wabanaki, who, as French trading partners and military
allies during the colonial era, had become Catholics. For
about half a century after the American Revolution, the
Penobscot and Passamaquoddy were without missionaries. Not until the 1830s were their reservation villages
finally served by Catholic priests, who were also needed

Wabanaki Indians and Catholic
Church officials standing in front
of Bar Harbor's Holy Redeemer
Church during the August 1913
celebration marking the 300th
anniversary of the founding of the
St. Sauveur Jesuit mission at Fernald
Point on Mount Desert Island.
(Courtesy of Our Holy Redeemer
Catholic Church, Bar Harbor.)

by the rapidly growing number of Catholic immigrants pouring in from Europe and Quebec—
cheap labor for the expanding lumber companies, sawmills, textile factories, railway companies,
granite quarries, and other businesses.

While Protestants on Mount Desert Island had few churches to choose from before 1875,
Roman Catholics had to go all the way to Ellsworth on the mainland for mass—except on rare
occasions when a priest from the Passamaquoddy reservation visited the Indian encampment.
The need to accommodate the growing number of Catholics on the island presented an opportunity for the Maine Diocese based in Portland to expand its religious footprint. Bishop James
Haley, who headed the Diocese, was the son of an Irish Catholic soldier and a mulatto slave in
Georgia. Setting his sights on the priesthood, he studied at a seminary in Paris and went on to
be ordained as a priest at Notre Dame Cathedral before coming to head the Maine Diocese in
1875. With this background, he was well aware of the historic significance of Mount Desert Island
as the chosen place where French Jesuits had planned a Catholic mission well before English

Protestants first arrived on the *Mayflower*. So, he ordered the building of a wooden chapel in Bar Harbor, dedicated to St. Sylvia and beautifully situated on Malden Hill at the base of Green (Cadillac) Mountain, overlooking Frenchman Bay.

Bishop Haley appointed Father James Madan, recently emigrated from England, as St. Sylvia's first priest. One reminiscence, describing Madan as "a true priest, absolutely devoted to his calling, and entirely self-sacrificing," mentions his occasional walks to Bar Harbor's Indian encampment, noting one incident in particular: "I remember a poor Indian woman who had just undergone a severe surgical operation, the result of which was more than doubtful. [Father Madan] prepared her for death, if it should come, and then sat by her side the entire night, never leaving her until the hour arrived for early Mass." In autumn 1881 Father Madan returned to England and later sailed for New Zealand, where he became a missionary to its indigenous Maori. [42]

Other Catholic priests succeeded Father Madan at St. Sylvia and the little church flourished. Many Wabanaki Indians attended. The following scene, described in 1886, must have been a common one during Bar Harbor's summer months, especially on Sunday mornings: "I remember we met an Indian maiden once upon her way home from mass, and, in her fashionably-made polonaise of ruby velvet, and Gainsboro's hat and plumages, she looked like a bird-of-paradise in a barn-yard, beside the island girls." [43]

After two decades, the number of Roman Catholics on the island outgrew the chapel. In 1907, it was razed and replaced by a much larger granite building on the corner of Ledgelawn and Mt. Desert streets. Staking out deep historical claims, the diocese decided to drop St. Sylvia and dedicate the new church to the Holy Redeemer (St. Sauveur), in lasting memory to Maine's first Catholic mission, established by French Jesuits at Fernald Point in 1613. In the summer of 1913, the 300th anniversary of the short-lived mission, the Diocese of Portland saw fit to celebrate this significant moment in the Church's Maine history. Several bishops were invited, as well as other dignitaries, including Cardinal Bonzano, the Papal delegate of the Holy See of Rome:

> The Maine Central Railroad furnished a special car for the party from Portland and the steamship *Norumbega* carried the group across Frenchman's Bay from Mount Desert ferry to Bar Harbor. The party arrived in Bar Harbor on Tuesday evening, August 5, and was received by the Rev. Fr. O'Brien, pastor of Bar Harbor, and General Edward deV.Morrell. Gen. Morrell was host to the Papal delegate and bishops attending. . . . At 10:30 a.m., the procession began, led by the crucifix; the candles were borne by priests on each side of the cross. Penobscot Indians, descendants of those who had first greeted Catholic settlers at St. Sauveur, next came in line wearing brightly colored festive costumes with feathers and medals of ornament.
>
> The sanctuary choir boys of the Cathedral of the Immaculate Conception at Portland sang during the dedication and Mass. After them, came the priests, more than 80 in number, from all parts of Maine and others from each New England State, Pennsylvania and Maryland. The streets near the church were crowded during the ceremony. . . . Following the dedication of the Holy Redeemer church, the personal representative of the Pope St. Pius X, John Cardinal Bonzano, was escorted to the church.

The choir sent forth the hymn "Unfold Ye Portals" as the Most Reverend Papal Delegate and the bishops entered. . . . At the close of the Mass, His Excellency bestowed the special papal blessing upon all the faithful present.

Two days later . . . [a] pilgrimage was organized and went by the Norumbega [steamboat] to the site of the first St. Sauveur mission near . . . Fernald's Point. . . . [There,] the bishop and all the company said the Our Father, the Hail Mary and Glory be to the Father. The priests in turn chanted the psalms and hymns of devotion to make the same hills resound with the identical sounds of the Jesuit fathers and the Indians who had chanted the Mass and Vespers there 300 years before. [44]

As a ceremonial performance in a most idyllic natural theater, this carefully orchestrated religious pilgrimage to the ancient site of St. Sauveur on the shore of Somes Sound was a resounding success—especially in the eyes of devoted Roman Catholics. Excluded from the Red Men Society and thus unable to show their patriotism by "playing Indian," they demonstrated that their church was older and therefore more American than Protestantism in the United States. Their inclusion of Wabanakis, in memory of the first Maine Indians to be converted to Christianity, underscored their argument. Whether this impressed any of the island's white Protestant rusticators is another story. And we can only guess what the Wabanaki thought about these competing white historical narratives, if they cared at all.

Going Home

Each year, come mid-September, New England newspapers typically ran headlines announcing, "Bar Harbor Summer Sojourners Going Home." The articles under such headings made a point of noting the departure and destination of each well-heeled cottager. As for Wabanakis, after a season of providing services and entertainment for summer tourists and cottagers, most went back to their reservations. Often, their hometown papers noted their return, as in this 1890 *Eastport Sentinel* newsclip:

Quite a delegation of returning summer visitors arrived from Bar Harbor by the Winthrop boat Monday; women of quiet, modest demeanor with touches of fashion about their traveling outfit, and sturdy looking men. . . . No member of the patrician families at Mount Desert Island could boast of purer American blood than they, and they enjoy an unusual advantage for visitors at a pleasure resort in bringing back more money than they carried away. Friends were on the wharf to meet them. . . . Doubtless, at their homes on Pleasant Point the events of the summer will be talked over in their own quiet way and plans made for another season, much as they will be in stately houses on Beacon Street and Fifth Avenue. [45]

CHAPTER FIVE

Peddling and Porpoising:
Wabanaki Summer Resources

In the old days, the Indians were privileged by law to enter upon any individual's 'wild' territory, in any section of the state, and peel his bark, cut walking sticks or ash for baskets, or bows and arrows, unmolested. (Albert Higgins, The Bar Harbor Times, 20 June 1934)

Beyond proximity to marketing possibilities for their arts and crafts, Wabanakis sought coastal campsites that gave them access to fresh drinking and cooking water, dry firewood, and, ideally, a range of other natural resources used for food and craft production. While it is true they arrived at Mount Desert Island with wares ready-made for market, they also gathered raw materials in the area for crafts made of wood, plant fibers, furs, and feathers. The cash they earned from sales enabled them to buy a wide range of food, drink, and other goods, including luxury items, in the town shops.

Ash, Grass, and Water

Wabanaki dependence on natural resources in the Mount Desert neighborhood is evident in various historical descriptions, including those about the Indian encampment situated next to the Parker's home at Clark Point in Southwest Harbor, dating back at least to the 1840s.[1] In one local reminiscence, Jesse Parker noted that the Penobscot families who summered there gathered sweetgrass "from the marshes at Bass Harbor. . . . [and] also cut some ash wood for use in making the wooden baskets."

A similar account provided by Southwest Harbor historian Nellie Thornton in 1938 mentioned that the traditional Indian "right" to cut brown ash trees for sturdy woodsplint baskets, as well as to gather sweetgrass for fancy baskets and other weavings, was "vouchsafed by the owners of the land as it was an unwritten law that Indians could have an occasional tree to use in their work from the land that, not so long before, had belonged entirely to them."[2] For drinking, cooking, and washing water, they depended upon the Parkers' well. This is known thanks to P.G. Rhoads of Wilmington, Delaware, who, around 1925, purchased property from the Parkers, built a cottage on the campsite, and henceforth referred to it as "the Indian Lot." Eventually, Rhoads acquired two historic items linked to the place: a 19th-century map that shows the location of the encampment, and a large ash-wood splint basket, which he tagged as follows:

> Basket bought by P.G. Rhoads from Mrs. Jesse Parker, who told him it had been given to the Parkers by Indians camping on Indian Lot in gratitude for permission to get fresh water from the Parkers. Told in 1966. Obtained June 25, 1967.[3]

Mount Desert Island resident Larry Closson remembered that "Indians in the Southwest Harbor-Bass Harbor area used to collect sweetgrass in a place we called 'the marsh' behind [present-day] Gott's Construction, which is behind Gott's Store—on the left [east] about two miles along the coast from Southwest Harbor."[4] And, according to Frank Stanley, "If you walk down the road [in Southwest Harbor] in the summer at the right time, you can smell sweetgrass. I've never found it, but I smell it."[5]

Whatever Southwest Harbor had to offer in terms of sweetgrass, it is clear that Wabanakis felt it was well worth a trip to obtain the sweetgrass growing on the neighboring islands. For instance, recently deceased Penobscot tribal elder Theodore "Ted" Mitchell (1919–2009) recalled that his great-grandfather (Sabbatis "Joe" Mitchell, 1829–1893), along with his sister and her family, camped at Southwest Harbor and collected sweetgrass at nearby Cranberry Island:

> They stayed over in Southwest Harbor in the summers. . . . selling baskets and getting sweetgrass for winter basketmaking. . . . My great grandfather died on the beach at Northeast Harbor coming back from picking sweetgrass at Cranberry Island. . . . They used to go down to the coast every spring, passing through those treacherous waters by Deer Isle. They had sea canoes. They'd go to Vinalhaven [in Penobscot Bay] and other islands picking sweetgrass. They went there for fish and clams during wintertime. They would salt the fish and bring it home for winter. Sweetgrass-gathering trips for the basket business evolved out of shore food trips. [6]

Mitchell's grandson, John Bear Mitchell (1968–), echoed his grandfather's comments about basket-making materials, citing oral history passed down in the family:

> During the summer, or during the times when [my ancestors] were actually there, residing at Mount Desert, my grandfather told me that basically you only took [tools] that you needed to make the baskets. You never took your materials. They were all right there. And when you got there you collected your materials, and then you just sat down and you started making your baskets, and pounding your ash. . . . Not only selling the final basket was worth making money on, but people would come watch you prepare the stuff to make the baskets and they'd give you a little bit of change here and there or take pictures of you making the basket. You know, splitting

Wabanaki encampment next to the Parker home at Clark Point, Southwest Harbor, 1880s. The campsite was used at least from the 1840s until 1925. (Photographer unknown—copy by W.H. Ballard. No. 5289. The Southwest Harbor Public Library Collection.)

Clark Point, Southwest Harbor, 1880s. The Indian encampment of tents and wood shanties is among the trees, just above the bowsprit of the schooner *Palestine*. (Photographer unknown—copy by W.H. Ballard. No. 5525. The Southwest Harbor Public Library Collection.)

This detail of the lower left-hand photo on the opposite page zooms in on the Indian encampment above the schooner bowsprit. (Photographer unknown—copy by W.H. Ballard. No. 5876, fragment of No. 5525. The Southwest Harbor Public Library Collection of Photographs)

The Parker family at Clark Point gave Wabanakis camping near their home access to fresh water. Reciprocating the good will, the Indians presented this large woodsplint basket to the family. (Private collection. Photo courtesy of the Abbe Museum.)

Wabanaki children (with a tamed red fox!) at the Clark Point Indian encampment, 1880s. (Photograph by Henry L. Rand. No. 5527. The Southwest Harbor Public Library Collection of Photographs.)

the wood, carving the ash and whatnot. And if you look at [the timing of] it, sweetgrass-picking season is . . . the beginning of July, and most of the sales were done in July and August. That's when [tourists] come to Maine. That's the best time to come. So there was always a market for the process and the final product.[7]

Ralph Stanley, renowned boat builder, local historian, and lifelong resident of Southwest Harbor, offered this boyhood recollection of a Passamaquoddy man who lived and hunted in the area and sold crafts for a living: "There was an Indian, Mr. Francis, I remember as a boy. He lived up in the woods somewhere. I have a birchbark model canoe he made for my grandmother. He got my father to take him out to Cranberry Island to shoot seal. My father had a sealskin belt he made. There are still descendants of the Francis family in Bass Harbor."[8]

Similarly, locals in Northeast Harbor and Bar Harbor have shared recollections of Passamaquoddy John Snow (1869–1937), who lived in both towns. Snow sold sweetgrass and woodsplint baskets all around Mount Desert Island, and according to numerous accounts, gathered sweetgrass for the work on Little Cranberry Island. (Snow is profiled in Chapter 9.) While Snow is still remembered by name, many other unidentified Wabanakis also gathered sweetgrass on Little Cranberry:

> Francis Fernald remembered that in the 1930s two or three [canoe] loads of Penobscots and, separately, Passamaquoddies, came to Little Cranberry each summer. 'They landed near the Marsh and collected sweetgrass there. Usually they slept on the shore beneath their canoes.' . . . [and] Lawrence Beal told of entering the Coast Guard's key post on Marsh Head [northeast end of Little Cranberry] only to find it filled with sleeping Indians.[9]

In Bar Harbor, the first historically described Wabanaki encampment linked to selling crafts to tourists was established in the early 1860s at the northeast end of the emerging town, between Birch Point and Newport House hotel. Albert Higgins, a lifelong Bar Harbor resident, recalled this campsite and others in his wonderfully detailed article "Good Old Days," written as an old man for the June 20, 1934 issue of *The Bar Harbor Times*. Beyond identifying the shifting locations of the Bar Harbor encampment, Higgins tells of Indians tapping into local resources—collecting natural materials for their crafts and hunting for porpoises:

> In the olden days, or from about 1860 to 1900, I well remember that in the early Spring, Indian encampments or 'villages' were the order of things in Bar Harbor, and indeed, when we saw the first of their little [canvas] tents being set up, and the hunters racing in the [Frenchman] Bay for porpoises, we were sure that the 'season' had really begun. The very first of these 'villages' that I recollect, was at the Newport [Cove] beach. They caught porpoises in their canoes, by shooting and harpooning, and then extracted the oil by some 'trying out' process, on a vacant isolated shore. These harmless people would gather here from Old Town and meet the Passamaquoddies from Pleasant Point near Eastport, by the hundreds. . . . I have seen hundreds, in former days,

of their tents at the lower part of Albert Meadow, at the point near the coal landing, the Athletic Field, West street, near Uncle Jake's Creek, and on Eden street, near Duck Brook. They had an aptitude for sitting on the grassy skin-covered floor of their little white cloth tents, and making all sorts of 'trinkets' to sell to the people who were wont to visit them. They always whittled with their sharp knives toward themselves, and would soon have an interesting supply of such articles to display, or carry about house to house, as canes, toy birch canoes, match safes, comb cases, bows and arrows, snow shoes and many other products of their ingenuity, and at one time their brightly finished walking sticks, with a ring neatly woven in at the top end, was very popular with summer tourists. They would always bring along a goodly stock of moccasions [sic] for ladies, children and gents, together with mits and gloves which they had made from skins of seal, otter, raccoon and other animals while at home through the long cold winter. Occasionally, these people would acquire a hall in town, if there was one, and give an interesting exhibition of war dances or 'pow wows' in language which was principally their own. However, the Penobscots and the Passamaquoddys were always very friendly, although of a different dialect. 'Joe' Lola was chief of the Eastport [Pleasant Point] Indians, and 'Big Thunder' that of those [Penobscots] from Old Town. Mary Dana, wife of Tomah Dana, and a sister of [Passamaquoddy] Chief Joseph Lola, lived to be very very old. In those days, the Indians were privileged by law to enter upon any individual's 'wild' territory, in any section of the state, and peel his bark, cut walking sticks or ash [trees] for baskets, or bows and arrows, unmolested. [10]

Brown ash trees (*Fraxinus nigra*) used to make woodsplint baskets could be found along low-lying streambeds and marshy areas within and beyond Bar Harbor. A 19th-century author writing about Wabanakis who camped on the edge of the village around 1890 likened them to wandering Gypsies (a comparison frequently made by white settlers since the 17th century), and had this to say about their harvesting of local materials to make baskets: "These gypsies are everywhere allowed to hew and hack the woods unchallenged. You can hardly turn off the road to the right or left without seeing some noble birch stripped of its bark to make knickknacks. . . . You meet them slinking about after nightfall with loads of basket-stuff on their shoulders. Their fathers knew how to split skulls; these fellows know how to split basket-stuff." To this derogative, yet informative, commentary, he added a brief note about natural dyes: "Apropos of basket-making, the Indians possess the secret of dyeing wood to a degree of perfection not yet attained by our most skillful workmen, though it is believed that the former make use of vegetable substances only. . . ." [11]

According to Mount Desert Island resident Innes MacPike, who was born in Northeast Harbor in 1905 and lived in Bar Harbor from 1918 onward, Passamaquoddy Frank Lewey (born in 1862) resided year-round in the Bar Harbor area and "traveled all around the bay with a canoe gathering sweetgrass to make his baskets."[12] Similarly, speaking of his parents' and grandparents' use of basket-making resources in the Bar Harbor area, Passamaquoddy tribal leader John Stevens of Indian Township commented: "They used to talk about the beautiful ash that grows around there and sweetgrass."[13]

Indian encampment at the foot of Bar (Bridge) Street on Bar Harbor's northern shore, ca. 1880, by Kilburn. From here, Wabanakis set out in their canoes to hunt porpoises in Frenchman Bay, as recalled by life-long Bar Harbor resident Albert Higgins. (Collection of the Maine Historic Preservation Commission.)

Frank Lewey and Stevens' ancestors probably ventured across Frenchman Bay to nearby Hancock Point, given this recollection by Lois Crabtree Johnson (1933–) of the Hancock Historical Society:

My mother (Lura Young) was born in 1892. She told of Indians coming to her family home [on Crabtree Neck near Hancock Point] every summer during her childhood [late 1800s-early 1900s] to get permission from her father to cut sweetgrass. They came by canoe up the Skillings River. (This I can swear, for my mother never told a lie or embroidered the truth. . . .) The house was on Crabtree Neck on the West Side Road (now known as Point Road) about 4.75 miles from Hancock Point. It's part of an area that since the late 1700s or so was called "Sweetland." No one has been able to figure out why it was called that, but it recently dawned on me that a likely reason is that it is where Indians came for sweetgrass. My great-great-grandfather Calvin Berry bought the land ca 1840 from heirs of my great-great-great-grandfather Stephen Merchant and it stayed in the family until recently. [14]

Other Wabanaki basketmakers who came seasonally to Mount Desert Island gathered sweetgrass in the Pretty Marsh area on the west side of the island. And, according to at least one reminiscence, they also set up camp there:

> Native Americans gathered sweetgrass from the marshy areas in Pretty Marsh, and other areas, with which to weave baskets for their own use and, in the late nineteenth and early twentieth centuries, to sell to local folk and summer visitors. Josephine (Gray) Doe [born circa 1900] remembers three Indian families who came to the meadow behind her house [between Round Pond and Squid Cove, by Indian Point Road] when she was a child, arriving with loud whoops and hollers. They set up their wigwams and went about their business of gathering, but felt free to enter the Gray's house to help themselves to pie or stew left by Josephine's mother—usually on purpose. [15]

Historic records show that Wabanakis continued to hunt deer and other wild game on Mount Desert Island at least until the end of the 19th century. By then, Maine state laws had imposed new restrictions, as documented in the following notices:

> Deer are still found in the mountains [of Mount Desert Island]. Last summer a Harvard student found a pair of antlers on Pemetic [Mountain].… Oldtown [Penobscot] Indians resort here every season to hunt them, in connection with the otter, fox, wild-cat, muskrat and mink. The law allows the deer to be hunted for three months, ending with the fifteenth of December. [16]

> Deer still roam the forests, and the Oldtown Indians come in the fall to hunt them in the three months' time allowed by law. [17]

> The Fish and Game Laws of Maine state the following laws now enforced. . . . Act for the protection of deer on the island of Mt. Desert. No person, except during… November and December, shall… hunt or kill any deer.… Indians are liable to the foregoing penalties the same as any other person. [18]

> The board of Fish and Game commissioners… decided… to prohibit… the taking of deer on Mount Desert Island for periods of four years. [19]

Fish, Fowl, and Sea Mammals

Following age-old traditions, Wabanakis also fished while encamped at Bar Harbor, setting weirs near the long sand bar, as well as line fishing from the piers and spear fishing in the shallows. This was still the case in the mid-1880s, according to this excerpt from an 1884 newspaper article: "Every Summer [Wabanakis] come to Bar Harbor in numbers of about one hundred and fifty.… Between peddling, swapping and fishing, they seem to get along first-rate." [20]

As Higgins recalled in his article, Wabanakis who camped on the island also hunted porpoise—a recollection corroborated by many others. For example, in 1875 the state-appointed

Passamaquoddy hunters shooting and spearing porpoises. These two drawings by M.J. Burns appeared with seven other engravings in an 11-page article, "Porpoise Shooting," *Scribner's Magazine*, 6 October 1880. (Authors' collection.)

Indian agent for the Passamaquoddy tribe noted in his annual report: "About 20 families are at Bar Harbor, selling their wares and catching porpoises." They pursued porpoises for food and, more importantly, for saleable oil used to fuel lighthouses and lubricate clocks and watches. It took considerable skill and experience to shoot and harpoon these small swift whales that measure up to six feet in length and can weigh more than 150 pounds.

Commentaries about Wabanakis camping, fishing, and hunting at other islands and mainland shores in the Mount Desert Island area include B.F. DeCosta's 1871 *Rambles on Mount Desert*, which places Indians at Mount Desert, Ironbound Island (in Frenchman Bay just east of Bar Harbor), and Grand Manan Island (a large Canadian island in the Bay of Fundy some twenty miles from the Passamaquoddy reservation at Pleasant Point). This brief excerpt from DeCosta's detailed descriptions tells of Wabanakis fishing and hunting, as well as making baskets and canoes for sale:

> At Mount Desert they occasionally find a good-sized shark or horse mackerel, but oftener the porpoise thus comes into the weir. Schools of these continually gambol about the bay for the edification of visitors, or as a prize for the Indians who hunt them for oil. I started once across Frenchman's Bay for their camp on Iron-bound Island to see them at home, paddling with an old trapper in his bark canoe; but when we got halfway over, a hard rain-storm set in, and we thought it best to return at once. Still the trip afforded an opportunity of testing the qualities of the 'bark' on the long ocean swell. No boat could have behaved more admirably. . . .

[Later,] we stepped upon the smooth shore of Indian Beach [on Grand Manan]. Here are the lodges of the Indians, built chiefly of bark, and kept in place by large stones laid on the roofs and against the sides. It was a windy afternoon and unfit for porpoise hunting. . . . At all seasons of the year the people are more or less scattered, being engaged in hunting, fishing and basket-making. . . . Here on the beach we found quite a colony. A part of them spoke English. Their canoes, finely built, and worth from 25 to 50 dollars apiece, were drawn up in a row on the sand. Some of the men were trying out porpoise oil, and others were making or repairing the various implements of their craft; while several children were playing with dogs. . . . I made inquiries about the porpoises and the mode of catching them. . . . Their custom is to shoot them with a rifle, and, before they have time to sink, paddle up and make fast with a lance, when the creature is dead taking him into the canoe. I afterwards saw them at their work. One Indian sat at the stern of the canoe, using his paddle as easily as a fish does his fins, and another, rifle in hand, stood at the bow. [21]

Among various descriptions of the derring-do that porpoise-hunting required, is this one, excerpted from Alexander Leighton's "The Twilight of the Indian Porpoise Hunters":

They set forth on the rising tide and met the porpoises coming in toward the rivers and estuaries in pursuit of herring and mackerel. As soon as a porpoise rose close enough, he was shot and then transfixed with the spear before he could escape or sink. The spear was never thrown, but held by the bow man, who rode his canoe like a horse and used the spear like a boar hunter. In a rough sea with a wild porpoise, both bow and stern man had to fight hard to keep the canoe right side up. To capsize miles from land, in [these waters] would have been fatal. When the porpoise was dead, he was pulled in over the side by the Indian at the stern—another difficult job, even in calm weather. [22]

Passamaquoddies beside porpoise skins and blubber that have been hung out to dry, Grand Manan Island, 1908. After drying, the blubber was boiled into oil and put into kegs. (Courtesy of Donald Soctomah.)

"Trying" (extracting) porpoise oil by boiling the blubber, 1880. Porpoise oil was in great demand in the 19th and early 20th centuries, especially to fuel lighthouses and lubricate clockworks. This drawing by M.J. Burns appeared with eight other engravings in an 11-page article, "Porpoise Shooting," *Scribner's Magazine*, 6 October 1880. (*Natural History*, June 1937; copyright © *Natural History Magazine*, Inc. 1937.)

Another description of Wabanakis camping, fishing, and peddling baskets in the Mount Desert neighborhood tells of a party of eleven Passamaquoddy tribesmen from Pleasant Point encamped on Saddleback Island between Deer Isle and Isle au Haut in Penobscot Bay during the late 1890s. The reference is particularly interesting because some of the individuals named also camped at Mount Desert Island:

> Saddleback Island is at present the home of quite a colony of Indians… from that highly civilized and cultivated band known as the Pleasant Point Tribe, residing in the vicinity of Eastport. They make daily trips to Stonington [Deer Isle] and their handiwork is being well exemplified by a number of rustic and ornamental chairs, settees, etc., purchased from them by many of our citizens.… They are devoting their time chiefly to the securing of gulls' breasts and such trophies and specimens as will turn over a dollar or two from some of the summer visitors who will be swarming along our romantic shores very soon.…The camp affords a very pretty scene with its unique combination of canvas and verdant canopy secluded among the rocky promontories of the island. There are four canoes each with a crew of two or three braves made up as follows. Joseph L. Dana, Gov.-in-chief of the Pleasant Point tribe, with his son Lolar Dana and a partner, Daniel Secovy; 2nd canoe, Sabbatis and Swissin Lolar, brothers with William Toma; 3rd canoe, Joe Soccabasi and Frank Francis; 4th canoe, Tom Pollis and Tom Loring. They are all genial and jolly fellows, and most of them speak English very fluently. [23]

Except for William Toma, the tribesmen mentioned in the Saddleback account appeared on the 1900 Federal census for Perry/Pleasant Point, ranging in age from 17 to 47. Focused on selling white tern and seagull breasts and rustic furniture at nearby Stonington, Deer Isle, it is likely that all of these tribesmen had many other skills. Surely, like most Wabanaki men of the day, all of them engaged in a variety of livelihoods beyond the single occupation each listed on the census, which ranged from "hunter," "basketmaker" and "picture-frame maker" to "Tribe governor" and "Tribe sheriff." [24] As for hunting and selling terns and gulls for their white plumage, the market value for the feather breasts the men secured on Saddleback Island was just peaking at this time, as evident in these citations referring to the ladies hat-maker industry:

> In 1899 a New York millinery dealer furnished Eastern Maine's Passamaquoddy Indians with guns and ammunition to kill gulls of all kinds. The dealers paid 40 cents each for adults, 20 cents for the brown immature gulls.… It is estimated that 5,000,000 gulls were killed each year for the millinery trade. [25]

> Frank Chapman, distinguished ornithologist, conducted a survey during two afternoon walks through the streets of New York. 542 heads out of a total of 700 had been decorated with feathered hats from 20-odd species, including terns, owls, herons, etc. [26]

> Sea gull breasts and wings are now in great demand by western buyers and the poor old fowl

now enjoys only little peace and quiet. The Indians are constantly on its tracks, and dozens upon dozens are shot each week. The breasts and wings, when cured, bring in a price of $3.50 to $6 a dozen." [27]

The price of gull wings and breasts has been steadily declining in the western market and now the business of shooting them is less productive. Now they hardly pay for the powder and shot, and the Indians do not spend the time to hunt them anymore because they are not worth anything. The seagull in the last few months was a fad of style. Now it is less of a fad. [28]

Notably, hunting gulls and terns for feather sales was hardly a new occupation. Records show that Wabanakis in the Penobscot Bay area began selling down and other feathers to European traders in the early 1700s. And they continued to do so nearly to the end of the 19th century. Residents on Isle au Haut in the latter 1800s also recalled that a "whole crowd of Indians," including Frank "Chief Big Thunder" Loring, used to come down to Isle au Haut from Old town in the summer to "kill the gulls for the feathers. . . . The government came in and put in a law to stop it. That hurt the Indians. It was a big business for them. . . . Those Old Town fellows were good guys. They used to ship those feathers to New York to trim hats. The feathers were as white as chalk. . . . Indians still came down after they couldn't shoot the gulls; they came to get porpoises for the oil." [29]

Wabanakis resisted gull-hunting restrictions, sometimes formally through government channels. Among those to do so was Louis Mitchell, who served several years as tribal representative to the Maine State legislature. As reported in one Maine newspaper, during one sojourn in the state capital, this Passamaquoddy leader left no doubt about his convictions that Indians should be "exempted from the operation of seagull laws," declaring that "his people are recognized and protected in their hunting, fishing, and fowling privileges by many different treaties between 1693 and 1777, which he believes to be properly in force at the present time. [30]

Folks on Eagle Island, just west of Deer Isle, had similar recollections of "small bands" of Passamaquoddies and Penobscots (including Frank "Chief Big Thunder" Loring) camping on their island in the 1880s and 1890s while "gathering shellfish, collecting gull's eggs, and obtaining sweetgrass from which to make baskets." Also according to the island's oral history, the Indians harpooned seals that "basked on the rocky shore or nearby ledges" and "at times also killed porpoises." [31]

Wabanakis also camped right on Mount Desert Island when hunting gulls, terns, and other seabirds for their feathers. In the Old Town paper, a June 1889 news item by Penobscot leader Joseph Nicolar about two fellow tribesmen announced: "Last Saturday John Bear [Mitchell] and Peal Sockose [Saukis] came home from Ar-bes-son-nuck, 'Mt. Desert,' with one hundred sea gulls as the result of a four weeks hunt." [32]

One can hardly overstate how important such seasonal coastal expeditions were for the emotional and financial well-being of Maine Indians bewildered and diminished

Passamaquoddy Horace Nicholas (born in 1866)—craftsman, guide, showman —and his hand-crafted rustic furniture, circa 1900, and Stonington, Deer Isle, resident Dorothy Sylvester, sitting on a rustic settee made by Indians on Saddleback Island in 1898. (Courtesy of Donald Soctomah; courtesy of Neva Beck.)

by the brave new world forced upon them—and pressing in upon them. Moving in sync with nature's seasonal rhythm offered a sense of the familiar in what was becoming an alien environment. One writer long acquainted with Wabanakis explained how the market demand for porpoise oil made it possible for hunting to remain part of their way of life and thereby allowed them to retain some of the sanity and equilibrium that tradition affords. As he put it, porpoise hunting helped a Wabanaki to

> possess his own soul and live pleasantly near European settlers. When the woods became pastures, when the salmon rivers spun saws, [Wabanakis] went out on the sea where there were no fences, axes or plows. They hunted porpoises and made oil which they sold to the white man to use in mowers, wagons, mills, and the unwanted hunting gypsy found a valued place for himself, profiting by the very machinery that had driven him and his game from the woods. [33]

Advertisement for ladies' feathered hats, 1896. With the enormous demand for bird plumage among hatmakers in the late 1800s, hunting gulls and other seabords for their feathers played an important part in Wabanaki livelihoods of the day. (The Delineator – specific date not known. Photo courtesy of the Abbe Museum.)

The Delineator. Autumn Millinery. November 1896.

CHAPTER SIX

Fancy Baskets and Toy Canoes at Tent No. 3: Selling Crafts, Telling Fortunes

The Indian encampment at… Bar Harbor will be found a pleasant place to wile away an hour or two. These [Indians] are expert with their canoes and at hunting and fishing. The village is composed of a score or two of little wood and canvas shanties, in which are sold a great variety of aboriginal trinkets, skins of seal and deer, baskets of birch-bark, moccasins, bead-work, snow-shoes, gulls' breasts, stuffed birds, clubs, carved sticks, bows and arrows, etc. (Chishom's Mount Desert Guide, 1888)

The Indian Encampment

From the 1860s onward, Wabanaki families set up camp on Mount Desert Island each summer primarily to sell handcrafted goods. Reflecting long-established marketing practices used all across Northeast America, Indians peddled their baskets and other wares door-to-door and set up simple booths to display their trade goods at boat landings. They also encouraged customers to come to their sale tents at the encampments. Over the decades, the location of Bar Harbor's seasonal Indian village shifted, but wherever it was it drew a stream of curiosity seekers and customers.

Before 1890, the Bar Harbor encampments featured a range of dwellings—from birch-bark wigwams to canvas tents to wooden shacks or shanties faced with strips of bark or wooden planks. The greatest number and variety of images and descriptions of the encampment date from the time it was located along the Frenchman Bay shore between Bar Harbor's steamboat wharf and the sandbar stretching between the town's north shore and Bar Island—although there are a fair number of drawings and photographs of the camp made during the years it was situated at locations a bit westward near Hamor's Wharf and the Eddy Brook outlet and southward at the Ledgelawn site.

Some members of the Wabanaki summer community slept in wooden shacks clustered near the sale tents. A few managed to rent rooms from locals in poor parts of town. Others slept in the back of their sale tents, either because they had no other place to stay or to guard their goods. Indians who were just passing through for a few days sometimes slept shoreside under an overturned canoe.[1]

Bar Harbor waterfront, ca. 1885. West End Hotel towers on the left. In the center, tiny houses built for workers have edged Wabanaki tents to the west side of Bridge St. (Collection of the Maine Historic Preservation Commission.)

A sturdy cloth made of long-fibered and closely woven cotton or hemp, canvas not only served as ship sails, but also as almost waterproof cover for cargo stowed on deck. For several centuries, fishermen and other seafarers also used their sails as protection against the elements—rain, snow, sun, and wind—whether staying on deck while anchored offshore or camping on a beach or in a saltwater cove. Canvas sheets were also cut and stitched to make tents for soldiers, shelters for horses, and a host of other things. Especially after the American Civil War (1861–1865), which created an enormous demand for canvas, growing numbers of Wabanakis began replacing their traditional birchbark-covered wigwams with canvas tents, many of which were probably used army tents or military surplus, and therefore easy and inexpensive to get. Moreover, by the mid-1800s, sport outfitters began selling canvas tents. It is not surprising to see these changes among Maine's Indians since, by this time, the traditional birchbark wigwams on the permanent tribal reservations had been replaced by wood-framed houses with clapboard walls and shingled roofs. By the 1880s, the last bark wigwams on the

small Mi'kmaq reservations across the Canadian border were also history—although for a few more decades some migratory families continued to live in them on their seasonal journeys.

During the summers when the Indian village was located along Bar Harbor's northern shore, its bleached canvas tents were clearly visible from the harbor and much of Frenchman Bay, from the upper stories of some of the hotels, and from the tops of some of the island's hills and mountains. As one writer noted in 1884, when the encampment was situated in a grassy shoreside field at the foot of Holland Avenue near Hamor's Wharf:

Wabanaki encampment along Bar Harbor's rocky north shore at the foot of Bar/Bridge Street, 1881. The greatest number and variety of images of the Bar Harbor Indian village date from the time it was located in this area. (Photo by Kilburn Brothers. Collection of the Maine Historic Preservation Commission.)

> The view from Green [Cadillac] Mountain is quite unique, the eye traversing ocean and land
> for forty miles in any direction; following the singularly serrated coast of Maine, the course of
> Somes Sound . . . and tracing the waving line of far distant mountain ranges. . . The clustering
> buildings of Bar Harbor appear like a child's playthings . . . the miniature vessels like seagulls

Shoreside view of Wabanaki Indian encampment at foot of Bar/Bridge Street, Bar Harbor, 1881. Note the canvas sale tent in background of the upper left corner and the bow and arrow held by boy in lower right corner. Adding to the family income, Indian boys earned money by shooting arrows at pennies and other small objects tossed in the air. (Photo by Kilburn Brothers. Collection of the Maine Historic Preservation Commission.)

just alighted; the white tents of the Indian encampment ludicrously suggest a laundry with big "wash" hung out to dry; and the whole scene looks as if viewed through the large end of an opera glass. [2]

Calling All Customers

Aiming to draw customers to their encampments, Wabanakis offered home delivery of goods purchased and did whatever they could to ease any qualms the public might have about shopping in their makeshift village. In Bar Harbor, this included arranging for electric lighting the very same year the town itself began the switch from gas to electricity. As announced by the local paper in the summer of 1884: "Arrangements are making to light the Indian encampment at the foot of Holland Avenue, by electricity. The new feature is due solely to Indian enterprise, Mr. Peter J. Gabriel being the leader of the movement." [3] Gabriel's leadership reached beyond bringing electricity to the camp. Hailing from Pleasant Point, this Passamaquoddy also served as his tribe's

representative to the Maine state legislature, elected to the two-year post in 1887.

As noted in an earlier chapter, Wabanakis not only abandoned their traditional bark wigwams, but also their distinctive traditional clothing, moccasins, and hats as part of the adjustments necessary to earn wages as seasonal laborers competing for jobs in mainstream American society. However, those depending on the sale of traditional indigenous medicines, handmade baskets, and other native arts and crafts recognized that dominant society's ambivalent racism provided them with commercial opportunity that could be enhanced by stereotypical self-fashioning. Conforming to the "American Indian" image then becoming popular with the general public; some began to dress the part, feathers and all. Often borrowing from Plains Indian styles popularized in Wild West shows, they donned neo-traditional garb. In addition, during the 1880s in particular, some tribal entrepreneurs attracted buyers by placing regular ads in the local papers, describing their wares and noting that the camp was "perfectly safe for anyone to visit." [4]

Path to sale tents at the Indian encampment along Bar Harbor's north shore at the foot of Bar/Bridge Street, 1881. Note frame, on right, used to stretch seal and other animal skins. (Photo by Kilburn Brothers. Collection of the Maine Historic Preservation Commission.)

Sale tents at the Bar Harbor Indian encampment at the foot of Bar/Bridge Street, 1881. The sign marks the tent of Passamaquoddy tribal leader Joseph Lola. (Photo by Kilburn Brothers. Collection of the Maine Historic Preservation Commission.)

Apparently, such efforts were successful, given the positive comments made by the state's Indian Agents in their annual reports concerning sales—and the soaring number of Wabanakis who descended upon Bar Harbor in 1885 when the local newspaper reported: "There are about two hundred and fifty Indians now in camp at Bar Harbor. They are of the Passamaquoddy, Penobscot, and St. John [Maliseet] tribe. They occupy forty tents at the foot of Holland Avenue." [5] We know that Mi'kmaqs, and probably a few Abenaki, Huron, and Mohawk Indians, were also present in Bar Harbor camps because intermarriage among Wabanaki and other Northeastern tribes was common. Moreover, the local press sometimes mentioned their presence, albeit less often than the other groups.

Who's Selling What Wares?

Beyond the remarkable number of Wabanakis marketing their wares at Mount Desert Island during the summer of 1885, individuals back on the Passamaquoddy's Pleasant Point reservation sent goods to the island, where other Wabanakis purchased them for resale. As reported in the The *Mount Desert Herald*:

> We had a pleasant call, Wednesday, from the Rev. John O'Dowd, Catholic priest in charge of the Passamaquoddy Indian Mission at Pleasant Point. He came to Bar Harbor on Monday, August 11, with a very large and choice selection of fancy baskets. These baskets were sold to the Indians – the proceeds to be used for repairing the Indian chapel at Pleasant Point. The baskets were furnished the Indians at wholesale rates (they were originally made by the Indians and contributed to the church,) and are now on sale at the Indian encampment. [6]

In addition to sweetgrass and woodsplint baskets, which were available in a wide array of shapes and colors, Wabanakis offered a great many other handcrafted items. The following, uniquely detailed description of the encampment offers a first-hand peek at these goods and how they were displayed, along with a visitor's view of some of the individuals selling their wares. Excerpted from a novel titled *Bar Harbor Days,* it is an informed piece of fiction—curiously, written from the vantage point of a dog visiting the encampment with its owner! Nonetheless, it provides a credible and verifiable account of the seasonal Wabanaki village as it was when located at the foot of Holland Avenue near Hamor's wharf in Bar Harbor during the mid-1880s:

Some Wabanakis promoted the goods and services they had to offer in Bar Harbor by placing ads in the local papers, such as this one which appeared regularly in the *Mount Desert Herald* during several summers in the 1880s. (Courtesy of the Abbe Museum.)

INDIAN ENCAMPMENT,

FOOT OF HOLLAND AVENUE.

Bar Harbor.

———

THE PASSMAQUODDY, PENOBSCOT AND MELISSA (OR ST. JOHN RIVER) TRIBES.

———

At this encampment may be found a great variety of

INDIAN WARES and *CURIOSITIES,*

COMPRISING

BASKETS OF ALL KINDS,

Gull's Breasts, Seal Skins and Deer Skins, Moccasins, Canoes and Birch Bark Ware.

———

The camp is open on pleasant evenings until half-past ten o'clock and will be found both quiet and orderly. *Perfectly safe for anyone to visit.* Goods purchased at this encampment will be delivered at any part of the village free of charge.

———

Bar Harbor Indian encampment just east of Hamor's Wharf at foot of Holland Avenue, ca. 1885. The rows of white canvas tents were visible not only from the harbor and much of Frenchman Bay, but also from the upper stories of some of the hotels and from the tops of some hills and mountains. (Collection of the Maine Historic Preservation Commission.)

On the morning of the third day there were symptoms of a change [in weather]. The fog took on a silvery lustre. We saw, over against Bald Porcupine [Island], the dazzle of white canvas where the sunlight settled on the sails of a yacht whose hull was still invisible. Green summits of the island next emerged from the void. . . . Longing for a row, we set out to go to the Indian wharf [Hamor's]. . . . When we pulled away from our dock the water was absolutely smooth. In ten minutes a flow of wind swept over the bay, ruffling its surface into long green ridges, capped with foam. . . .

Having failed to reach the Indian encampment on that occasion, we walked there the next day.... It was a pleasant walk across the bluff leading to the Indian camp. So many wild-roses grew there, amid thickets of sweet-fern and vanilla grass, that the air was embalmed with odors. Approaching the settlement in the rear, we saw more of their inside life than in front, where all is swept and garnished for customers. Old women hovering over pots and kettles; girls up to their elbows in dye-stuff; old men mounting birds, curing seal-skins, or hanging upon lines the

dyed splints to be woven into baskets; dogs and babies without number…. In religion many of them are Catholics, attending on Sunday the little Church of St. Sylvia nestling beneath the crest of Malden Hill at Bar Harbor. We met an Indian maiden once upon her way home from mass, and, in her fashionably-made polonaise of ruby velvet, and Gainsboro's hat and plumages, she looked like a bird-of-paradise in a barn-yard, beside the island girls.

With these Penobscots unite certain Passamaquoddies in the business of supplying Bar Harbor visitors with their wares. Their dwellings, half tent, half booth, are erected to leave a well-swept carriage-road between the lines, and here, every day during the season, come throngs of people. . . . Within the booths are draperies of red and blue and orange calico, or bunting. Broad shelves, serving as counters, present a charming medley of harmonious colors. Baskets of every shape and tint are piled into glowing masses. Seal-skins and deer-skins, pipes and sticks fashioned from distorted roots, canoes and paddles great and small, snow-shoes, lacrosse-bats, bows and arrows, moccasins and caps—what do not their skillful fingers put into captivating guise to witch away the money of the idler? Then there are gulls' breasts and wings, stuffed owls, pearly grebe plumage, and, their latest novelties, wood-baskets and flower-pots of birch-bark, etched with a frieze of native scenes.

Lola, the queen, [7] is a sovereign of generous proportions, living in a circular tent, around which are planted vines of the California cucumber, and sunflowers. We found her that day sitting on a low splint-bottomed chair, knee to knee with a gossip in shawl and bonnet, suggesting Betsy Prig. Fast as her hands could fly she was shaping a waste-paper basket of deep, soft yellow, braided with vanilla [sweet] grass. . . . My mistress bought of Lola a flat basket to hold handkerchiefs, then passed on to a tent where the proprietor, a stately old fellow, wore a clean gauze undershirt, with brand-new slop-shop trousers. At his feet sat the prettiest little maid, with ripe red lips, and dusky hair tied up with a knot of crimson! They had dressed her in a petticoat of yellow stuff and a dark-blue jersey. Spite of the visitors who came and went, she kept busy with the playthings in her lap – a china doll, some shells, some bits of silk and ribbon packed in a small tin box. . . .

In another tent we found a pretty young woman, helping her husband to dispose of the sweet grass baskets, for which they were particularly famed. The man, a good-looking fellow, wore a smart red shirt, with [ribbon] bands of Indian work, and an embroidered belt. It so happened that every basket of which my mistress asked the price was valued at "one-dollar-half." While waiting for her to make selection, the young [woman] heard a sound we had not noticed in the rear tent, darted in there, and presently reappeared carrying in her arms a rose-bud of a baby.

Passamaquoddy "Queen Lola," as depicted in *Frank Leslie's Illustrate Newspaper,* 23 August 1884. According to the article accompanying this image, Lola was "the largest" Indian in the camp and "must have weighed 300 pounds; she wore a man's hat and shoes, carried a stout staff and sat on a bench complacently smoking a T.D. pipe." (TD pipes were old-fashioned white clay pipes manufactured in England and the Netherlands—and popular trade items among Wabanakis from the time of early contact through the American Revolution.) Although Wabanakis smoked dried native tobacco, they often preferred the stronger imported varieties grown in the south and which they bought in stores or received as part of their annuities.

"Oh! What a beauty!" exclaimed my mistress. "I suppose you will sell him, too, for one-dollar-half."

"Not for all the money in the world!" answered the mother, her stolid face becoming suddenly aglow with feeling, as she hugged her treasure close. It was a pretty little scene.

My mistress bought a square basket, then a long basket, then a round basket, a basket with a lid, and a basket without a lid. Everybody does the same at Bar Harbor. When visitors prepare to go away the agony of packing these fragile acquisitions is met by the Indians, who put them in barrels, to be sent to distant points, often across the ocean. And thus it is that in a hundred homes remote from the Maine island arises at midwinter the fragrance of summer walks in fields beside the sea. Let the wind rave as it lists, the sleet dash on the window panes, a whiff of sweet grass brings back Mount Desert! [8]

A close look at a Wabanaki family inside their Bar Harbor sale tent. Most likely this photograph was taken when the Indian encampment was located just east of Hamor's wharf at the foot of Holland Avenue, 1884–86. (Photo by Bryant Bradley. Collection of the Maine Historic Preservation Commission.)

Another excerpt from the same narrative mentions one Wabanaki tribesman stopping by the sale tent of another looking for news of his nephew, who had been guiding at Moosehead

FAMOUS BOWMAKER NEWALL AND WIFE

Lake. Located at the headwaters of the Kennebec and Penobscot rivers, that large lake area became popular with white sport hunters and fishers from the mid-1800s onwards. Familiar with Maine's northern woodlands as hunters and trappers, some of these Indian guides were Abenakis, others Maliseets, Passamaquoddies, or Penobscots, who lived with their families in the lakeshore's town of Greenville or at the foot of Mount Kineo. Some of these Moosehead Indian families had close family ties to Wabanakis frequenting Mount Desert Island and a few actually camped there, too. As told in an earlier story about eleven Passamaquoddy men hunting seagulls on Saddleback Island, it was common for Wabanakis who summered at Mount Desert Island to have relatives frequenting other popular tourist resorts. Among numerous other examples, Andrew Nicholas, a guide born in Greenville

Wabanakis who spent the summer on the reservation sometimes sent supplies of baskets to relatives camped at seaside resorts. They also sold their wares on the home front—at the local wharf or railway station, or on the reservation itself. At Old Town, it was quite common for tourists to come over to Indian Island in the tribe's hand-rowed bateau ferry and find some Penobscots selling baskets and other crafts from wooden stalls, canvas tents, or bark wigwams set up beside their houses or on the slope of lawn that stretched between the boat landing and St. Anne church. Here we see members of the Newell family ready to welcome customers with bows, arrows, hides and baskets, ca. 1900. (Authors' collection.)

at Moosehead Lake, spent the summers of 1894 and 1901 (and perhaps other summers in between) at the Bar Harbor encampment, where, among other things, he offered guiding services. Over the years, his wife, Mary Francis Nicholas, gave birth to three children during their Mount Desert Island sojourns—twins Lewis and Mary in 1894 and Annie in 1901. It is likely that Mary was the daughter of the much-touted Passamaquoddy fortuneteller Elizabeth Francis, known as "Queen Francis" or "Madame Francis."

More than Meets the Eye

More details about the Bar Harbor Indian encampment while it was located at the foot of Holland Avenue near Hamor's wharf come from an 1884 newspaper article:

> Every summer [Passamaquoddies] come to Bar Harbor in numbers of about one hundred and
> fifty, and tempt dollars from the tourists by their display of wonderfully-made baskets, minia-
> ture canoes, and all sorts of things which might come under this sign's meaning:
>
> JOSEPH NICHOLAS
> Dealers in all kind Birch Bark things, Fancy Baskets and Toy Canoes, at tent No. 3.
>
> There is another "industry," as will be noticed by the following copy of a second sign:
>
> The Great Fortune Teller,
> By MADAME FRANCIS.
>
> This means that for twenty-five cents Madame Francis will tell you how your luck will "pan out"
> in the future. [9]

Offering readers a behind-the-scenes peek at the Wabanaki encampment, the journalist of this article continued: "All the cooking is done out-of-doors, just in the rear of the tents, on rusty cook-stoves set up on a few boards. The menu is not tempting, but there is lots of it."[10] Pans would have been filled with frybread, likely cooked in lard that came from the annual distribution of annuity goods provided by the state to Penobscots and Passamaquoddies as part of its ongoing obligation to the tribes for land obtained from them in the 17th and early 18th centuries. For frying fish, Wabanakis favored seal oil. Cast-iron pots and kettles, blackened by years of cooking on smoky open fires, held stews, sometimes made with muskrat, which were common in the island's freshwater and saltwater marshes, lakes, ponds and streams. And, given descriptions of porpoise hunting in Frenchman Bay and "unpleasant odors" wafting through the camp, porpoise meat was surely on the menu. It was said that "many Indians, especially the Penobscot," disliked it due to its "rank greasy smell." However, Passamaquoddies, headquartered at Pleasant Point by a saltwater bay and specialized as sea-mammal hunters were "extremely fond" of porpoise meat. The same was true for the saltwater Mi'kmaq of Bear River, Nova Scotia, on the opposite shores of the Bay of Fundy. Typically, these Wabanakis cut porpoise meat into steaks and roasted it directly on fire embers.[11]

Some of the pots that boiled behind Wabanaki shacks and tents were filled not with food but with dyes used for basketmaking. After dipping each slender strip of ash wood into the hot bright brew, women draped the long strands over lines to dry in the island breeze, creating colorful curtains of blue, red and green. Traditionally, Wabanakis turned to nature's storehouse to color their splint baskets, as well as the porcupine quills and moosehair strands they used to embroider birch bark crafts and animal skin clothing. Among their dyes, a range of reds came from speckled alder bark, bloodroot, hemlock root, stiff marsh bedstraw, Solomon's seal (eel berries), and cranberries. Blueberries were used to make a (quickly fading) reddish-pink, and hemlock bark yielded a reddish-brown. Beech bark created blue, while sugar maple bark produced violet. Several plants provided shades of green: princess pine root, Canada yew leaves, and white cedar leaves and bark (sometimes combined with American elm bark). Yellow dyes came from goldthread (especially strong, clear, enduring) and white ash bark. Ochre, charcoal, and clamshells were also used for color, ground and mixed with egg as a binder for painting leather or bark. [12]

As the commercial market for fancy baskets and other Wabanaki goods soared, those who made their living selling handicrafts began using commercial dyes. In 1893, a long article about Cushing's Dyes appeared in the *Lewiston Journal*, making specific note of Penobscots selling crafts in Bar Harbor and providing the following overview of craft production and the shift from traditional dyes:

> In all matters relating to Indian life on salt or fresh water, in wood craft, hunting, trapping and imitating nature, the Penobscot Indian leads the red men of the world. Hiawatha never made a canoe so firm and true as those of the Penobscots. They know the fibres of wood as book-keepers know the pages of their ledgers, while the women, in basket work of wood are far beyond . . . all other workers in these lines. The Penobscots can go into the woods and cut ash logs; go to the salt water marshes along the sea coast and pull sweet grass, and then with the aid of a pocket knife can produce from these materials which they color with Cushing's dyes, hats that are eagerly purchased by the wives and daughters of the millionaires who visit Bar Harbor and Kineo in summer; make ornamental pieces such as an anchor and shield, picture frames, card and photograph holders, napkin rings and all known shapes and styles of basket work.
>
> The men even weave fishing nets from roots and they color, with Cushing's dyes, the strands a dark purple, giving them, to the telescopic eye of the fish, the exact hue of water. They blend shell and basket work beautifully, decorate plain birch bark on the brown inside with animals of the forest and fish of the lakes. . . .
>
> Once they took alder bark from the shores of the stream for a red color, white [sugar] maple bark for purple, sumac for brown, white birch bark for a cross between orange and yellow, cedar boughs for green and butternut bark for black. . . . [Today they] have the 70 colors of Cushing's dyes and the exhibit which they will make with the colors at the World's Columbian Exposition at the Chicago World's Fair will astonish visitors. . . . To use the expression of an old Indian who first took me to the [Penobscot Indian Agency store in Old Town], "you see basket stuff the squaws make. Everything looks like peacock." [13]

But most white visitors to the Indian encampment did not witness the dyeing process. Typically, they stuck to the front of the tents, waiting to be invited, often in broken English, to step inside and survey the array of goods being offered. Much of the actual weaving of baskets happened within or in front of the tents in full view of the public, for this often helped to promote sales.

The range of people visiting Bar Harbor's Indian village spanned the social ladder, from

lower-rung folks who stayed in more modest hotels to upper-rung cottagers. Regardless of social rank, most left with mementos—and included mention of their purchases in letters to friends and family members about their holidays. For instance, in the summer of 1882, Mabel Bell, wife of telephone inventor Alexander Graham Bell, wrote to her mother-in-law: "Mama and the rest had a very good time in Mt. Desert in praise of which they are enthusiastic. . . . She brought back pretty Indian basketry, sea gull's wings, etc." [14]

A decade later, nine-year-old Eleanor Roosevelt (future wife of Franklin D. Roosevelt, 32nd president of the United States) wrote to her father telling him about her visit to the Indian encampment. It was not her first trip to Mount Desert Island. Members of her family had been going to Bar Harbor for years, beginning with her aunt Anna Roosevelt Cowles in the 1870s. Eleanor's uncle, Theodore Roosevelt (26th president of the U.S.) had courted his wife Alice Lee in Bar Harbor during the summer of 1880. Clearly delighted with her 1894 visit, little Eleanor had this to say to her father, Elliott Roosevelt:

> Dear Father: I hope you are well. I am now in Bar Harbor and am having a lovely time. Yesterday I went to the Indian encampment to see some pretty things. I have to find the paths all alone. I walked up to the top of Kebo mountain this morning and I walk three hours every afternoon. . . .We eat our meals at the hotel and . . . I have lessons every day with Grandma.

Penobscot sale tents at the Bangor Fair, 1928. The sign on the right announces "Palmistry" and the one in the center "Penobscot Indian Baskets." As indicated in this photograph, beyond selling handmade wares, some Wabanakis also offered fortune-telling for a fee—often in conjunction with selling traditional medicines. The woman on the left, sitting in a hand-crafted rustic chair, is Mary Irene Nicolar Lewey (1893–1936), great-niece of the famous Penobscot leader Joseph Nicolar who authored *The Life and Traditions of the Red Man* (1893). As a teenager, she spent time at the Bar Harbor encampment with Passamaquoddy Frank Lewey and his wife Delphine, who were long-time summer residents there. That may be where Mary Irene met John Charles Lewey (1892–1953), whom she married in 1918. John attended the Carlisle Indian School in Pennsylvania, founded in 1879 as the first off-reservation boarding school in the country. Over the generations, several Nicolars from the Penobscot reservation and Nicholases from the Passmaquoddy's Pleasant Point reservation frequented Mount Desert Island. (Authors' collection.)

Eleanor's father, stereotyping the island's Wabanakis as generic "Indians," responded:

> When you go to the Indian encampment, you must say 'How' to them for your old father's sake,
> who used to fight them in the old claims in the West, many years before you opened those little
> blue eyes and looked at them making birch bark canoes for Brudie ["little brother" Gracie Hall]
> and Madeleine [the children's governess] to go paddling in and upset in the shallow water, where
> both might be drowned if they had not laughed so much. . . . [15]

A half century later, when First Lady Eleanor Roosevelt attended the christening of a U.S. Maritime Commission barge at the Camden Shipyard in Maine, Penobscot singer Lucy "Watahwaso" Nicolar made her an honorary member of the Penobscot Tribe—giving her the name *Owduleesul* or "Many Trails." Mentioning this in one of her "My Day" articles, Roosevelt wrote: "The Penobscot Indians who build life boats for these wooden ships, were on hand to take me into their tribe and sing a song for my safety on far trails. They presented me with a wonderful sweetgrass basket and beaded headband." [16] By this time, Eleanor was also familiar with Wabanakis who lived on the Passamaquoddy reservations near Campobello Island in Passamaquoddy Bay, another summer resort popular among well-to-do folks in the 19th and early 20th centuries. There, since childhood, her husband had passed many a summer in his family's cottage. (In 2009, Passamaquoddy tribal historian Donald Soctomah coauthored *Remember Me,* a children's book about FDR's relationship with Tomah Joseph, a Passamaquoddy elder and former chief who made his living as a guide, birchbark canoe builder, and basketmaker. Today, the beautifully decorated birchbark canoe that Joseph made for FDR is in the collection of the Roosevelt Campobello International Park.)

In all likelihood, when Eleanor Roosevelt visited the Bar Harbor Indian encampment as a young girl, she saw Wabanaki children her own age. Numerous written and oral sources show that it was common for Wabanaki children to be there with their parents—or simply with their mothers. Because Wabanaki men were often busy elsewhere with other tasks, such as river driving or guiding sport hunters and fishers, it was not at all unusual for their wives to spend at least part of the summer running the family sale tent on their own, with children in tow. This prompted numerous non-Native observers to refer to the camp as "Squaw Hollow." In 1912, one historian described the situation like this:

> The [Penobscot] Indians of Old Town Island are . . . among the most skilled and faithful of all
> the twenty-three hundred registered guides of Maine and are always in demand among visit-
> ing sportsmen who make the canoe trips of hundreds of miles down the vast waterways of the
> Maine woods. During the summer while the men are pursuing this avocation one who visits any
> of the seashore resorts along the coast of Maine and Massachusetts will see Indian women and
> girls, many of them comely and attractive, in little stalls, selling Indian baskets and moccasins,
> miniature war clubs, canoes, snow shoes and a hundred and one similar trinkets, useful and
> ornamental, which they have made during leisure hours in their homes in their little village on
> Indian Island in the Penobscot River." [17]

July 10th 1894

Dear Father

I hope you are well. I am now in Bar Harbor and am having a lovely time. Yesterday I went to the Indian encampment to see some pretty things. I have to find out the paths all alone. I walked up to the top of Nebo mountain this morn. Ned are mild to ring and I walk three some other hours every afternoon we get. I have Brudie walks from lessons every day 4 to 5 miles every day, with Grandma. Please write to me with a great deal of ____ soon. We eat our meals at the hotel and the ____ names off the things we get to eat or to ____ Washington please am ____ love Ta your little daughter. Nell

Over the generations, quite a few Indian babies were born in the inter-tribal encampments at Mount Desert Island. For instance, Passamaquoddy tribal leader John Stevens of Indian Township (who played a leading role in the 1980 Maine Indian Claims Settlement) notes that his mother, Maria Lewey Stevens, was among those whose lives began on the island. She took her first breath in the summer of 1909 when the encampment was located at the Ledgelawn site by the present-day athletic field at the southern end of Bar Harbor. Margaret "Dolly" Apt, a Passamaquoddy living at Pleasant Point, tells this story about her great aunt Margaret Basset:

Excerpt from nine-year-old Eleanor Roosevelt's letter to her seriously ill father Elliott Roosevelt, telling him about her time at Mount Desert Island, including a visit to the Indian encampment in Bar Harbor. He died shortly after responding to this letter.

In August 189[6] my great aunt Margaret Basset Nicholas was born in Bar Harbor. . . . In the early 1980s [when she was about 90], I was in Bar Harbor with her for the Native American Festival sponsored by the Abbe Museum. She told me, "I want you to know I was born right here in this ballfield." My cousin Lisa Altvater remembers Margaret saying she was born on third base in that ballfield. Lisa has a picture of Margaret pointing to the spot. Margaret told her there used to be a big white mansion that you could see from the ballfield when she was a girl. A lot of the Indian women worked in that house over the years. Margaret said people called the encampment at the ballfield "Squaw Hollow" because there were so many women and children there. [18]

Nancy Sopiel with her parents Mary Francis Neptune and Selmore Sopiel, circa 1904. Mr. Sopiel is holding a traditional "war club" carved from a birch tree root—one of many hand-crafted items available to visitors who came to the camp with curiosity in their heads and money in their pockets or purses. These clubs were highly symbolic, with root ends sharpened to a point or carved with animal and human forms. Beyond weaponry, they were used in ceremonies and dances. When Nancy Sopiel grew up, she married Penobscot Jessie Ranco. Her own daughter Gertrude married David Soctomah, father to Passamaquoddy tribal historian Donald Soctomah.

The marketing of handmade goods at Mount Desert Island (and other resort areas) was so important to Wabanakis from the latter half of the 1800s until the 1920s that a slow summer season at the coast (due to such uncontrollable forces as weather or illness at the encampments, both of which discouraged buyers from coming), spelled financial hardship for reservation families for the entire year. As noted by one of Maine's Indian agents:

> The summer trade of the Indians is, in a small way, a
> sort of commercial barometer, indicating whether the
> general money market is easy or tight, and the readings of
> this barometer can be inferred quite correctly, by noting
> the number of new and improved dwellings among our
> [Penobscot Indian] island friends. Judged by this stan-
> dard, the readings were [this year] of mean height and the
> money market not easy. [19]

"*An Indian Mother,*" 1872. Drawn by Sol Eytinge, Jun., from a sketch by R. Emmet. The family shown in their "summer lodge" at Niagara Falls is identified only as "belonging to a Canadian tribe." Natives from various tribes, not only Iroquois but also Wabanakis, camped there in canvas tents. Regardless of the specific tribal identity of this trio, the scene gives a sense of how life was for a small Wabanaki family inside their summer tent at Mount Desert Island. Notice the various baskets and the scattered woodsplints used to weave them. (*Harper's Weekly,* 2 March 1872. Authors' collection.)

Passamaquoddy Margaret Basset Nicholas, 1988. Margaret is pointing to her 1896 birthplace "on third base" in the ballfield at the old Ledgelawn Avenue Indian encampment site in Bar Harbor. (Photo courtesy of the family.)

Even with these fluctuations, summer trade offered Wabanakis the greatest potential for financial gain during this era. While marketing handmade goods was the primary focus at their Bar Harbor encampment, many other entrepreneurial activities happened there or in the vicinity—from traditional medicine and fortune telling to leasing canoes (with an Indian paddler and guide) and hiring Indian guides for hunting expeditions.

CHAPTER SEVEN

Mighty Tippy:
Canoe Services and Sales

There are Indians here of the genuine summer-resort variety. . . ; guides and boatmen, whose grammar is as piquant as their hands are brown and their hearts are true; and the usual regalia of grandeloquently-named points for excursions in the immediate environs. (Moses Foster Sweetser, Picturesque Maine. Portland, Chisholm Bros., 1878, p. 40)

Most rusticators took advantage of Mount Desert Island's boating opportunities, which, for the more adventurous, included sport-hunting from a canoe. Those without boats could rent them, and authentic birchbark canoes made by Wabanaki Indians were particularly prized. Built for hunting seal and porpoise in open water, these swift saltwater canoes were about eighteen feet long, sometimes more.[1] In 1881 it cost 35 cents an hour to hire a canoe—extra for a guide. As noted in a guidebook of the day, "Indians have the principal share of [the canoe] business, and are thoroughly capable and trustworthy."[2]

Wabanaki Indians were determined to maintain a hold on canoe renting in Bar Harbor, so much so that in 1880 they petitioned the Maine legislature, saying: "We also ask the State to make a law that no white man shall rent canoes at Bar Harbor, Maine. This ought to belong to Indians. Some white men buy lots of canoes and rent them; and Indians cannot get jobs." Emphasizing their point that they did not want to be edged out of the few remaining livelihoods that at least echoed their age-old traditions, the petitioners added: "We also ask you that Indians have the right to kill deer anytime and let the white man kill sheep or cows."[3]

As with marketing crafts, Wabanakis sometimes announced their canoe services in newspapers:

> Birch-Bark Canoes—Louis Mitchell of the Passamaquoddy tribe of Indians will have during
> the season, at the shore between Suminsby's and Steamboat Wharf, Bar Harbor, a number of
> Birch-Bark Canoes, in which he will take parties to the several Islands in the bay and around

Passamaquoddy Louis Mitchell, circa 1885. Mitchell gained notoriety for paddling his canoe all the way around Mount Desert Island—60 miles—in just 12 hours. (New Brunswick Museum, St. John, NB, #1987.17.461.)

Mount Desert island. Carrying sporting parties to places where porpoise and seal may be shot. Guns and ammunition furnished when desired. Reliable and experienced paddlers will be provided. [4]

The Most Expert Canoeists

Numerous examples of Wabanakis retaining canoeing skills and paddling endurance appear in written records of the 19th and early 20th centuries. For instance, in 1881 the *Mount Desert Herald* reported that Passamaquoddy "Lewis [Louis] Mitchell recently paddled his canoe entirely around the island of Mt. Desert, a distance of sixty miles, in twelve hours."[5]

Several years later, a popular Mount Desert Island guidebook noted: "The Indian boatmen of the island sometimes make an adventurous voyage by taking their boats up to Eagle Lake, and crossing that sheet of water; carrying over the portage; and descending to Jordan's Pond, and so on down to Seal Harbor; whence they return to Bar Harbor by the sea." [6]

Zoologist Addison Emery Verrill, who grew up in Maine and did maritime fieldwork in Passamaquoddy Bay, introduced his son Hyatt (1871–1954) to the Passamaquoddy. Hyatt, who became a prolific author, illustrator, and naturalist, wrote about his experiences with them—including his observations of their seafaring skills. He noted, "I have seen Passamaquoddy canoes, far out to sea, manned only by a woman and several youngsters, scudding home from the fishing banks, with a blanket for a sail, when the fishing schooners were making heavy weather of it under double-reefed sails. One old Indian of the tribe actually paddled and sailed his canoe from Eastport to [Bridgeport,] Connecticut—'merely to see my father'—and thought nothing of the feat." Verrill also wrote about a steamship captain seeing an Indian wildly signaling him from a canoe out of sight of land. Assuming he was in trouble, the captain stopped his ship, only to find that the Passamaquoddy paddler simply wanted matches to light his pipe.[7]

Similarly, a writer recounted this story about Mi'kmaq porpoise hunters, told by a Bay of Fundy fisherman:

> He said he had been a cabin boy on a coastwise schooner that was beating up the bay one windy afternoon in 1885. It was a blustering day of sudden gusts and heavy sea, with no land visible. One of the sailors, who was gazing idly over the side, suddenly called his attention to the astonishing sight of two red Indians in a long canoe. The fisherman said that at first he thought they were ghosts, for they soon vanished behind the high waves. But they appeared again nearer, paddling against the wind, working desperately, and drifting backward. . . . They were hailed and taken aboard and, although properly grateful, were less concerned about their predicament than were the sailors. They said they were porpoise hunters who had been swept out and down the bay by the wind. As evidence they showed their three porpoises in their canoe and, out of gratitude, presented one of them to the sailors. . . . The next morning was calm and sunny, and despite all protests the Indians put their canoe overboard and paddled away on a gleaming sea unfringed by land. [8]

A much briefer but equally telling recollection came from an Isle au Haut old-timer talking about Penobscot Frank "Chief Big Thunder" Loring: "I remember Big Thunder. . . . I used to borrow his canoe to go up to the pond. Mighty tippy. He never minded. A birch canoe was a good boat if there was an Indian in it. Took their canoes [across Penobscot Bay] right out to Matinicus [Island].[9]

Rent a Canoe and Paddler, Too

An 1888 guidebook noted these details about Bar Harbor boating activities and services on Frenchman Bay:

> . . . boatmen have more than a hundred rowboats and canoes, and a score or so of yachts, besides three or four small steamers, for lease. There are also catamarans, Rob-Roys, canvas-boats, cat-boats, and all manner of small craft, insomuch that the harbor is at times fairly crowded with little shipping. The rates for row-boats are thirty-five cents an hour, or seventy-five cents with a boatman. People unacquainted with these waters should take boatmen with them, for the rocks are scattered about inconveniently; and there are occasional unexpected squalls, attended with little or no danger to one familiar with the place, but hazardous for strangers. Cat-boats and yachts, with competent skippers, can be hired for longer voyages up and down or across the bay, to the lower Heads, Egg Rock, Ironbound, the Ovens, South Gouldsborough, Winter Harbor, Sullivan, or Sorrento. The most expert of the canoeists, naturally, are the Indians, who carry visitors in their frail boats around the harbor and islands, or even on longer and more daring voyages. [10]

Wabanaki canoeists awaiting customers on the shore between the steamboat wharf and the Indian encampment, circa 1881. Photo by Kilburn Brothers. (Collection of the Maine Historic Preservation Commission.)

Frank "Chief Big Thunder" Loring was probably best known of all the Wabanakis who leased canoes and provided paddling and guiding services. As noted by the *Bar Harbor Record* in 1896, "Every visitor to Bar Harbor knows 'Big Thunder,' the ancient Indian, who for years has canoed the children of summer visitors, and the parents oft-times themselves when they were children, about the points of interest in the bay."[11] For some years, Loring ran a canoe concession next to the steamboat wharf. Perched above the narrow "Boats and Canoes to Let" sign of a boathouse, his big two-sided sign announced, "FRANCIS BIG THUNDER CANVAS AND BIRCH CANOES."

Perhaps the most detailed accounts of what it was like to head out in a canoe with a Wabanaki guide appear in letters written by Caroline Briggs. This Massachusetts widow of relatively modest means stayed at Rockaway House on the Bar Harbor shore every summer from 1881 until her death at age 73 in 1895. Repeatedly, she wrote about venturing out in the care of Big Thunder or his son Mitchell, describing the men as well as the cherished outings. A small sampling:

> Almost every day canoeing. Big Thunder is always our guide, and one could have no more fitting companion. I wish you could see this charming old man and his son. Two finer types of youth and age you will rarely see.

Yesterday we went out with Mitchell and stayed all the morning. The water was gray and the fog was drifting about, and the sea made our little canoe dance like a cockle-shell. Great swells carried us grandly on their backs; the birds swooped and gave strange cries, and the breakers on the islands came in with a voice of thunder. The rocks played with the water, and it dashed back on them with great mountains of spray.

Rusticators and Wabanakis making arrangements for a guided canoe tour on shore between the steamboat wharf and the Indian encampment, circa 1881. Photo by Kilburn Brothers. (Collection of the Maine Historic Preservation Commission.)

We often go out in Mitchell's canoe: at morning when the sun is sparkling and surf dashing at the feet of the beautiful islands; at sunset when the ocean looks like a melted opal, out into the darkness with all its mystery, only the stars twinkling overhead and the drip of the paddle – then this world and the next seem to meet, and the soul stretches away into the infinite without boundary line. It always costs me a little struggle to come back.

We have paddled with dear old Big Thunder, when the waves rocked us in his little canoe, and when we glided like shadows, while twilight fell around us so softly that one felt like a baby in its mother's arms. [12]

Penobscot Frank "Big Thunder"
Loring, a well-known figure for
decades on Mount Desert Island,
had a canoe concession by the
steamboat wharf in Bar Harbor.
His two-sided sign, touting "birch
and canvas canoes," sat atop a
pier-side boathouse. Circa 1890.
(Collection of the Maine Historic
Preservation Commission.)

A Canoe of One's Own

Owning one's own Indian-made birchbark canoe was a status symbol on Mount Desert Island, so the boats were in considerable demand. It took considerable skill and time to make one, but the financial rewards provided enough incentive for Indian craftsmen. The best were made of one large flexible sheet of paper birch bark, ideally more than one-eighth-inch thick and tightly sewn or lashed with very long, thin, and durable roots of black spruce, or sometimes deer sinew, to the hand-hewn gunwales, the ends of which were nailed and also securely wrapped with spruce. The well-rounded bottom was framed with flat, wide spruce or cedar sheathing and ribs. For structural strength, these canoes usually had five thwarts, the ends of which were mortised into the gunwales and also fastened with spiral lashing. To make the bark cover completely watertight, all seams and "sewing" were coated with spruce gum. The paddles were usually carved from hard maple wood. Some tribesmen engraved or dyed their personal mark, their family's animal totem, or some other stylized figure on the bow of their canoe. [13]

If selling a birchbark box or wood-splint basket was comparable to snaring a rabbit, selling a birchbark canoe was like bringing down a bull moose—a family could live off the proceeds for quite some time. As noted in an 1881 local paper: "Birchbark canoes made by the Indians at Bar Harbor sell at prices ranging from $25 to $40. [$530–$850 in 2009 dollars] *And they are very nicely made too."* [14]

Another notice, appearing in a Bangor newspaper, showed that birchbark canoes were in demand well beyond Mount Desert Island: "The canoe has become so popular a craft among sportsmen and tourists, even indispensable with the former class, that the building of this light and graceful craft is now quite an important industry in Maine, especially on the Penobscot River. . . . Thirty-five dollars, the usual price, is none too much for a good canoe." The article continued with a description of the process and particular challenges of making these canoes:

Nowadays, the [big, clear, straight] birches are from twenty to one hundred miles distant from up-river towns, and two suitable trees are seldom found within sight of each other. . . . In winter [the bark's] inner side has reddish brown coat, but in summer it is smooth and yellow. The winter bark is preferred because it is tougher, and because of the opportunities for

Frank "Big Thunder" Loring and boy sitting by boatshed just west of the Bar Harbor steamboat wharf, ca. 1890. (Collection of the Maine Historic Preservation Commission.)

ornamentation. . . . The canoe builder fells a white birch which is at least one foot in diameter eighteen feet from the butt, allowing it to fall across some small logs to keep it from the ground and then strips off its outer coat. The bark must be warmed, toasted as it were, before it can be straightened out and rolled up in proper shape for transportation. . . . The builder drives stakes into the ground and thus forms a frame the shape of his canoe. The bark, after more toasting, is smoothed out and fitted to the frame, after which the gunwales, strips of spruce or cedar, are put in place and the top edge of the bark secured to them by copper nails. Then the whole inside of the birch is lined with lengthwise strips of thin shaved cedar, and next, about fifty cedar timbers are 'sprung' into place over these, and the ends being secured under the gunwales. All cuts made in bringing the bark to the required shape are sewn up with cane threads and gummed over with a paste composed of resin and oil. Ash thwarts, very narrow, are put in, strips of canvas glued on over the ends of the canoe where the two sides of the bark meet and the craft is done. Paddles are shaved from poplar, maple and ash. [15]

Passamaquoddy Peter Joe Dana (a.k.a. Nicola Denis, circa 1820–1889) was one canoe-maker linked to Bar Harbor in the historic record. Adney and Chapelle's well-known book on canoes includes this description of a canoe Dana built "sometime between 1890 and 1892" for his son Francis, "who used it at Frenchman's Bay":

The outside of the canoe was painted red, the inside was pale yellow, the gunwales and middle portions of the thwarts were cobalt blue, the ends of the thwarts were red. The *wulegessis* [16] was blue, and the 'canoe mark' was a painted representation of the spread eagle of the United States seal, the border being in black and white and the eagle in black, yellow, and white, holding a brown branch with green leaves. The whole panel was outlined in red. On the side of the canoe, near the stern, was a white swallowtail pennant on which was lettered 'Frenchmans Bay' in black capital letters. This canoe was used for fishing and also for porpoise and seal hunting. [17]

Peter Dana's son carried on the canoe-building tradition—and continued to paddle Frenchman Bay, as noted by a journalist in 1893: "Francis Dana, a well-known Indian hunter and guide whose home is at East Machias, having built a 16-foot birch canoe, started out last week to find a customer for it. He put to sea Friday in his frail craft, and having no sail paddled to Bar Harbor, where he disposed of the canoe, and returned home by Saturday's steamer. The distance is sixty miles, and the water was rough." [18]

Among Mount Desert Island rusticators, a growing fascination with canoeing led to the founding of the Bar Harbor Canoe Club in 1886. Incorporated the following year, the club initially had its boathouse at the Pendleton & Roberts Wharf and a clubhouse on Bob Sproul's property at Albert Meadow. In 1888 both were combined at a Bar Island site visible from Bar Harbor's Main Street shore. [19] The follow passage from Richard Hale's 1949 book about the town offers a good summary of the club, including the role Wabanakis played in its activities:

> The ever-useful Rodick family [of the Rodick Hotel fame] had a site on Bar Island on which was established a canoe house, safely away from the waterfront of West Street and to be reached at low tide by a walk or carriage ride, at high tide by a fee and a ride in a hired boat. At the Club House were established the ever-present Indians of the Penobscot and Passamaquoddy tribes, who would give instruction in the fine art of paddling or themselves furnish propulsive power. And at least thrice a year, the ladies of the Canoe Club would entertain at tea, sending out engraved cards to announce the event. [20]

Once established, Bar Harbor's canoe club grew steadily, reaching a peak of 300 members in 1900. A year earlier newspaper magnate Joseph Pulitzer hosted a lavish party for club members

"Peter Joe at Work," a drawing from Tappan Adney's "How an Indian Birch-Bark Canoe is Made." *Harper's Young People*, supplement, 29 July 1890. (Courtesy of *Harper's Magazine*.)

Maliseet canoe-builder Nicholas Lola (with wife and child), scraping slats for the interior of the birchbark canoe. July 1875, Houlton, Maine. (National Anthropological Archives, photo no. 01100400.)

at Chatwold, his luxurious cottage estate on Ocean Drive. According to one reminiscence:

The unforgettable highlight of the party [was] a parade of canoes in the sheltered cove on the ocean side of *Chatwold*. . . . Most of the canoes, handmade from birch bark, had been purchased at the Indian Village off lower Main Street . . . where Penobscots from Indian Island came many years to camp, bringing for sale the products of their winter's handiwork. The Indians also supplied members of the Bar Harbor Canoe Club with hand-carved individual paddles with the owner's initials etched into the wood, and many of the braves were employed to instruct the children of the rich in the art of paddling the fragile craft over Frenchman's Bay. Each canoe in the spectacular parade was dazzlingly decorated with lighted Japanese lanterns. The great line of illuminated craft, carrying splendidly attired passengers, moved rhythmically around the cove to the background music of dozens of strumming banjos, while a full moon shed its glory on the breathtaking scene. [21]

Given the Wabanaki's recognized expertise as canoeists, rusticators took great pleasure in seeing their paddling skills displayed. A regular opportunity for that came with the annual canoe races sponsored by the Mount Desert Canoe Club. In 1893, onlookers were especially pleased to see a popular Penobscot, well-known at Mount Desert Island, wield his paddle and take the lead:

Friday's races given in front of the Mt. Desert Canoe Club house were as always an event of much interest to the crowd who attended and who watched from the neighboring shores and

boats. A unique part of the programme was the canoe races by a company of Indians from the Passamaquoddy [and Penobscot] tribe[s] who are encamped just outside the village. There was a shout of triumph when [Penobscot] Mitchell Loring was seen to come ahead in this race for he is the club steward and a great favorite with all Bar Harbor residents. He is the son of Big Thunder who is as much a feature here as Green Mountain [Cadillac Mt.]. He is a handsome young fellow, over six feet in height and he looks as if his name ought to be Hiawatha. [22]

Henry Richards (in stern, foreground boat) with family members in a birchbark canoe purchased in the 1870s. Richards, a young architect at the time, was traveling to Mount Desert Island by steamer to supervise construction of a summer home for Mrs. Charles Dorr. On that same large steamboat, an unidentified Wabanaki was carrying a small fleet of bark canoes to rent to Bar Harbor's burgeoning rusticator population. Before disembarking the steamer, Richards bought this canoe and two paddles for $30. It remained in his family until 2006, when his grandson presented it as a gift to the Abbe Museum. (Abbe Museum Collection.)

How ironic that this Maine Indian tribesman with the rather commonplace European name of Mitchell should be romantically imagined as Hiawatha—the "noble savage" invented by Henry Wadsworth Longfellow in the mid-1800s. For the sake of euphony, Longfellow gave his *Algonquian* Indian hero the name of a legendary Mohawk chief who founded the *Iroquois* Confederacy, an alliance of nations traditionally feared and hated by their Algonquian enemies, including the Penobscots.

A few years later, two Wabanaki tribesmen at Mount Desert Island were disqualified in a canoe race in Frenchman Bay at the occasion of "Eden's Gala Day." A 28-year-old Passamaquoddy was declared the winner, but fellow tribesmen "J.M. Loring and Francis Dana were barred because of their modern canvas canoes." [23] Were they removed because they ruined the romance of being Hiawathas in Eden?

CHIEF BIG THUNDER PENOBSCOT TRIBE OLD TOWN ME
COPYRIGHTED 1912 A F ORR OLD TOWN ME

Frank Loring, popularly known as Chief Big Thunder, ca. 1890s. Even death did not dent the fame of this Penobscot showman, storyteller, hunter, guide, medicine man, and tribal leader, who collected and sold Wabanaki relics and crafts. This postcard was published in 1912, six years after he died. (Abbe Museum Collection.)

CHAPTER EIGHT

Everyone Knows Chief Big Thunder: Notable Wabanakis

Every visitor to Bar Harbor knows 'Big Thunder' the ancient Indian, who for years has canoed the children of summer visitors, and the parents oft-times themselves when they were children, about the points of interest in the bay. (Bar Harbor Record Centennial Souvenir Edition, July 1896)

Between the 1840s and 1920s, a total of several thousand Wabanaki men, women, and children spent their summers at encampments in Bar Harbor and other places on Mount Desert Island. Among them were some truly remarkable characters who appealed to imaginations and inspired stories. One of the most notable was the Penobscot Frank Loring, known to the public as Chief Big Thunder. Because of his high profile, literally as well as figuratively, journalists and non-journalists alike delighted in telling stories about him. This chapter is devoted to profiles of Big Thunder and selected other Wabanaki personalities to help us picture the real people who inhabited "the Indian encampment."

Frank "Big Thunder" Loring (1827–1906)

Born in 1827, Frank Loring was the youngest of eight children. His mother was an itinerant Penobscot Indian doctress. She died before he reached the age of twelve, and he and his sisters took up basketry to survive. They traveled around Northeast America, from Maine to Pennsylvania, hawking their wares. Growing up to be well over six feet tall, Frank was strong, handsome, and imposing. Some referred to him as "Big Frank."

By the late 1840s, Frank Loring had added public showmanship to his survival strategy. Soon thereafter, still in his twenties, he married Mary Lola Socoby, a Passamaquoddy often referred to as Mary Old Soul. Together they had at least seven children. Frank was often away from Mary and their brood, producing, directing, or acting in Indian "entertainments" throughout New England,

as well as hunting or guiding. But as the children got older, they and Mary often accompanied him on his travels and even appeared with him on stage. In 1860, for example, he and Mary did an eight-month stint as headliners in an "Indian Exhibition" at P.T. Barnum's American Museum on Broadway in New York.[1]

Frank "Big Thunder" Loring, pencil on paper, 1899. By West. (Courtesy of the Penobscot Indian Nation Museum.)

A consummate showman, "Big Frank" was a leader among fellow Wabanakis who, in the course of the 19th century, resorted to commercializing their public identity in order to make a living.[2] His name appears in dozens of newspapers and historic records across New England, especially in Maine—and very often in the Mount Desert area.[3]

A memoir by a young Mainer who was adopted and raised by Mi'kmaq Indians in Nova Scotia tells of meeting Frank Loring in Boston in 1851:

> One day as I was passing down Washington St., I met an Indian who accosted me, and asked me if I had ever traveled with a company giving entertainments. I told him I had never traveled with any company, but had often danced for the amusement of the people. He said that he would give me a chance, and would pay my fare to New York, where we should hear in regard to the rest of the company.[4]

After this chance meeting, Loring took his new companion back to Panawahpskek, the head Penobscot Indian village on Indian Island, Old Town, to hire a handful of fellow Wabanakis for their troupe and gather some "dresses and outfit"—costumes, canvas tents, and other basic supplies for their traveling "Indian" show. Before leaving Old Town, Frank purchased a pair of young "pretty tame" black bears to enhance the theatrical road shows he had in mind. Transporting the young bears, props, and other luggage by railway to Bangor, they traveled from there by steamship to Boston, and then on to New York: "As soon as we arrived at New York, we commenced to travel. The [circus] proprietor's name was Horn, and Loring acted as agent for the company, there being twelve of us in number. . . . Our tent would accommodate some three thousand, having a stage and curtain at one end, where we performed."[5]

Their program included the popular story of Pocahontas, with Frank playing her father, the Virginian Indian Chief Powhattan: "Big Frank was finely formed, and of massive proportions, which gave indications of Herculean strength, and being painted in Indian style, he looked extremely savage, while the tall black plumes in his head-dress gave him the appearance of being somewhat taller than he really was. The audiences were rather awed by his formidable appearance."[6]

The earliest suggestion of Frank Loring's presence on Mount Desert Island comes from a reminiscence about a group of Indians putting on shows in Southwest Harbor four years before he began the tour described above:

> In the year of 1847. . . . came a tribe of [Penobscot] Indians from Old Town, some fifteen or twenty,
> and camped on the salt water shore opposite Parkers [at Clark Point]. The chief said they had
> been rehearsing their old customs and would like to give exhibitions if we had a hall large enough.
> The woolen factory [in Somesville] was the only place and in the winter there was no use for it.
> The carding machine being in one end was partitioned off and that left a very large hall. Crowds
> flocked to those Indian shows. . . . They stayed all winter, hunting, fishing and giving shows. . . .[7]

Although Frank Loring is not mentioned by name in this passage, it appears that Penobscot fiddler Johnny Newell and members of his family were among the performers. Historic records show that Loring occasionally traveled with the Newells—a family known for practicing medicinal and musical skills in concert with selling baskets and other crafts.[8] Seasoned performers by this time, the Newells probably took the lead, while Frank, then about twenty years old, honed his showman skills.

If the performers spent the entire winter of 1847 at Mount Desert and the Somesville mill was indeed the "woolen factory" mentioned here, it is likely the Indian troupe not only camped at Clark Point, a six-mile trek to Somesville, but that they also camped at least part of the time closer to Somesville, at sites long used by Wabanakis—near Somes Pond or at Round Pond between Indian Point and Squid Cove, where they may have beached their bark canoes after their fall hunting season.[9]

In the next three decades, Frank Loring played theatrical "Indian" roles in traveling road shows, including the circus, throughout North America. Somewhere along the way, Big Frank became Chief "Big Thunder," a name more befitting an Indian entertainer who had to compete

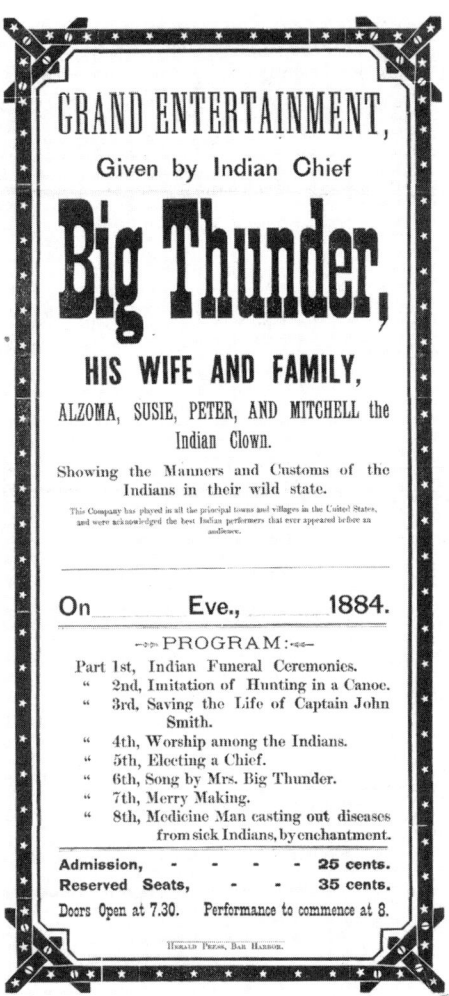

Frank "Big Thunder" Loring in his crowd-pleasing feather-skirt and spectacular ostrich- or rhea-feather headdress, photographed about the same time as this 1884 placard promoting one of his shows in Bar Harbor. (Authors' collection; Acadia National Park Archives.)

with other tribesmen performing in popular Indian medicine shows, Wild West shows, and sportsman's shows with romantically appealing "primitive" names such as Black Hawk, Charging Bear, Lone Cloud, or Rolling Thunder.

In the summer of 1882, Loring gave at least one performance in Bar Harbor. As reported in the local newspaper: "Big Thunder, the famous Indian Chief, gave an exhibition at the pavilion on West Street last evening. He was supported by his wife and family. The exhibition consisted of an exemplification of Indian customs and relics." [10] Two years later, again in Bar Harbor, he had a flyer printed to promote another "Grand Entertainment" starring himself and his family "showing the manners and customs of the Indians." [11]

While recognized far and wide as an entertainer, Loring was also known for his knowledge of traditional Wabanaki medicines and as an outdoorsman and sport-hunting guide with considerable "bush savvy." According to historical notes collected by a niece of Adelma Somes Joy:

Professional doctoring was hard to come by, so the mothers had their own remedies. At one time they had help from an Indian, Big Thunder, who had a camp [on Mount Desert Island]. For a sore throat, he would put pepper in a pipe and blow it down over the tonsils. Tansy worn in a bag around the neck was a good preventative for worms. The children gathered and dried pennyroyal, good for many troubles. Baked onions in a bag on the chest were used for pneumonia. Skull cap was used for medicinal tea. [12]

Two generations later, Frank Loring's granddaughter Hattie Gordius, who lived her long lifetime on Mount Desert Island (in Bass Harbor), told a journalist that her father gargled with goldenseal for a sore throat. In the same interview she touted the virtues of tansy with an enthusiasm echoing that of her great-grandfather: "Dry tansy will 'drive out the measles' she said. 'I wish someone would use my tansy; I've got a whole field of it.'" [13]

In Bar Harbor, Loring's presence was so well established that the *Bar Harbor Record Centennial Souvenir Edition 1796–1896* featured a big head-to-toe picture of him, captioned: "At the Bar Harbor wharves are all kinds of sailing craft, which can be hired for a moderate sum. Every visitor to Bar Harbor knows 'Big Thunder' the ancient Indian, who for years has canoed the children of summer visitors, and the parents oft-times themselves when they were children, about the points of interest in the bay." [14] And a big sign atop the boathouse of a boat concession near Bar Harbor's steamboat wharf announced "Francis Big Thunder Birch & Canvas Canoes."

Throughout most of his long traveling life, Loring's home base was the Penobscot reservation. In the nineteenth century, several islands in the tribe's stretch of the Penobscot River were inhabited by indigenous families. In the 1880s Loring's family and a few others resided on Olamon Island, about thirteen miles north of Old Town. In 1889, after his wife Mary's death, Frank moved his family to Indian Island. Sixty-two years old by this time, he continued traveling, mostly in New England, to give performances, guide white hunters, and sell crafts and paddle "summer people" at Mount Desert Island.

Loring, like so many of his Wabanaki contemporaries who came to Bar Harbor in the summer, did not simply go back and forth between the reservation and Mount Desert Island. As their ancestors did when traveling, they often stopped at other places en route, following whatever opportunities might crop up—be it settling in for a while with groups of Wabanakis encamped near a train station or steamboat wharf making and selling crafts or temporarily joining up with fellow Indian hunters who crossed their path. Because of this, Wabanakis frequenting Mount Desert Island also spent time at other offshore islands or seacoast towns. For example, now deceased residents on Isle au Haut recalled Loring camping seasonally on their island to hunt terns, seagulls, and porpoises for the hat-feather and oil markets. [15]

Folks on Eagle Island, just west of Deer Isle, had similar recollections of "small bands" of Passamaquoddies and Penobscots—including Loring—camping on their island in the 1880s and 1890s as a base for gathering shellfish, gull's eggs and sweetgrass, as well as for hunting seal and porpoise: "Harold Ball, son of Capt. John Ball [the lighthouse keeper from 1883–1898], recalls several of the Indian visits. The [Penobscots], led by Chief Big Thunder, whom Harold

Frank "Big Thunder" Loring. While Loring was a real hunting guide, he was also a performer. In these two photos we see him as an authentic sport hunting guide and as a be-wigged fellow showing off as an Indian guide. The lefthand photo appeared in the *Bar Harbor Record Centennial Souvenir Edition*, 1896, with the caption: "Big Thunder, The Indian Guide." The other was taken ca. 1900, photographer unknown. (Collection of Acadia National Park; authors' collection.)

came to know personally, landed in Lighthouse Cove and came to the light to get permission from Capt. Ball to camp on the island. . . . The Indian chief took Capt. Ball and his wife out for a ride in a large bark canoe."[16]

Wherever he ventured, Frank Loring was known as a great storyteller—a man who filled someone's ear whether selling a basket, paddling a canoe, entertaining on stage, or just sitting on the stoop of the little relic shop he established on Indian Island in the last years of his life. The birchbark sign out front read: "Big Thunder, Relics and Traditions of the Penobscot Tribe." He did just what the sign said: selling "relics" and telling stories about Wabanaki traditions (often partially invented or imaginatively improved for the sake of dramatic effect). [17] His oratory skills as a public performer also served him well on the reservation, where even in his twilight years he played an important role. For instance, during the 1898 inauguration of Joseph Francis as the Penobscot tribe's newly elected chief, Loring acted as master of ceremonies and had the honor of administering the official oath of office. An on-the-scene observer described Loring's role like this:

[Big Thunder's] honesty of purpose, public spirit, good sense and ripe judgement [sic] have gained for him the confidence of the whole tribe. He is a man of large and powerful frame, and as he stood in the assembly dressed in the ancient costume of the tribe, his face striped with black paint and red, his head covered with a mass of iron-grey hair on which rested a head-dress of eagle plumes, his appearance was extremely picturesque. And when in a sonorous voice— deep and strong, yet melodious—he delivered his address of congratulation and admonition to the young chief, the effect was impressive. . . . Big Thunder . . . led a company of men in the shot-horn dance and the snake dance to weird chants sung by the dancers.[18]

A year or so later, Loring gave several interviews about his decision to appeal directly to U.S. President William McKinley (1897–1901) concerning the plight of Penobscot people—perhaps in relation to new state laws restricting traditional Indian hunting, fishing, and fowling rights. As reported, "Lamenting the condition of his people," the old chief embarked in "an old-time birch canoe . . . with deerskin costume and birch wigwam." As if to underscore his role as a brave champion for age-old Wabanaki rights, Chief Big Thunder took a pair of traditional fire-making sticks on board! How far he actually made it after paddling downriver beyond the sight of onlookers is anyone's guess.[19]

At age 74, two years after his avowed seacoast journey to the nation's capital, Loring was officially elected vice chief (lieutenant governor) of the Penobscot Nation, having already served in various other capacities, including wampum keeper (tribal historian and orator). With this, Big Frank's long-practiced theatrical role as "Indian chief" finally became political reality. Eleven months before his death in April 1906, Loring was working on a new "Indian Play" to be performed in the town hall

Postcard picturing Frank "Big Thunder" Loring at his place on Indian Island, Old Town, ca.1890s. Loring also sold wares (and told Wababaki war stories) when back on the reservation. The sign reads ,"Big Thunder, Relics and Traditions of the Penobscot Tribe." (Authors' collection.)

of Lewiston. An article about the event appeared in the *Lewiston Journal* under the headline "Big Thunder, Mighty Medicine Man, Chief of the [Penobscots]." Loring, well aware that journalists were capable of spinning fancy yarns to sell newspapers just as he had entertained his audiences to put bread on the table, must have chuckled when he read this line in the article: "It is to Big Thunder that the young Indian who would know of the greatness of the [Penobscots] goes for information. To him, too, go those members of the tribe who wish to retain a knowledge of the customs of the days when the [Penobscots] ruled Maine from end to end."[20]

When Frank Loring died the following year at age 79, Penobscots buried him in Indian Island's Catholic cemetery. Numerous newspapers ran obituaries heralding his celebrity, and his death was front-page news in the *Old Town Enterprise:* "Not since the passing away of Molly Molasses," the paper declared, "has the Penobscot Tribe of Indians lost from its midst such a famous personage. . . . 'Big Thunder' . . . bears the record of being the last of the old chiefs of the Penobscot tribe."[21]

Elizabeth "Queen" Francis (1839–ca. 1915)

In 1884, at the entry to her canvas tent near the foot of Holland Avenue in Bar Harbor, a 45-year old Passamaquoddy businesswoman from Pleasant Point posted a sign that read: "The Great Fortune Teller, by Madame Francis." Inside, according to one journalist of the day, "For twenty-five cents Madame Francis will tell you how your luck will 'pan out' in the future." [22] Journalists and locals usually referred to Elizabeth Francis as "Queen Francis." At least two other Passamaquoddy women were called "Queen" in the 19th and early 20th centuries—"Queen Lola" and "Queen [Mary] Mitchell" (ca. 1820–1910). But neither is noted with the frequency and pomp given to this enterprising Indian lady from Down East. Yet, few details about her life have been unearthed.

The 1900 Federal census shows that Elizabeth, born at Pleasant Point in 1839, was married to Passamaquoddy basket maker Edmond Francis (born 1840). She knew how to read and write English, but her husband did not. Of the nine children she bore, four had survived as of 1900. One of her daughters, Mary Francis Nicholas, continued the family tradition of coming to Bar Harbor to market Native wares, often with her husband Andrew Nicholas, a well-known guide. Mary gave birth to several of their children during summer sojourns there.

Newspaper accounts make it clear that Elizabeth was a well-known figure in Bar Harbor for some twenty summer seasons, from 1877 (if not earlier) through at least 1896. Among Mount Desert Island news bits about her is this one from 1883: "The Indian 'Queen Frances' was out riding yesterday in full gala day costume. The queen and her party occupy four tents near Hamor's wharf and have a fine lot of baskets and small wares. This is her seventh season at Bar Harbor." [23]

In August 1889, when Elizabeth's grandson nearly died in a hunting accident in Sorrento, just across Frenchman Bay, the story was especially interesting to Bar Harbor residents because the child was related to her. As reported in the local newspaper:

A sad accident occurred Saturday at Sorrento. A little Indian boy, grandson of the queen
Elizabeth Francis was over there gunning [porpoise hunting?] with his father and accidentally

FORTUNE TELLING

discharged the gun in such a manner that the bullet passed through his right lung. He was brought home and at last accounts, was suffering intensely and the doctors had no hope of his recovery. . . . A very pleasant party went over to Sorrento, Sunday morning, on the little steamer *Sorrento* to hear the Rev. H. Bernard Carpenter. . . . Mr. Carpenter, before commencing his discourse, spoke of the little Indian boy who met with the accident at Sorrento, and in whom the Sorrento people have shown a deal of interest. He was glad to tell them, he said, that the boy was having excellent care and that the doctors reported each day a very little gain. . . .[24]

Passamaquoddy Elizabeth "Queen" Francis reading palms at the Bar Harbor Indian encampment near Hamor's wharf, 1884. (*Frank Leslie's Illustrated Newspaper,* 23 August 1884, p. 5. (Authors' collection.)

A month later, mixing up the tribal names of Penobscot and Passamaquoddy and confusing Elizabeth with a slightly older Penobscot woman of the same name,[25] the newspaper announced her death—only to run a correction the following week:

Elizabeth Francis, an aged [woman] of the Penobscot tribe, known to Bar Harbor people as 'Queen Francis' was burned to death on Thursday morning of last week in her house in

Oldtown, which was totally destroyed, together with that of her son next door. The cause of the fire is a little mysterious, but it is surmised that it took from a tobacco pipe, as Mrs. Francis was a habitual smoker. The unfortunate woman had just finished her summer business of basket-selling at Bar Harbor and returned home. [26]

It now appears that the Indian woman, Elizabeth Francis, who was burned to death at Oldtown recently, was not 'Queen Francis' but another Elizabeth Francis [born 1835], who summered at Southwest Harbor. Queen Francis is yet at Bar Harbor. [27]

Like Frank Loring, Queen Francis figured significantly in Bar Harbor's 1896 centennial celebration. The festivity included a parade featuring Maine's first peoples. As noted in the *Bar Harbor Record:* A week from tomorrow begins the most important event in the life of Eden and Bar Harbor—the centennial. It will continue two days. . . . Mr. Fennelly, the chairman, is rapidly completing the make-up of the procession. One of the features will be Queen Francis of the Passamaquoddy tribe and several Indians in their original costumes. [28]

The federal census for 1910 shows that Elizabeth and her husband Edmond were still alive, she at age 71, he at 70. Neither appears on the 1920 census.

Louis (Lewis, Louie, Lewey) Mitchell (1847–1931)

No matter how one spells his first name, Passamaquoddy Louis Mitchell of Pleasant Point was a well-known figure on Mount Desert Island and well beyond. Like Frank Loring, he epitomized the versatility of many Wabanakis of his era. He was an expert hunter, canoeist, and guide; a tribal representative in the Maine State legislature; an outspoken advocate for traditional Wabanaki hunting and fishing rights; an ace pitcher in baseball games; and a rich source for historians, linguists, folklorists, and early anthropologists interested in tribal lore and traditional Passamaquoddy ways and beliefs. Notably, he provided a handful of well-known scholars valuable cultural and historical information in both written and oral form. [29]

Born at Pleasant Point in 1847, son of Peter Mitchell Neptune, Louis Mitchell married Bridget (born ca. 1855), who could speak English, but did not write or read. They had their first child, James, in 1881, followed by Susan (ca. 1883), Nichola (ca. 1888), and Evelyn (ca. 1897). All of their children learned to read and write in English.

By 1881, at age 34, Mitchell was a well-established figure in the Bar Harbor summer scene—known, among other things, for his business acumen and for the remarkable feat of paddling his bark canoe Mount Desert Island's entire sixty-mile circumference in just a dozen hours. He used this achievement to good effect in the recurring ad he posted in the local paper that year:

Birch-Bark Canoes—Louis Mitchell of the Passamaquoddy tribe of Indians, will have during the season, at the shore between Suminsby's and Steamboat wharf, Bar Harbor, a number of Birch-Bark Canoes, in which he will take parties to the several Islands in the bay and around Mount Desert island. Carrying sporting parties to places where porpoise and seal may be shot. Guns

Louis Mitchell, Passamaquoddy tribal representative to the Maine State legislature, ca. 1880s. (New Brunswick Museum, St. John, N.B. #1987.17.464)

and ammunition furnished when desired. Reliable and experienced paddlers will be provided. Mitchell recently paddled his canoe entirely around the island of Mt. Desert, a distance of sixty miles, in twelve hours. [30]

Evidently, Mitchell's entrepreneurial spirit was already in action, for the ad suggests that he solicited work for several "experienced paddlers" in addition to himself. The reputation he earned as an expert canoeist stayed with him for many years, prompting the author of the most comprehensive guidebook to Mount Desert Island to describe him as one of the "expert . . . aboriginal Argonauts." [31] Sometimes Mitchell's adventurous spirit reached the point of audacity. At age 52 he made headlines when he and fellow tribesman Xavier Francis attempted an all-but-impossible canoe feat. A summary version of a full-length story about the event read as follows:

The canoe in which Lewis Mitchell and his partner Francis, of Pleasant Point, attempted to shoot the falls at St. John [River] was at the International Wharf [in Eastport] and attracted

Louis Mitchell, ca. 1915. While noted as a politician, culture-keeper, and business man, Mitchell usually referred to himself as a basketmaker. (Courtesy of Donald Soctomah.)

a good deal of attention. The canoe is a canvas affair and was none the worse on this foolhardy trip, which cost Francis his life and came near being fatal to Mitchell also. Lewis said a few years ago he could have performed the feat successfully, but was now too old for such a trial. [32]

When the widely traveled author and lecturer Charles G. Leland, then living in Philadelphia, came to Mount Desert Island seeking information on traditional Wabanaki lore, Mitchell proved to be a valuable resource, earning this acknowledgment in Leland's 1884 book *Algonquin Legends:* "To this gentleman I am greatly indebted for manuscripts, letters, and oral narrations of great value." With such an endorsement, it is not surprising that when Columbia University professor John Dyneley Prince followed in Leland's steps to Bar Harbor in 1887, he, too, met with Mitchell. They discussed Passamaquoddy language and traditions, including the *Wapapi Akonutomakonos* or Wampum Records concerning the formation of the Wabanaki inter-tribal alliance centuries ago and a description of its ceremonial protocol and the functions of wampum belts and strings. Publishing on the subject a decade later, Prince commented, "I obtained the Wampum Records at Bar Harbor, Me., in 1887, from a Passamaquoddy Indian, Mr. Louis Mitchell, who was at the time a member of the Maine Legislature." Mitchell's manuscript, Dr. Prince added, "contained both the Indian text and a translation into Indian-English." [33]

Fannie Hardy Eckstorm of Brewer also sought out Mitchell in her Wabanaki historical research. They corresponded on a range of topics—from the origins of indigenous family and place names to traditional stories and songs to oral history of Wabanaki involvement in the American Revolution. He also assisted Miss Mary Cabot Wheelwright (1878–1958), a wealthy Bostonian who summered on Sutton Island, just south of Northeast Harbor, in her collection of Wabanaki oral histories and artifacts. (Wheelwright's remarkable collection of artful Wabanaki handicrafts, ultimately donated to the Abbe Museum in Bar Harbor, includes moccasins, beadwork, baskets, birchbark work, powder horns, and crooked knives.) In a 1930 letter to Eckstorm, Mitchell wrote:

I have few relics for Miss Wheelwright such as old crooked knives and rattle, or powder horn, and the original stick used with Indian quick-step dance, very old. Also I know where I can get 3 silver Breast Plates, 5-inch, decorated, and a French Hatchet, used by Indians probably 300 years ago and 2 of the Indians can sing Indian Songs yet, such as Love Songs, Salutation Songs, very interesting, Dancing Tunes – these ought to be preserved. [34]

On the political front, Louis Mitchell served several terms as the Passamaquoddy tribal representative to the Maine State legislature in Augusta between 1880 and 1911. His political activities were commonly recounted in newspapers around the state, including in the *Mount Desert Herald,* which in 1888 reported that: "Passamaquoddy representative Lewis Mitchell requested from the Maine state government that the Indian agency at Calais would be removed to Eastport [much closer to the Passamaquoddy village at Pleasant Point], and that a subagency would be created in Princeton [not far from the Passamaquoddy village at Peter Dana Point], because of the difficulty Passamaquoddies had to get their state aid in the form of food and money and permissions in times of sickness." [35] While concerned with an array of issues, he was especially committed to challenging Maine state game laws that made it increasingly difficult for Wabanakis to rely on hunting as a key means of subsistence. His efforts to convince state officials in Augusta that game laws ran counter to aboriginal treaty rights were frequently chronicled in various newspapers. For instance, a paper reported in 1891:

An interesting question has come up before the Maine Governor and his Council, in relation to the treaty rights of the Indians in this State. It will be remembered that not long ago Lewis Mitchell, one of the brightest of the Passamaquoddy Tribe, made the point that his Tribe should not be subjected to the restrictions of the game laws of this State because the treaty which his Tribe signed especially stipulated that the Indians should have the uninterrupted right to hunt and fish at their pleasure in the State. . . . Mitchell has been to Massachusetts studying the archives. . . . The effect of allowing the claim advanced by Lewis Mitchell might have a widespread effect upon the sporting interest of the State." [36]

Mitchell's efforts were ongoing. A decade after the previous newspaper account, the following appeared:

One of the picturesque figures about the capital in Augusta last week was Lewis Mitchell, the Representative of the Passamaquoddy Tribe. . . . Mr. Mitchell is anxious to have Indians exempted from the operation of seagull laws. He declares that only about 50 of his people are engaged in the hunting of gulls. He declares that men who gather the eggs of the birds are the ones who do the most to destroy them. He declares that his people are recognized and protected in their hunting, fishing and fowling privileges by many different treaties between 1693 and 1777, which he believes to be properly in force at the present time. [37]

When verbal protests failed, Mitchell turned to civil disobedience, even while serving as tribal representative to the Maine State Legislature. The following newspaper excerpt chronicles an incident that occurred in 1902:

> The old claim of the Maine Indians that they have certain inalienable rights not accorded their paleface brethren is to be again thrashed out in the courts. Game warden Miller recently seized a box containing 13 dozen pairs of gull's wings shipped from Eastport to Boston. Lewis Mitchell was arrested, tried, and adjudged guilty of having thus violated the game laws. He was sentenced to pay a fine of five dollars and costs and to serve 10 days in jail. Mitchell appealed his sentence, claiming that under the treaty with the Indians, he had a perfect right to kill the birds. The case will be tried at the January term of court. Hon. Hanson of Calais is counsel for Mitchell. [38]

Remarkably, Mitchell was still at it two decades later at age 74, as per this news clip:

> Lewis Mitchell and Thomas [Joe] Lola from Pleasant Point reservation at Perry were before US commissioner Reid in Bangor Friday on charges of unlawful possession of certain migratory birds and offering them for sale, contrary to the convention entered into between US/Great Britain and in accordance with the act of Congress. It was charged that the men had taken gulls and were selling the breasts. They entered pleas of not guilty through their Council [sic], Edward Murray. Probable cause was found and the respondents were held in $500 each for their appearance at February term of court. [39]

While Louis Mitchell was a man with many skills, he identified himself as "basketmaker" to census takers. But, as with the rent-a-canoe/rent-a-paddler business he established in Bar Harbor, when it came to baskets he was an entrepreneur with an eye for expansion. As the following news clip shows, he became a middleman in the basket trade, sometimes providing basket makers with raw materials needed for their work:

> Lewis Mitchell and Joe Dana [b1852], who are noted for their thrift and enterprise, and who do an extensive business in baskets and other Indian wares, are making great preparation for the coming season's trade, having recently received a carload of [brown] ash logs from Houlton via the railroad, which is to be converted during the winter months into baskets of various designs. Mr. Mitchell's industry is a great benefit to the Tribe, furnishing them, particularly the female population, with means of earning a livelihood during the winter months. The industry is a lucrative one, both men said to be laying a generous competence [compensation?] for old age and rainy days. [40]

Beyond selling fancy baskets in Eastport and resort areas such as Mount Desert Island, Mitchell capitalized on the needs of sardine-packing factories for work baskets. In 1888 the *Eastport Sentinel* reported the growing demand for "sardine baskets," noting, "The Pleasant Point Indians have supplied a large part of the demand. . . . Lewy Mitchell who is interested in the manufacture of the goods says that there have been probably $6000 worth made and disposed of since last fall at the Point." [41] By 1902 Mitchell was busy shipping both types of baskets to his clients, as noted in this newspaper excerpt:

> Basket making is a rushing business this winter, $100 worth of baskets being brought to Eastport and shipped to other factory towns weekly. Lewis Mitchell, one of the largest dealers, has mostly sardine baskets, while shipments to the west are fancy baskets. The industry is a growing one and of great value to the village, as it provides labor and income to most of the residents of Pleasant Point. [42]

In August 1918, Mitchell's wife died at age 62, after 46 years of marriage. He appears on the 1920 U.S. census for Pleasant Point as an 83-year-old widower living with daughters Susan Dana and Evelyn, along with Evelyn's newborn son Aloysius. His profession is still identified as basket-maker. In 1930 we find him living with Evelyn and her Passamaquoddy husband John Newell (born 1890), along with their children Aloysius and Margaret (born 1912). Again, Mitchell is listed as a basketmaker. In his last known letter to Eckstorm, written in early 1931, Mitchell commented that he was old and sick. Soon thereafter, on 15 March 1931, he passed away, having lived a long and remarkable life.

Joseph Lola (1830-ca.1900]

Passamaquoddy Joseph Lola (also spelled Lolah or Lolar) was a regular at the summer Indian encampment in Bar Harbor. He wore his hat low, nearly covering his eyes, but he was not shy about marketing his wide array of Indian crafts. He believed in signage and the handmade "Joe Lola, Passamaquoddy Indian Wares" sign that he posted by his tents and shanties over the years is visible in at least three photos taken at the town's shifting encampment sites. In addition to posting a sign on location, Lola sometimes solicited business by placing ads in the local paper. During the summer of 1885, the following ad ran weekly in the *Mount Desert Herald*:

> PASSAMAQUODDY INDIAN BASKET SALE, At the INDIAN ENCAMPMENT near Hamor's wharf, BAR HARBOR. Commencing Friday, July 3, and to continue until the end of the season. – A large assortment of INDIAN WARES of all kinds, Baskets of every description. A very fine assortment of Sea Fowl Feathers. Toy Canoes, Bows, Arrows, etc. Please call and examine our wares. JOSEPH LOLA & Co. [43]

Elected Passamaquoddy tribal governor at Pleasant Point in 1888, Lola was equally innovative when it came to finding or creating year-round markets for his crafts. Sometimes he traveled long distances to do so, as seen in these two wintertime newspaper excerpts:

> Joseph Lola, Governor of the Passamaquoddy tribe of Indians was in Boston, Monday, to sell baskets and other articles of Indian manufacture. He visited the State House and

Joe Lola outside his tent at the Bar Harbor Indian encampment, ca. 1881. (Detail of Kilburn Brothers photo. Collection of the Maine Historic Preservation Commission.)

exhibited a handsome sealskin prepared for a mat, which he said he desired to send to President Harrison as a Christmas greeting, and wanted information as to how it should be directed and sent. The information was supplied by Secretary Pierce and Joseph departed, happy at the thought that his little contribution would reach the Great White Chief. [44]

While Joe Lola was in New York City he created some excitement in city hall. He is a man with long black hair and a dark complexion who was carrying a mysterious looking canvas bag under one arm. He came into the corridor and walked around for a while, peering into doorways and looking suspiciously at everyone who approached him. He wore no overcoat, his trousers and coat were two sizes too big for him, and his black hat was pulled down so low on his head as to conceal his piercing black eyes. When policemen and janitors and a scrubwoman began to gather around him he clutched his canvas bag nervously and began to speak his native language, which no one could understand. Then everyone moved back a few steps and looked at the canvas bag and thought he may have dynamite. Finally, a big policeman who was passing by in the hallway, after listening to him for a while makes out he was looking for the mayor's office. Then most of the crowd felt for sure that he had dyna-mite in his canvas bag. A second big policeman and the mayor's messenger stopped Lola just outside the mayor's door and demanded to know the contents of the bag. With evident reluctance, Lola started to pour out his bag onto the floor and again the crowd scattered. Chattering away in his native tongue, he poured out a pile of wonderfully designed and constructed little baskets made of bark and painted red, white, blue and old gold colors. After much effort he made the crowd understand that he was an Indian from Pleasant Point Reservation in Maine and had come to the city to sell his baskets. He said, in English, his name was Joseph Lola and he was a member of the Passamaquoddy Tribe. He wanted to find the mayor to get a license to sell his baskets on the streets. He was referred to the mayor's marshall. [45]

John Leonard Snow (1868–1937)

John Leonard Snow's life began on the Passamaquoddy reservation at Pleasant Point in 1868, [46] but he spent at least half of his life on Mount Desert Island, making and selling crafts to locals and visitors. He appears on the 1900 Federal census for Bar Harbor as a resident of dwelling #266 at the Ledgelawn Indian Camp. In all likelihood, it was not his first summer there. That year he came with his wife of two years, Penobscot Mary Ann Fransway Francis Snow (ca. 1855–1946)—both listed as basketmakers. Over the next four decades he became a well-known figure all over Mount Desert, especially in Northeast Harbor and the Cranberry Isles. In 1910, we find him listed twice in Federal records: on the Northeast Harbor census (recorded 23 April) as a married man living alone, owning his own house, and employed in "general work," and on the Indian Island/Old Town census (recorded 6 May) as a married man living with his wife Mary Ann on the Penobscot reservation as boarders in the Sapier household. [47]

Sometime between 1910 and 1919, John and his Penobscot wife parted ways and he fell in love with Alice Sockabasin from his Passamaquoddy home reservation at Pleasant Point. In 1919, she gave birth to their daughter Susan in Bar Harbor. Alice (earlier separated from Mitchell Francis of Pleasant Point) was also a basketmaker and like other Passamaquoddies had boarded with John Snow on Mount Desert Island. The couple settled in at Northeast Harbor, and had three more children together—Phillip (born 1920), Bertha (1922), and Juanita (1921). As year-round residents, all of the children attended the local school. Alice's children by Mitchell Francis (Josephine/1903, Lewey/19??, and Daniel/1915) sometimes lived with them in the small wooden house by the intersection of South Shore and Manchester roads, within sight of the old steamboat wharf. Susan Snow later remembered the place as "camp-like" with "about four bedrooms," and recalled that they used the front room or living room for basket-making in the winter and as a storefront in the summer. Heat came from a woodstove in the kitchen and a potbelly coal stove in the living room. It was cold in the house in the winter, but, noted Susan, "us kids never complained. I guess we were used to it. We never got up in the morning until after my father got the heat going." [48] She and her siblings grew up well aware of nature's food offerings in the area— clamming and fishing near the wharf, and collecting dandelion greens and wild berries that grew in nearby fields.

Passamaquoddy John Snow, ca. 1905. (Collection of the Abbe Museum.)

Alice made most of the fancy baskets John sold, often with help from her daughters and any Wabanaki women who might be visiting. John prepared the ash and collected the sweetgrass for their work and made numerous crafts himself—including birchbark boxes, frames, and toy canoes, as well as sealskin moccasins. His primary sweetgrass-gathering place was Little Cranberry Island. He was not the only Wabanaki to get basket grass there. According to one oral history, told by a Little Cranberry Island resident as she showed some of Snow's work to her granddaughter:

> In the summertime [during the early 1900s] Passamaquoddy Indians would come around the Islands and sell all these kinds of baskets and woven napkin rings and so forth. Not expensive. They came door-to-door. . . . These are John Snow's baskets. He was a Passamaquoddy who lived with several other Indians in Northeast Harbor. . . . He used to come out to [Little Cranberry] and pick sweetgrass. They'd even come up from Eastport in big canoes to pick it. [49]

As for basket ash, he often obtained it from fellow Passamaquoddies at Pleasant Point. (In the 1900s ash wood was a line item in the tribal budget managed by the state's Indian agents. Suitable brown ash trees had become scarce around the reservation, so ash "sticks" were brought in by boat and made available to basketmakers. In addition, Snow likely obtained ash from Louis Mitchell, the tireless tribal entrepreneur who brought it in by train from Aroostook County.) But even when using imported basket wood, Snow pounded and prepared it himself. As Susan recollected, "I used to hear him pounding ash when I was running home from school. We could hear that all over Northeast Harbor. People used to say, 'Oh, that's John pounding ash.' It's kind of noisy . . . but it had a good sound to it."

John also turned to fellow Wabanakis for the sealskins he needed to make moccasins. Getting the skins was not a problem, said Susan, because "there were a lot of men from Pleasant Point who used to go seal hunting." John usually tanned them himself, but when fellows from the reservation showed up on his doorstep, he hired them to help. Among them was Sabbattis Lola. Speaking of him, Susan commented, "He used to come to Northeast Harbor and work with my father. That is *work* for my father, like tanning sealskins and pounding ash. . . . I remember when I was young, when I was a kid, he came there. Stayed for the whole summer working with my father."

John Snow sold crafts throughout the Mount Desert Island neighborhood—from Seal Harbor to Otter Creek to Bar Harbor to the Cranberry Isles. And, according to daughter Susan, many people came to the little storefront shop in his house: "He used to have a lot of company. All kinds of people [came], you know, white people, to talk to him. And you know he *liked* to talk to people. I imagine he got used to all that, being with people, on account of his work—you know, peddling baskets *all* the time. He met thousands of people. . . . I don't want to brag, but he was very good doing what he did."

Susan Snow's view matches the fact that so many Mount Desert Island residents can still call up memories of her Passamaquoddy Indian family. Some recall how her father John seemed to grow larger with each passing year. Among numerous examples, Polly Bunker of Little Cranberry noted that when he came to gather sweetgrass at "The Pool," he stopped by her parents' house and her mother served him lunch. She described John Snow as a "big man, friendly and quiet." An elderly Bar Harbor resident recalled that her husband bought a sweetgrass whisk from John in 1934. Asked who it was for, the husband replied "My wife." "Is she sweet?" John wanted to know, "because this is sweetgrass." Walter Schurman, who hung out with Snow's son Phillip in their boyhood years, recalled watching John Snow making sealskin belts and vests in a dark corner of the house and wondering how such a big man managed to catch seals. [50]

Another resident summed up John Snow's work like this: "Mr. Snow made beautiful sweetgrass baskets, picture frames of birch bark and sweetgrass, toy birchbark canoes, and many other items, which he sold door to door with his children, mainly to our summer residents. He also dug clams and chopped wood for locals and summer residents alike. The children were enrolled in school and one of the boys, Phillip "Porky" Snow, was in my mother's class at Stetson School." [51]

Beyond being a hardworking Passamaquoddy craftsman, salesman, general laborer, and frequent employer of other Wabanaki artisans, John Snow collected, told, and wrote down traditional Wabanaki stories—in Passamaquoddy and English. When asked what it was that made her father so memorable, his daughter Susan told about his storytelling:

> Well, he had a pretty good personality. He used to tell stories too. Indian stories. And he'd translate them in English. . . . I remember [when I was about 10 in 1929] we went to this BIG house in Northeast Harbor and this lady – we all sat out back in her garden. It was so pretty there. Well, *rich* people. So we all sat in back. I was with my father. And my father was reading her the story. I don't even remember what the story was about. It was all Passamaquoddy language. . . . After that he translated to her in English. . . . He wrote it down and gave it to her [in] both languages. He sold it to her.

Susan Snow did not remember who the woman was who bought the story, but it may well have been historian Fannie Hardy Eckstorm or her wealthy friend Mary Cabot Wheelwright, who had a summer home at Northeast Harbor and collected Indian folklore and artifacts. One of Passamaquoddy Louis Mitchell's many letters to Eckstorm opens up this possibility:

> I received your letter Saturday. . . . Also I received a letter from John Snow. . . . He came to see me about three weeks ago with about 20 pages of Kluskap Stories and one Indian Love Song, both in Indian and English. He claims the stories to be straightening out. He says some Indian words in the stories [still needed] to be translated in English, which I did. . . . He also says to me that you cannot understand my spelling on some words, but did not tell me the words. I will gladly explain them to you. I can read my own writing. [52]

Maine writer Elizabeth Coatsworth (1893–1986), whose family purchased a carved wooden cane from John Snow in his later years, wrote down this recollection of his storytelling:

> In his mind the old stories and traditions lay in dimmed and broken images; yet, as a sort of gypsy dweller beside the white men's houses, he still remembered something of the tales, which his mother had told him as a little boy. He remembered about the great sea monster, and about the small people known as Pukwudgies. They stood no higher than a man's waist, and their heads were long, or so said the few who had seen them, for they were shy, and hard to get a glimpse of. They would visit a hunter's camp while he was away, and if they were in good humor they might cook him a dinner and leave it for him to find simmering in his pot over the coals of a fire; or they might scrap a hide for him, or do some other kindness. But if something had happened to put them in bad humor, they would upset all his things, throw his supplies in the bushes, hide his blankets – there was no end to their mischievous tricks. The Pukwudgies were childish, but they were very wise. They knew the future, and if one approached them properly they would answer questions. As a man, John Snow remembered that his mother had once taken

him as a little boy to a rock near the mouth of Machias River. There were old marks on it [petroglyphs] . . . [and he remembered] that he and she stood by the rock, and that she called out a question and that the Pukwudgies answered it. [53]

Passamaquoddy John Snow with a basketful of baskets to sell, alongside two little rusticators, ca. 1910. (Photo by W. H. Ballard. Authors' collection.)

The place Snow visited as a boy is Picture Rock, a ledge near Machias Falls on which Wabanaki ancestors carved more than 500 petroglyphs. Located along an ancient canoe route that led to Mount Desert Island, it is the largest concentration of Native American rock carvings along the East Coast. Some of them are several thousand years old. In 2006, the Passamaquoddies (re-)acquired a six-acre area around Picture Rock from the Maine Coast Heritage Trust in exchange for a conservation easement on 300 acres. These drawings in stone tell of caribou, deer, hunters, and shamans. Tribal historian Donald Soctomah, who helped spearhead the exchange, describes them as "our storybook of the last thousands of years."

JOHN SNOW

Passamaquoddy John Snow during
his later, heavyset years, ca. 1920.
(Collection of the Northeast Harbor
Library.)

In 1934, Alice Snow decided she wanted to return to Pleasant Point, so John built a home there for the family. Over the next few years they spent winters on the reservation and summers in Northeast Harbor. Their Mount Desert Island home continued to be a stopover place for other tribespeople—until John Snow's death in 1937. His strong ties to Northeast Harbor remained evident even after death, for he is buried there in Forest Hill Cemetery.

What drew John Snow to Mount Desert Island and ultimately prompted him to settle at Northeast Harbor? Clearly, the island provided him and other Wabanakis with income needed to support their families. But much more than economics was involved. There was also an aesthetic pleasure and, no doubt, a deep spiritual dimension to their lives that guided them to the area. And age-old Wabanaki place names and petroglyphs—words and images that stirred ancestral memories—must have played a role in drawing them toward the site of Chief Asticou's birchbark wigwam encampment, to an island where Wabanakis past and present have relished and relied upon nature's wealth and beauty.

CHAPTER NINE

Where Moose Bones Turned to Stone: Folklorists and Conservationists

When I first put my mind to this subject [of Wabanaki folklore], I went to Bar Harbor, the summer rendezvous for all Indians in the country, and began work.
(Charles Godfrey Leland)

The rise of tourism on Mount Desert Island in the second half of the 19th century coincided with the emergence of American anthropology. Early anthropologists bought into the era's popular myth of the "Vanishing Indian"—the idea that Indians were primitive relics of a bygone age destined to be destroyed along with their primeval wilderness home in the name of "progress." Mourning the expected disappearance of America's indigenous peoples (not entirely irrational given their decimated population due primarily to foreign diseases), folklorists, linguists, and early anthropologists interviewed Native elders. Salvaging information concerning cultural traditions prior to the European invasion and reservation confinement, they collected myths, legends, and oral histories.

Given the large number of Wabanakis who came to Mount Desert Island each summer to market their goods and skills, it is not surprising that scholars committed to "salvage ethnography" sought them out there. These researchers included Charles Godfrey Leland, John Dyneley Prince, Albert Samuel Gatschet, Fannie Hardy Eckstorm, and Frank Speck. It is also quite likely that 19th-century Penobscot tribal leader and author Joseph Nicolar spent time at Mount Desert Island, for his now classic book, *The Life and Traditions of the Red Man* (1893), features detailed descriptions of this seacoast area long frequented by his own ancestors. Moreover, written records place various members of Nicolar's extended family there during and after his lifetime.

Nicolar and the non-Indian scholars who were so intrigued by the traditional lifeways

Joseph Nicolar, Penobscot tribal leader and historian, ca. 1893. He served many years as the Penobscot representative to the Maine state legislature and authored *The Life and Traditions of the Red Man.* (Courtesy of Nicolar's grandson, Charles Norman Shay.)

of Penobscots and other Wabanakis, all investigated and wrote about the Wabanaki culture hero, Glooskap. Like most other hunting, fishing, and gathering communities, Wabanakis saw everything in their world—the sky, land, sea, animals, and plants, as well as invisible spirit beings—as an organic whole. From generation to generation, they sustained themselves by seeking to thoroughly understand their place in the environment and acting in a cycle of give-and-take with fellow creatures—plants and animals alike. This indigenous world view is expressed in many cultural ways, including ancient creation stories featuring Glooskap. Larger than life, this giant hunter-shaman lived in the Wabanaki homeland at the beginning of time itself. Mount Desert Island formed part of his vast mythological hunting domain, and ancient legends about the place memorialize Glooskap as the first and greatest sea- and landscaping artist, who helped shape the dramatic beauty of the place. Such stories were part of the cultural repertoire gathered and relayed by Nicolar and the early non-Native scholars profiled in the following pages.

Joseph Nicolar (1827–1894)

Joseph Nicolar was a keen witted and much respected man whose reputation reached well beyond the shores of the Penobscot reservation at Indian Island, Old Town.[1] Born in 1827 to Tomer Nicola and Mary Malt Neptune, he hailed from a notable line of Penobscots. His maternal grandfather, Lt. Governor John Neptune, was one of the most impressive Penobscot chiefs of all time. On his father's side, his great-grandfather was the famous "half-arm" Nicola, who survived the 1724 English attack on the Abenaki village of Norridgewock on the upper Kennebec, which cost him a limb and earned him his nickname.

Intellectually ambitious from childhood, Joseph attended school in several Maine towns, while traveling with his mother, known as Mary Malt, a famous Penobscot doctress. It was said that he had the best education of all Maine Indians of his time. At age 31 he served his first term as the Penobscot tribal representative to the state legislature, an elected position he held with distinction and won more often than any other Penobscot to this day. People on and off the reservation referred to him as the lawyer of the tribe. They also called him the tribe's scribe, for he often wrote short news items about Penobscots as well as feature stories about their crafts, traditions, and history for various newspapers. Last but not least, he wrote *The Life and Traditions of the Red Man*. Published in 1893, this classic book is rich in detail concerning the Wabanaki culture hero Glooskap and his adventures. It also tells how, after Glooskap's departure, his Indian children in the Land of the Dawn fought against enemies and then made peace.

Articulate and dignified, Nicolar frequently received invitations to lecture about Penobscot traditions. On top of this he did a bit of land surveying and proved highly successful at growing crops. For a while he served as superintendent of farming for the tribe, submitting written reports, which the Indian agent included in his annual report to the state. Moreover, like most Penobscot men of his day, Nicolar hunted and fished "for the pot" and helped market baskets made by his wife and three daughters. He saw to it that his daughters received formal schooling and classical music training in addition to being well versed in Native traditions. His middle daughter, Lucy, grew up to be a nationally recognized performance artist known as Princess Watahwaso. Trained in opera, she sang on the stages of New York concert halls and recorded for the Victor Talking Machine Company, in addition to presenting popular renditions of American Indian music and stories all across the country on the traveling Chautauqua Circuit. She and her younger sister Florence were political activists who devoted much of their energy pressing for Native rights for Penobscots.

Their mother, Elizabeth Josephs Nicolar, was a Penobscot of part Huron descent. About 21 years younger than their father, she was known as Lizzie. Described by a local newspaper as "respected," "intelligent," and "superior in many ways," Lizzie was "a power for good" in "all the doings" of her people.[2]

Joseph Nicolar's many public lectures included one given in 1892 in partnership with fellow tribesman Frank "Big Thunder" Loring. Together they hired Old Town City Hall for a performance that presented the customs of their people. In their twilight years, these two mates both still commanded attention—Nicolar as a dignified presence accustomed to writing seriously about Penobscot traditions and speaking on behalf of his people in the halls of state government, and Loring as a seasoned entertainer who could package any tradition and bring it to life for public consumption. Their joint city hall performance, as described in the local paper, showcased their contrasting skills and personalities: "Mr. Nicolar" gave "an articulate" lecture and "Big Thunder" quickened everyone's pulse with his "very amusing" enactment of Indian customs. We can assume Nicolar appeared in a suit and tie while Loring donned an Indian costume, including a showy headdress—either a Plains Indian–style warbonnet or one made of ostrich plumes.

After Nicolar's premature death in 1894, his name and reputation lived on—in large part thanks to his book, published the year before he died.[3]

Charles Godfrey Leland (1824–1903)

Leland, a folklorist and lecturer, wrote some fifty books, including *Algonquin Legends of New England—Myths and Folk Lore of the Micmac, Passamaquoddy, and Penobscot Tribes* and several classic texts on English Gypsies and Italian witches. Born into a well-to-do Philadelphia family, his fascination with folklore and the supernatural began early in life. According to his biographer, as a baby, "he was carried up to the garret by his old Dutch nurse, who was said to be a sorceress, and left there with a Bible, a key, and a knife on his breast, lighted candles, money, and a plate of salt at his head"—a rite intended to bring him luck and help him "rise in life and become a scholar and a wizard." Such influences continued as he learned about fairies from an Irish servant and voodoo from a black woman who worked in the kitchen.

Although born and raised in Philadelphia, Leland came from a family with deep roots in New England. As he later wrote: "When I was a boy my happiest moments were spent in

Charles Godfrey Leland, folklorist, ca. 1900. Author of *Algonquin Legends of New England—Myths and Folk Lore of the Mimac, Passamaquoddy, and Penobscot Tribes*, 1884, researched, in part, at Mount Desert Island. (Photo in authors' collection.)

the rural scenery of Massachusetts."[4] After graduating from Princeton at age 21, he sailed for Europe, traveled around Italy and then went on to Germany, where he continued his graduate studies. Venturing to Paris in 1847 and renting a room in the *Quartier Latin* near the Sorbonne, he got caught up in the same revolutionary events that toppled the monarchy. On 24 February 1848, 23-year-old Leland even participated in some fighting. His time in Paris overlapped with that of other romantic foreigners such as the German poet and essayist Heinrich Heine and his philosopher friend Karl Marx.

Upon returning to Philadelphia, Leland studied law, passed the bar, and in 1851 opened his own office. Meanwhile, he continued to write, contributing to leading magazines in New York and Philadelphia. But law did not have his heart, and he increasingly devoted himself to writing. Beyond journalistic work, he translated Heine's poems, winning praise for this literary effort from Henry Wadsworth Longfellow in 1855, the very year Longfellow published his own epic poem "The Song of Hiawatha." According to a friend who wrote to Leland after having dinner with the famous poet, "Longfellow spoke in the highest terms of your translation, both of the poetry and the prose. . . . He further said that when he had completed his examination, with the care that it deserved, he would write you his views in full."[5]

Moving to Boston in 1861 to work for the Republican magazine *The Continental,* Leland got to meet Longfellow personally, along with other literary figures, including Ralph Waldo Emerson and Oliver Wendell Holmes. It was there, during the U.S. Civil War, that he became one of the voices advocating the emancipation of enslaved blacks in the southern states. In 1863 Leland joined the Union Army and participated in the Battle of Gettysburg. Soon after the war ended end, he was invited as a journalist to ride the new railway about to span the entire North American continent. In November 1866, he boarded the train in Philadelphia and traveled westward in comfort to Fort Riley, a military outpost in the Great Plains. There, he encountered armed Cheyenne, Kaw (Kansas), and other mounted tribesmen trying to stop the railroad from slicing through their buffalo-hunting territories.

In the late 1860s, Leland moved to England, where he began his studies of Gypsy society and lore. After ten years, he returned to Philadelphia in 1879, and completed his book, *The Gypsies* (1882). In this work, Leland frequently draws comparisons between American Indians and the Gypsies, explaining, "Ask me why I haunt gypsydom! It has put me into a thousand sympathies with nature and art, which I had never known without it. The Romany, like the red Indian, and all who dwell by wood and wold as outlawes wont to do, are the best human links to bind us to their home-scenery, and lead us into its inner life." But, he added, "there are perishing with the wretched fragments of the red Indian tribes mythologies as beautiful as those of the Greek or Norseman."[6]

Meanwhile, having heard of the Indian encampment in Bar Harbor at Mount Desert Island, Leland began to inquire about Wabanaki legends and stories. In spring 1881, he noted in a letter: "Expect to go to Mount Desert, Maine, in July. Injuns live there who take you out in their canoes!" [7] He continued this pursuit for three years and, according to his niece and biographer, he developed a "close alliance with the peaceful Passamaquoddies weaving their baskets in the pine woods of Bar Harbor and Campobello." [8]

After each summer trip to the Maine seacoast, Leland returned home to Philadelphia with a load of birchbark boxes, perhaps as gifts for friends. He also carried notebooks filled with precious Wabanaki lore, which he reworked and published in his 1884 book, *The Algonquin Legends of New England; or, Myths and Folk Lore of the Micmac, Passamaquoddy and Penobscot Tribes*. Leland "cordially dedicated" this work to "Miss Abby Alger, of Boston," who had been his assistant. As reported in the *Mount Desert Herald* in 1884:

> Charles Leland who during the past three summers has lived among the Indians of the Passamaquoddy with the view to learning their traditions, superstitions and national songs, is now engaged in compiling his material preparatory to publishing it in book form. "When I first turned my mind to this subject," he said, "I went to Bar Harbor, the summer rendezvous for all the Indians in the country, and began work. At first my efforts were fruitless. Do what I would, the Indians would not confide in me, and after spending the entire summer among them, I found that I had learned nothing of their traditions. Their reticence was not without reason. The Indians live among the commonest white people, who take no interest whatever in their legends and superstitions; and besides, the Indians being Roman Catholics, are taught to regard legends as superstition, and as such must be forgotten. Now while they by no means forget them, they are averse to relating them broadcast. Somewhat disappointed with my Bar Harbor results, I turned to Campobello, New Brunswick, in the summer of 1882. There I became acquainted with three Passamaquoddy Indians, men who traveled a great deal and were quite intelligent. They were Peter Gabriel [of Pleasant Pt., born 1841], his son, and Toma-quhah (Tomah Joseph) [of Indian Township, born 1839]. Winning the confidence of these men, I was delighted at discovering the existence among the Indians of a real mythology and folklore, and cycles of legends and traditions. . . . [9]

In the front pages of this book, under the heading "Authorities," Leland identified in a single list the scholars and Wabanakis he consulted in writing the work. Of the Indians listed, at least three spent summers in Bar Harbor (Tomah Joseph(s), Peter Gabriel, and Louis Mitchell):

> *Tomah Josephs*, Passamaquoddy, Indian Governor at Peter Dana's Point, Maine; *John Gabriel*, and his son *Peter J. Gabriel*, Passamaquoddy Indians, of Point Pleasant, Maine; *Noel Josephs*, of Peter Dana's Point, alias *Che gach goch*, the Raven; *Joseph Tomah*, Passamaquoddy, of Pleasant Point; *Louis Mitchell*, Indian member of the Legislature of Maine. To this gentleman I am greatly indebted for manuscripts, letters, and oral narrations of great value; *Sapiel Selmo*, keeper of the Wampum Record, formerly read every four years at the great fire at Canawagha [Mohawk reservation]; *Marie Saksis* of Oldtown, a capital and very accurate narrator of many traditions; *Noel Neptune*, Penobscot, Oldtown, Maine.

Tomah Joseph (1837–1914), one of several Passamaquoddies who collaborated with Leland, served as tribal governor at Peter Dana Point, Indian Township reservation. He made his living as a canoe and hunting guide, and as an artisan especially known for his etched birchbark work. (Collection of the Abbe Museum.)

One of these informants, Marie Saksis (also spelled Saukees/Sakis/Sokes), was Frank "Big Thunder" Loring's niece. It is likely that she was Leland's source for "The Story of Glooskap as told in a few Words by a Woman of the Penobscots," which relays how moose bones turned to stone:

Glus-gahbé gave names to everything. He made men and gave them life, and made the winds to make the waters move. The Turtle was his uncle; the Mink, Uk-see-meezel, his adopted son; and Monin-kwessos, the Woodchuck, his grandmother. . . . At Moose-tchick [the moose's rump – Cape Rosier] he killed a moose; the bones may be seen at Bar Harbor turned to stone. He threw the entrails of the Moose across the [Frenchman] bay to his dogs, and they, too, may be seen there to this day, as I myself have seen them; and there, too, in the rock are the prints of his bow and arrow. [10]

Another story gathered by Leland and directly connected to Mount Desert Island concerns an unnamed Indian doctress with "m'teolulin" (magic or spirit power), whom he encountered in Bar Harbor:

Women are sometimes *m'teolulin.* There is one at Psesuk [11] ("Clambake place"/Bar Harbor) now, this summer. You have met her. She is _____'s wife. [12] If you offend her she can hurt you in strange ways. She is a good doctor. Once she cured a man. When he got well he could not pay her for the medicine. His name is Louis_____. She asked for her money . . . many times; she could not get it. He was going to the woods, far away, to trap; he said he would pay her when he returned, but she wanted it then. She said, 'I will never forget this; I will be revenged.' He went far up the St. John River with his traps; he set them in the stream for beaver. All he caught that winter was sticks, and sometimes an eel. Then at the end of the day he would say to his man, 'It is of no use.' And then they could hear the witch laughing behind the bushes, and tittering when he came home. So it went on long. Then he was sorry, and said, 'I wish I had paid that woman what I owed her.' And at once they heard a voice from the bushes, or rocks, say, 'Louis, that will do. It is enough.' And the next day they caught two beaver, and every day two, and so on, till the season was over. This happened in 1872, in the Miramichi [New Brunswick, Canada] Waters. [13]

Not long after *Algonquin Legends* was published, Louis Mitchell of Pleasant Point informed Leland that there were other narratives and poems quite different from those already in the folklorist's possession. Among these precious indigenous documents was a history of the Passamaquoddy Tribe, illustrated with numerous designs of "the birch-bark school of art." Since Leland had returned to Europe and was occupied promoting folklore studies there and pursuing his passion for Gypsies, he passed this valuable Wabanaki material on to his friend Dr. Daniel G. Brinton, then professor of American linguistics and archaeology at the University of Pennsylvania. [14]

Back in Europe, Leland became founding president of the English Gypsy-Lore Society in 1888, and the following year he served as president of the first European folklore congress, held in Paris. Thanks in good measure to him, folklore became a respectable field of study. A colleague in England even asked him: "Why not an American corresponding Society of Gypsies, started with the help of Miss Alger?" [15]

After his friend Brinton's death in 1899, Leland realized that the ancient Wabanaki legends he had collected and transcribed as prose were, in fact, poems "chanted as a tale." [16] Wanting to revisit *Algonquin Legends*, he contacted the linguist Dr. John D. Prince, then a young professor at Columbia University. Both men shared a keen interest in foreign languages (including Romany), folklore, and, last but not least, Algonquian cultures. When first contacted by Leland, Prince had already established his own personal contact with Louis Mitchell at Bar Harbor in 1887. Soon afterwards, both scholars collaborated on the Glooskap cycle, rendering it poetic English. In 1902, they published the Glooskap poems. Leland mentioned these poems—and the value of Indian lore in one of his last letters:

> I have had a great part of the proofs of the Epic of Kuloskap, Glusgabe – Glooskap. *Do* keep an eye on the book—it will be out soon. And try—try to collect Indian poems. It is a new field, and I recommend you to collect them and correspond with Prof. Prince. Go at it earnestly, be among the first. For I foresee that sooner or later every scrap, good or bad, will be studied and admired to a degree of which no one now living has any idea whatever, and men will wonder that among all the scholars of our age so few cared for such a marvelous record of the vanished race. [17]

In this same letter, Leland also lamented the recent death of his devoted wife Isabel, who had stood by him and his work for nearly fifty years: "I *miss* her who was my only company for so many years and entered so into every little consultation and deed of life that to have nobody and be *responsible* to no one . . . is as bewildering and new to me as if I myself had died!" Within a year of Isabel's passing, Leland died in Italy. His sister and her husband, the Rev. Wood, were by his side and made sure that his ashes were transported across the ocean and placed in a grave alongside Isabel's. [18]

Albert Samuel Gatschet (1832–1907)

Born in Switzerland, Albert S. Gatschet was trained as a linguist at universities in Bern and Berlin. Coming to the United States in 1869, he helped pioneer the study of Native American languages. In 1877 he became ethnologist of the U.S. Geological Survey and in 1879 a member of the newly organized Bureau of American Ethnology at the Smithsonian Institution in Washington, D.C. He remained on the Bureau's staff for nearly thirty years, retiring in 1905, two years before his death.

Like other folklorists, linguists, and anthropologists who did research on Mount Desert Island, Gatschet worked especially with Passamaquoddy Louis Mitchell. But he also gathered information from at least two other Passamaquoddies: Newell Salomon Francis (born 1840) and his brother-in-law Lewis Soctomah (1833). About Soctomah, Gatschet noted, he "knows all about old local names; over 70 years old. Lives in Pleasant Point." [19]

Gatschet also consulted with Francis in Washington, D.C., while Francis was in the capital helping fellow Passamaquoddies Joe Tomah and Francis Lola work on an exhibition for the newly founded Smithsonian National zoological park in Washington D.C. Commonly known as the National Zoo, its natural landscape was designed by Frederic Law Olmsted and originally envisioned as a protected natural enclave where endangered American animals could breed in captivity and the public could be educated about wildlife. The idea to invite three "vanishing Indians" from the Maine seacoast and pay them to reconstruct their "primitive" bark wigwams in a Zoological Park conformed entirely to popular American ideology and is detailed in the following newspaper excerpt:

> The *Washington Post* of March 25th has the following description of an old-time Passamaquoddy
> Indian hut, recently built in that city by two Passamaquoddy Indians, Joe Tomah, who now
> lives in Rockland, Maine [overlooking Penobscot Bay], and Francis Lola of Pleasant Point, who
> is still in Washington, D.C. The Indians were employed for this work on the recommendation
> of Prof. Gatschet who spent last summer in eastern Maine. The primitive birch bark wigwam,
> which has been in course of construction during the past winter at the Zoological Park, is
> now practically completed and is probably the only one of its kind in existence today. It was
> constructed under the supervision of the Bureau of Ethnology as an attraction for the visitors to
> the Zoo. . . . The structure is 15 feet long, 13.5 feet broad and 9 feet high. The Indians first drove
> tall stakes of arbor vitae into the ground for each side of the building. These were bent over at
> the top in a half circle and tied together with thongs of split ash. Other poles were driven at both
> ends of the building and then smaller poles were tied across these after the manner of slats in

a shingle roof. The birch-bark was put on in large square pieces and sewed together with split spruce root. The sewing of these pieces of bark is the most attractive part of the work, and was accomplished with a needle made of bone. . . . The bark is turned with the outside exposed and renders the wigwam impervious to the severest rains. Inside, just as you enter, there is a small square space divided off by poles laid upon the ground. Inside of this space the floor is bare earth and here is the fireplace directly beneath the opening in the roof. All around next to the walls little branches of spruce are spread and this is used for the sleeping place. . . . [20]

Although Newell Francis is not mentioned in the above article, Gatschet described him as "builder of the Indian wigwam in the Zoological Park, District of Columbia, in January 1897"…He and Francis met on several occasions over a period of at least three months, and Gatschet made use of these sessions to continue his linguistic and ethnographic work. [21] Francis, like Louis Mitchell and some of Gatschet's other Passamaquoddy collaborators, helped the linguist with words and phrases in their own language as well as with those in Penobscot. Given the long-time association among Wabanaki groups, extensive intermarriage and shared seasonal encampments, such multi-linguistic versatility is not surprising. As noted by linguist Philip Lesourd: "Many Passamaquoddy speakers in the last decade of the 19th century had a good knowledge of Penobscot and at least some familiarity with Western Abenaki. Some thirty years earlier, Eugene Vetromile, an Italian Jesuit missionary who ministered to the Indian population of Maine, noted that 'the Passamaquoddy Indians generally know the Catechism in Penobscot language." [22]

Fannie Hardy Eckstorm (1866–1946)

Graduating from Smith College in 1888, Fannie Hardy was among a privileged group of women in her day who gained a formal education beyond high school. Moreover, she was well educated by her life circumstances as well as by a keen intellectual curiosity that drove her to explore the depths of the fragmented Wabanaki communities that comprised part of her world. As the granddaughter of fur trader Jonathan Hardy, who was in regular contact with Penobscot Indians on the seacoast and in Maine's Bangor/Brewer area, she had a unique opportunity to look into the lifeways of Maine's indigenous peoples. [23] Her father, Manly Hardy, grew up well connected to Wabanaki traditions and woods lore. He passed on much of what he absorbed to Fannie, who continued and deepened the association as a prolific writer of Wabanaki history and culture. In the words of Fannie's biographer, Elizabeth Ring, Manly Hardy "counseled [his daughter] to win and deserve the confidence of the Indians, to learn their language and the meaning of their nomenclature, and to study their tribal customs." [24] This she did, and her resulting contributions to our understanding of 19th-century Wabanaki cultures in particular are considerable—ranging from commentaries on the region's natural and industrial history to an ambitious investigation of Wabanaki place names in Maine to a collection of folklore and songs to biographical writing about individuals whose lives were emblematic of Native communities in Maine.

Fannie Hardy grew up in the Penobscot River town of Brewer, about a dozen miles down-river from Indian Island. Living there among her father's Wabanaki friends and associates in the

Fannie Hardy Eckstorm,
historian/folklorist, ca. 1893.
(Collection of the Maine
Historical Society.)

heyday of Maine lumbering and shipping, she saw first-hand the lumbering industry's impact on the Native population and their habitat. Her father was a naturalist and she roamed the woods with him countless times until her 1893 marriage to Protestant minister Jacob Eckstorm in 1893:

> These years that preceded her marriage were the genesis of her later work. As she tramped the woods with her father, she learned the habits of mink and of coon . . . . wolf [and] otter. . . . He encouraged her to keep wildlife notes. In her later life, as other interests crowded out her study in this field, she would note the records of trappers with an appraising eye and compare them with those made years earlier by her father. When down on the Cranberry Isles, where she would go on a hunt for ballads or to note Indian landmarks, she would absorb the stories of Indian trappers and later recall them at will. [25]

In addition to meeting with Wabanakis on the Cranberry Isles, Eckstorm also visited Indians on Mount Desert Island. She met with Passamaquoddy artisan John Snow in Northeast Harbor— perhaps when calling on her Boston friend Mary Cabot Wheelwright who summered there or during the time she collected a version of the ballad "The Indian Elopement" from Mrs. Rose Robbins, who also lived in the village. [26] In addition, Eckstorm may be the woman who bought a Passamaquoddy story from Snow at a circa 1929 social gathering in Northeast Harbor recalled by his daughter. We know she and Snow were in touch thanks to a letter Passamaquoddy Louis Mitchell wrote to Eckstorm. [27] Mitchell and Eckstorm were in frequent contact by mail, and probably first met on Mount Desert Island, in all likelihood at the Bar Harbor's Indian encampment. [28] Their exchanges center on Indian "relics" he was acquiring (mostly for Eckstorm's friend Wheelwright) and information he offered in response to her queries. For example, here are excerpts from letters they exchanged in May 1930:

> Dear Madam,
>
> When I look over my letters, some Questions you asked for I did not answer. . . . One of the Neptunes your father mentioned, Sabattis Mitchell['s] father-in-law, he was John Francis Neptune. He was Chief of the Passamaquoddy Tribe for 30 years. He died in 1872. He was the son of Francis Joseph Neptune of the Revolutionary War. His grandfather Bah-gal-wett, also of the Revolutionary times; his Christian name is Jean Babtist Neptune. Both the Neptunes fought under Col. John Allan. . . .
>
> I have few relics for Miss Wheelwright. . . . If you want more place names I can get them now the weather is warmer, such as marks on Roque's Bluffs. The Indians go by the place on their seal-hunting trips. If Miss Wheelwright come home please let me know. . . .

> My Dear Mr. Mitchell,
>
> Your letter came at just the right time; for I was thinking of writing today to Miss Wheelwright's Boston address to find out whether she was home yet and to ask when she wanted me to send her the stories I got from you last winter. . . .
>
> I have not been able to get the meaning for M'jelm't, the name you gave as nickname of old John Neptune. Oldtown [Penobscot] Indians say they did not know he had any nickname.
>
> Though I never heard the story of the Mohawk who lived here, I knew that there were Mohawks in our Tribe. In Revolutionary times they went by the name of Cook – Joseph Cook was one. My father used to go muskrat hunting with Joe Mary Mohawk, a man older than himself.

Upon marrying Reverend Eckstorm in 1893, Fannie moved to Boston with him and took up motherhood and editing work. But the marriage lasted only six years—until his death in 1899. After his passing, she moved back to Brewer with their children and began a career of research and writing that continued for the rest of her life. Her important publications include *Indian Place Names of the Penobscot Valley and the Maine Coast*, first published in 1941.

John Dyneley Prince (1868–1945)

In the summer of 1887, some 20,000 visitors came to Mount Desert Island. [29] Among them was the gifted linguist Dr. John Dyneley Prince. This young professor of Semitic languages at

New York's Columbia University was also keenly interested in Algonquian Indian languages and in Romany as spoken by Gypsies.[30] While in Bar Harbor, Prince also met Passamaquoddy tribal representative Louis Mitchell from Pleasant Point, and they discussed Passamaquoddy linguistics, oral traditions, and the *Wapapi Akonutomakonol* or Wampum Records.[31] Mitchell gleaned these records orally from Passamaquoddy wampum keeper Sopiel Selmo (also spelled Selma or Selmore).

After a return trip to Mount Desert Island the following year, Prince wrote "Notes on the Language of Eastern Algonkin Tribes," noting in the conclusion that "it was solely from the mouths of the Indians in Bar Harbor . . . that I gathered the above information."[32] In the years that followed, Prince kept returning to the island for his linguistic research among the Passamaquoddy and Penobscot.

In 1899, Prince brought with him the latest in high-tech sound equipment: a wax cylinder phonograph,[33] which he used to record "six tales of witchcraft" told in Passamaquoddy by 60-year-old Newell S[alomon] Francis of Pleasant Point,[34] one of many Wabanakis at the Indian encampment that summer. The next year Prince published his transcriptions and analyses of these texts in the American Philosophical Society's *Proceedings* under the title "Some Passamaquoddy Witchcraft Tales." He continued to work with Francis for some time, probably during his subsequent trips to Bar Harbor.[35] In a 1902 article on Penobscot and Canadian Abenaki dialects, he reported, "The Penobscot material used in this treatise has all been gathered orally from Indians in Bar Harbor, Maine." Significantly, among the examples of Penobscot sentences given in this paper we see the following: "I know your language a little. I learned it at Bar Harbor."[36] In his 1910 *American Anthropologist* article, "The Penobscot Language of Maine," Prince commented that the stories, phrases, and glossary included "the whole of Penobscot material, which I have obtained orally from Penobscot Indians at Bar Harbor, Me., during the past ten years."

Prince also collaborated with fellow scholars, co-publishing *Kuloskap the Master, and Other Algonquin Poems* with Charles G. Leland in 1902, and three articles on the Pequot-Mohegan language in 1903 and 1904 with his Columbia University undergraduate student Frank Speck, who later went on to write many works concerning Wabanakis.

In 1906, Prince entered politics, becoming a member of the New Jersey State House of Assembly for three years, serving as Speaker of the Assembly in 1909 and then as state senator from 1910 to 1912. From 1921 to 1926 he held the post of U.S. Minister to Denmark. In 1926 he became U.S. Minister to the Kingdom of the Serbs, Croats & Slovenes—a position that was changed to U.S. Minister to Yugoslavia in 1929. He left this appointment a year early in 1932, after being passed over for the post of U.S. Ambassador to the Netherlands—where he had ancestral roots. His richly varied life came to an end in 1945, at the age of 77.

Frank Gouldsmith Speck (1881–1950)

In the introduction to his 1940 book *Penobscot Man: The Life History of a Forest Tribe in Maine*, an important anthropological study of the Indian Island community at Old Town, Dr. Frank

Anthropologist Frank Gouldsmith Speck with two Indian companions in 1913, the year he interviewed Maliseets Louis and Caroline Francis at Bar Harbor. Dr. Speck authored the important book on the Wabanaki tribal community headquartered at Indian Island, Old Town, titled *Penobscot Man: The Life History of a Forest Tribe in Maine* (1940). (Collection of the American Philosophical Society.)

Speck described his "systematic attempt to investigate the long-neglected [Wabanaki] bands . . . in northern New England and eastern Canada. Attention was first directed to the Penobscot in northern Maine. . . . Beginning with the summer of 1907, the succeeding summers through 1912 were spent mostly in contact with the people at home and in their summer camps," in addition to winter visits to reservations. [37]

The Speck family owned a summer cottage in Gloucester on the Massachusetts coast. Details about Speck's activities on Mount Desert Island are scant, but some of his research took place there. As noted by his former student Dr. Edmund Carpenter: "Speck often went to Bar Harbor" and he "went there for Indians." [38] And Speck himself, in a footnote on sources for data on Maliseet personal animal nicknames, mentions being there: "This material was first brought to my attention by [Maliseets] Louis Francis and his wife Caroline Francis, in 1913, at Bar Harbor, Me., both of them reliable informants of the old school." [39]

Stories about Dr. Speck passed down among Wabanakis paint a picture of a man fully at ease in Indian communities. According to Gilbert Ketchum, a Penobscot whose adopted father Jim Lewis guided the young scholar on an ethnographic artifact search along the coast, "Frank Speck, he's a good one. . . . He liked the Indians, and he could talk Indian as much as I could."[40]

Frank Speck's interest in North America's indigenous peoples began early in life. From age eight to fifteen, he spent summers in a small Mohegan Indian community in Connecticut. His parents sent him there for doses of healthy living with Fidelia Fielding, an old widow and family friend and one of the last speakers of her Native Mohegan-Pequot dialect. Fielding taught young Frank her language and shared a wealth of traditional knowledge with him. His experiences with the Mohegan led him to study at Columbia University under professor John Dyneley Prince, who had a reputation as one of the most prominent linguists of American Indian languages at the time. As an undergraduate at Columbia University, Speck surprised his mentor by offering some specifics on Pequot, an Indian language thought to have been dead. [41] Mrs. Fielding, meanwhile, served as the chief informant for Speck and Dyneley's linguistic studies. [42] After doctoral fieldwork among the Yuchi in Oklahoma, Speck went on to become a well-known anthropology professor at the University of Pennsylvania. There he helped build a great department, which he chaired until his death. His office was a lively place where "an ever-changing cast of colleagues, students, friends, Indian delegations, and strangers gathered . . . to work, visit or participate in seminars," and sometimes present "spontaneous 'recitals' of traditional Indian songs." [43]

A tireless fieldworker with a special interest in Algonquian tribes of the Eastern Woodlands, in particular Wabanaki and Innu (Naskapi-Montagnais of Labrador), and able to speak Penobscot and several other Algonquian languages, Dr. Speck authored numerous publications and collected ethnographic artifacts for a dozen museums in the U.S. and abroad. He became critically ill when attending a traditional Seneca Indian mid-winter ceremony at Cold Spring Longhouse in upstate New York, dying soon thereafter at the age of 68.

Birth of Acadia National Park

While some scholars journeyed to Mount Desert Island in an effort to preserve a record of Wabanaki legends and languages, others came with an eye toward documenting and preserving its still largely unspoiled habitat. A catalyst in Mount Desert's natural conservation effort was Charles Eliot (1859–1897), son of Dr. Charles W. Eliot, a professor of chemistry and president of Harvard University from 1869–1909. In the summer of 1880, the younger Charles visited Mount Desert with some fellow Harvard College students. Establishing the Champlain Society to study the island's many scientific aspects, they pitched camp on the eastern shore of Somes Sound, just above the home of Asa Smallidge. Inspired by this sojourn, Charles wrote to his parents, pressing upon them to buy a tract of land for a family summer home on the coast between "our campground on Somes Sound and Seal Harbor. Somewhere on that line you will find a site that will suit you—a site with beautiful views of sea and hills, good anchorage, fine rocks and beach and no flats." [44] And so they did. Little more than a year later, the Eliot family moved into their summer cottage, Blueberry Ledge.

Participating in the Champlain Society's Mount Desert expeditions two summers in a row sparked young Charles' interest in environmental management. After graduation in 1882, he apprenticed with Frederick Law Olmsted, the "father of American landscape architecture," famous for designing New York City's Central Park (1859) and many other well-known urban

parks. In 1883, when a Maine entrepreneur wanted to develop a planned "summer colony" on Cushing Island, his privately owned offshore island in Casco Bay, Maine, he commissioned Olmsted's firm, which had just relocated from New York to Brookline, Massachusetts, to

George Dorr (left) and Charles W. Eliot, known as Acadia National Park's founding fathers, at Jordan Pond, Mount Desert Island, ca. 1905. (Collection of Acadia National Park.)

design that small island's landscape. Although Olmsted was familiar with the Maine coast because his family had owned a summer cottage at Deer Isle in Penobscot Bay for many years, he gave the assignment to his young apprentice, Charles Eliot. Two years later, Charles left Olmsted and journeyed to Europe to see the famous public gardens with his own eyes and study natural landscape designs.

In 1886, he returned to Boston, opened his own landscape architecture office and quickly garnered commissions. By this time, he was a man with a keen vision, articulated in an 1890 article in *Garden and Forest Magazine* in which he outlined "a strategy for conserving [natural] areas of scenic beauty in the same way that the Boston Public Library held books and the Museum of Fine Arts pictures." This landmark publication prompted a conference on the preservation of scenic beauty at the Massachusetts Institute of Technology. The conference, in turn, resulted in the State of Massachusetts passing legislation in 1891, creating the Trustees of Public Reservations, charged to "acquire, hold, protect and administer, for the benefit of the public, beautiful and historical places."

Having quickly gained national notoriety as a landscape designer, young Charles accepted an invitation from Olmsted in 1891 to become a full partner in Olmsted's firm. Tragically, four years later Charles died of meningitis. He was just 37 years old. [45] Yet, while his own work was cut short, his vision did not die.

In the summer of 1901, apparently inspired by his son's vision as a nature conservationist, Dr. Eliot called a meeting among fellow rusticators from Northeast Harbor, Bar Harbor, and Seal Harbor to discuss the idea of establishing "reservations at points of interest on this Island for the perpetual use of the public." The group organized the Hancock County Trustees of Public Reservations, and within a year and half this corporation had tax-free status and a charter that stated its purpose: "To acquire, by devise, gift or purchase, and to own, arrange, hold, maintain or improve for public use lands in Hancock County, Maine, which by reason of scenic beauty, historical interest, sanitary advantage or other like reasons may become available for such purpose." [46] Among those attending the first meeting in 1901 was George B. Dorr, whose father built Old Farm, one of the earliest grand cottages in Bar Harbor. Driven by the idea of preserving the natural beauty of the island that had been his seasonal home since boyhood, Dorr devoted over four decades of his life—and most of his family fortune—to the effort.

By 1913 the corporation had acquired 6,000 acres. This included Green (Cadillac) Mountain, "centerpiece of the emergent park," [47] quietly purchased for the cause by the railway magnate and Bar Harbor cottager John S. Kennedy just before his death in 1909. Dorr, hoping for national park status, offered all of the corporation's land holdings to the federal government. He achieved partial victory in 1916 when U.S. President Woodrow Wilson announced the creation of Sieur de Monts National Monument.

Dorr continued to acquire property and held to the goal of obtaining full national park status for the expanding preserve. In 1919 Wilson signed the federal law establishing Lafayette National Park, the first national park east of the Mississippi. Dorr became its first superintendent. Ten years later, it was renamed Acadia National Park. [48] By then, John D. Rockefeller, Jr., whose 100-room cottage, Eyrie, sat on a wooded granite ledge in Seal Harbor, was well on his way to completing his most extraordinary contribution to the park: an extensive network of carriage trails that he designed and financed. Commenced in 1913 and taking more than two decades to complete, it features 17 stone bridges and nearly 50 miles of gravel roads that weave along the natural contours of the land, here and there offering sweeping vistas. They are lined with rough-cut granite stones that serve as guardrails—fondly referred to as "Rockefeller's teeth".

The founding of the park was a remarkable achievement. However, for Wabanakis of the day it imposed just one more layer of restrictions in the natural environment where their ancestors had ranged freely for thousands of years. Its creation even impacted their encampment at Ledgelawn Avenue, which in the early 1920s was converted into a short-lived auto camp for park visitors. Eventually, park administrators and Wabanakis developed a mutual appreciation and even engaged in collaborative efforts. But that did not happen for many years.

Birth of the Abbe Museum

Dr. Robert Abbe, Bar Harbor rusticator and founder of the museum that bears his name, in a birchbark canoe in Duck Brook, ca. 1920. (Collection of the Abbe Museum).

For many decades, residents and summer rusticators in the Mount Desert Island area engaged in "recreational" Indian artifact-hunting in local shell middens—seriously damaging, or even completely destroying, many of these ancient indigenous camping sites in the process. Wealthy people placed their findings on fireplace mantels or in display cases. Those of lesser means displayed them on windowsills—or sold them to boost the family income. And so it was that one day in 1922, long-time Bar Harbor rusticator Dr. Robert Abbe took a walk down Cottage Street, saw a window display of a dozen prehistoric tools, and decided to buy the collection for study. Over the next few years, this acclaimed New York surgeon and medical pioneer bought other collections and committed himself to protecting and displaying such artifacts to ensure public awareness of the region's original inhabitants and to prod contemplation about life as it was long before the onset of industrialization. Prodding others to add to the collection, Dr. Abbe also raised funds to build a trailside museum in Mount Desert Island's newly established national park to showcase the artifacts. His goal was not to amass a vast inventory. Rather, in his words, he hoped to "fix indelibly a fact of incontrovertible history on the minds of the large and rapidly growing traveling public. My aim has been to create a permanent classic 'one show' historic incident in the path of the 'Madding Crowd' and

Dr. Robert Abbe's drawing of the museum he conceived. He sent out a refined version of this sketch as a Christmas card in 1927, the year before his death and the museum's inauguration. (Collection of the Abbe Museum.)

to make it as perfect as possible," a place where people might "linger and dream over this small and unique collection."

Dr. Abbe received considerable help from his friends George Dorr and Charles W. Eliot, the founding fathers of Acadia National Park, who envisioned an Indian artifact museum as a complement to the park's offerings. In a remarkably short time Abbe's dream was realized in a lovely trailside museum situated at Sieur de Monts Spring. Founded in 1927, the museum opened in the summer of 1928. Its dedicatory ceremony also served as a memorial for Dr. Abbe, who died in March of that year. Beyond gathering the collection housed in the new building, he had created maps and drawings for its displays. Shortly before his death, he painted a small watercolor of the museum.

Dr. Abbe's absence on opening day was conspicuous, but it appears people in the crowd failed to notice that he was not the only missing person invested in the artifacts on display. Wabanakis, whose ancestors had made and used the items in the museum's collection, were not part of the inaugural event. Their absence, coupled with the museum's original full name—The Lafayette National Park Museum of Stone-age Antiquities—underscores the common mainstream assumption that Indians in Maine were part of the past, not the present. Even Dr. Abbe, it seems, bought into the

idea of the "vanishing Indian." Had he lived another fifty years, he would have been surprised—not only by the survival and cultural resurgence of Maine's Wabanaki tribes, but by the supportive role the museum he founded would have in that revitalization.

Opening day at the Abbe Museum of Stone Age Antiquities, 1928. (Collection of the Abbe Museum)

CHAPTER TEN

A Perfect Shame:
Bar Harbor Village Improvement Association

With the advent of a Village Improvement Society certain new-fangled and disturbing ideas as to sanitary conditions obtained a hearing, and the Indians were banished to a back road out of the way of sensitive eyes and noses.

(F. Marion Crawford, "Bar Harbor," Scribner's Magazine Vol 16: 3, pp. 271-72, 1896)

From its first location on Bar Harbor's north shore, east of Main Street, in the early 1860s, the Wabanaki summer village of white canvas tents and shanties made of wooden planks and bark strips gradually shifted westward, making way for the construction of wharves and hotels. By 1881, the camp had inched to the foot of Bar/Bridge Street. With a cottage-building boom underway and hotels swiftly expanding in size, number, and amenities, land values were rising and white middle-class tolerance for a sprawling Indian encampment in plain sight of visitors landing at the wharf or strolling through town was falling.

In mid-July of that year, Bar Harbor town officials tried to push the Wabanakis out of sight, forcing them to relocate their camping site. As noted in the local newspaper: "Contrary to the usual custom of the [red] race, the Indians of Bar Harbor have gone South instead of West. The hauling of their bark-roofed houses through the streets of our village created quite an excitement." Three days later the paper announced, "The Indians are much pleased with their new location." Whether this claim was true or not, we do not know, but the new location may well have been Albert Meadow, on the town's eastside shore near Balance Rock.[1] Early Bar Harbor settler A.L. Higgins mentioned this meadow as one of the Indian encampment sites he personally remembered from the island's "olden days from 1860 to 1900."[2]

Where Will the Indians Go?

At summer's end in 1881, townspeople dubbing themselves the Bar Harbor Village Improvement Association adopted a constitution late one evening "at an adjourned citizen's meeting,

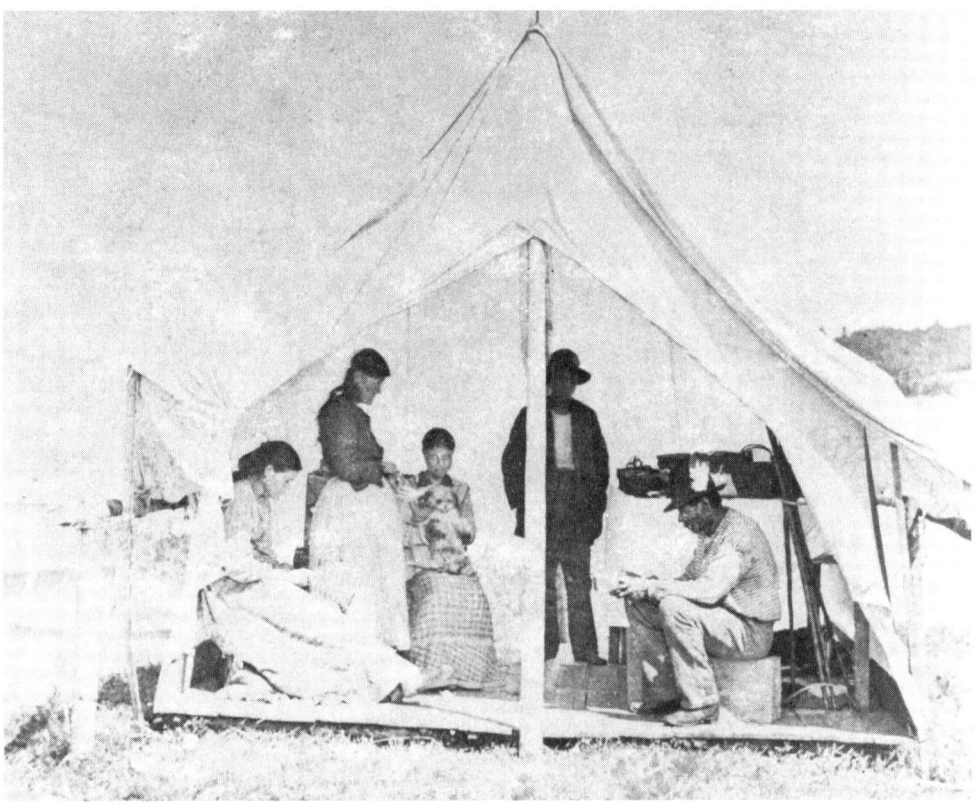

held at the Cottage Street school-house." Apparently, an agenda item for the association in its nascent year was the banning or relocation of the Indian encampment. Records suggest the issue remained unresolved, for the following summer the local paper reported:

Close view of one Wabanaki sale tent, ca. early 1880s. (Photo by B.W. Kilburn. National Anthropological Archives, photo no. 00930700).

> Just now the question is 'Where shall the Indian go this summer?' Otter Creek, one of the Por-
> cupines, Kebo road, and many other places have been suggested, but no decision reached. Some
> of the Aborigines, tired of waiting, have already encamped on the shore near Hamor's wharf,
> not far from their old [Bar/Bridge Streeet] camping ground. The authorities should look after
> this important matter at once.[3]

An item in the newspaper the following month shows that Mount Desert Island's seasonal visitors were not in agreement with what appears to have been a movement to ban Indians from Bar Harbor:

> Now that the Indians have not been allowed to come here, we begin to appreciate their value.
> Summer guests say they 'think it a perfect shame' that there is no Indian Camp here. 'It used to
> be one of the unique attractions of the place.' We are afraid there will be a general outcry among

the fairer sex, if the Indians are not allowed camping ground. Hundreds of people visited them every day and considered it great fun to look over and purchase the wares of the aborigines. [4]

For Wabanakis, such mixed signals—indicative of the ambivalent racism they had come to expect from their white neighbors—meant the door to vitally important summer trade remained at least partially ajar, so they continued to come. In late July the paper announced: "On Friday there was quite a large arrival of Penobscot Indians, who located near Hamor's wharf. Eight tents." [5]

Published news items about the Bar Harbor encampment from 1883 to 1886 place it "at the foot of Holland Avenue, near Hamor's Wharf"—an area some referred to as the "Devil's Half Acre." A handful of written descriptions and illustrations reveal a somewhat formalized public sales area with market stalls that were "half tent, half booth . . . erected to leave a well-swept carriage-road between the lines. [6] But the backside of this area was a more chaotic collection of wood shanties along the shore."

The Hamor's wharf location proved to be short-lived due to the growing value of and demand for prime real estate along West Street (now extended to Holland Avenue). As noted in the centennial souvenir edition of the *Bar Harbor Record* in July 1896: "In 1887 there appeared a speck on the horizon in the form of a land boom. . . . Land companies sprung up in a night. Stories of fabulous sales and rise in land values were spread like wildfire. A strip of land surrounding the old Hamor Wharf and called the 'Devil's Half Acre' arose in fictitious value till they saw millions in it. Men mortgaged their land to buy more. . . ." Before long, the boom went bust, but on its heels came "a strong, steady, healthy growth which has continued and will continue."

The year the boom began, Wabanakis were instructed to relocate their camp westward from "Devil's Half Acre" to "the rear of Mr. A.W. Ells store at Eddy Brook." [7] An 1887 map locates the Ells' store just east of Eddy Brook on the south side of Eden Street, and a photograph shows the Wabanaki encampment extending from behind the store down the slope toward the shore where the brook spills into Frenchman Bay. [8] A brief narrative written in 1888 that describes the place, its inhabitants, and the goods they offered for sale:

Bar Harbor Indian encampment near Hamor's wharf at the foot of Holland Avenue. A shoreside view of this encampment is shown in the next photograph. (*Frank Leslie's Illustrated Newspaper* 8/23/1884. Authors' collection.

THE CAMP

MAINE. — THE PASSAMAQUODDY INDIAN ENCAMPMENT AT BAR HARBOR.
FROM A SKETCH BY C. UPHAM.

The Indian encampment at the outlet of Eddy Brook, just north-west of Bar Harbor, will be found a pleasant place to wile away an hour or two. These [Indians] are of the Penobscot, Passamaquoddy, and St. John River [Maliseet] tribes ... expert with their canoes and at hunting and fishing. The village is composed of a score or two of little wood and canvas shanties, in which are sold a great variety of aboriginal trinkets, skins of seal and deer, baskets of birch-bark, moccasins, bead-work, snow-shoes, gulls' breast, stuffed birds, clubs, carved tusks, bows and arrows, etc. [9]

At first glance this looks like the Bar Harbor Indian encampment when it was located at the foot of Bar/Bridge Street. But it actually shows the village as it was when located along the shoreline and field near Hamor's wharf, ca. 1885—a place some referred to as the "Devil's Half Acre." Two rows of sale tents (and booths) were located in the field just above these wooden structures. (National Anthropological Archives.)

For the Convenience of the Village

The Wabanaki encampment remained at the Eddy Brook site through the summer season of 1889. That year the Village Improvement Association, which had become rather laissez-faire, regrouped with renewed determination, as indicated in several notices in the local paper:

A meeting was held at the St. Sauveur hotel last Saturday forenoone, for the organization of a Village Improvement Association. Mr. Parke Godwin, of NY, was chosen chairman, and Joseph Wood, of Bar Harbor, secretary. The meeting was addressed by Messrs. Parke Godwin, Morris K. Jesup, Charles T. How, Joseph Wood, C.S. Leffingwell and L.B. Deasy. A committee on organization was appointed consisting of Messrs. John T. Higgins, Fountain Rodick, Elihu

Part of the Bar Harbor Indian village, ca. 1889, when the Wabanaki encampment was situated near Eddy Brook outlet between the shore and Eden Street. Indian families set up their sale tents and living quarters here during the summers of 1887–89. A boardwalk ran from Eden Street behind Ells' Store and along the row of canvas tents that extended toward the shore. (Collection of the Maine Historic Preservation Commission.)

G.T. Hamor, B.S. Higgins, Fred A. Shaw, Morris K. Jesup, William R. Rice, Charles T. Howe. . . . The meeting then adjourned to Sat. July 27. [10]

At the adjourned meeting of the Bar Harbor Village Improvement Association held at Hotel St. Sauveur on Sat. July 17, a constitution was adopted and . . . officers were elected. . . . From this board are to be formed a committee on Finance and an Executive comm., inspection comm., entertainment committee, water front committee, and suggestion committee. [11]

Now that the Bar Harbor Village improvement Association has emerged from its dormant condition and been newly organized for business, it will be of interest to all Bar Harbor people to know just what the society is and what it proposes to do. This information can be given in no better way than by publishing its Constitution and By Laws, and we take pleasure in laying them before our readers.

"Constitution: Preamble. Whereas it is evident to all who are interested in the village of Bar Harbor that some method of united action is needed in order to preserve the natural beauties of the place, and to encourage artificial improvements, by the ornamentation of the streets and public grounds of the village; by planting and cultivating trees; erecting tasteful buildings, clearing and repairing sidewalks, lighting streets and doing such other acts as shall tend to beautify, adorn and be for the convenience of the village. . . ." [12]

The goals of Bar Harbor's revitalized Improvement Association, combined with real estate development along Bar Harbor's north flank, had direct consequences for Wabanaki families who were relocated yet again in the summer of 1890. This time they were moved to a site at the southern edge of town, near Cromwell Stream on the east side of Ledgelawn Avenue, near the intersection of Cromwell Harbor Road and what came to be Ash Street. School Street had not yet been extended that far south, so it did not separate the encampment from a large swatch of land owned by the Rodick family on the west side of lower Main Street—a piece of property that in the early 1900s became the town's athletic field. The first known written indicator of the "Ledgelawn Indian encampment" comes from a description published in 1891, probably describing the scene as it was in 1890:

> The winding shore path leading to Cromwell's Cove is still as charming a promenade as ever. You enjoy the open sea-view, the bracing air, the splash of the waves at your feet, the gliding sails, the tasteful cottages. . . . I found it quite different, however, when walking in the street [Main St.] skirting this fine bit of shore. Here the inhospitable warnings, 'No Thoroughfare,' 'No Trespassing,' or 'No Passage,' stare one in the face as often as some inviting by-way tempts one to turn aside. . . . In going a little farther on I ran up against the ill-favored camp of some peripatetic Indians. . . . [13]

The new Indian village at the town's southern end featured two central rows of wood-walled platform canvas tents with wide double-doors that families opened to indicate they were open for business. Although pictures do not show it, surely there were other tents and wooden shanties scattered about beyond these neat rows, probably closer to Cromwell Stream. Apparently, being relegated to a location away from the shore did not discourage Wabanakis, who depended on sales in Bar Harbor for their livelihoods. As noted by the *Mount Desert Herald* in the fall of 1890:

> The *Eastport Sentinel* of September 17 . . . chronicles the return of Indians to their winter home at Pleasant Point. Quite a delegation of returning summer visitors arrived from Bar Harbor by the *Winthrop* boat Monday. [14]

About this time, *Scribner's Magazine* featured an article about Bar Harbor. While devoting most of his words to the weather and social activities of tourists and cottagers, the writer offers this peek at locals and Indians—including the impact Victorian taste was having on the traditional arts of the Wabanaki:

THE INDIAN VILLAGE, BAR HARBOR, ME.

Arthur Livingston, Publisher, New York. 413

This photograph of Wabanaki sale tents at the Ledgelawn Indian village is probably the most circulated picture of any Indian encampment on Mount Desert Island. Printed and reprinted during the early 1900s, it was marketed as a postcard. (Collection of the Maine Historic Preservation Commission.)

Wandering through the streets of the little village [of Bar Harbor] one is struck again and again by the sharp contrast between what may be called the natural life of the place and the artificial conditions which fashion has imposed upon it. In some of the streets almost every house is evidently meant to be rented, the owners usually retiring to restricted quarters at the back, where they stow themselves away and hang themselves up on pegs until they may come into their own again. Here and there a native cottage has been bought and altered by a summer resident, and over the whole there is the peculiarly smug expression of a quarter which is accustomed to put its best foot foremost for a few months of the year. But in the back lanes and side streets there are still the conditions of the small New England community, in which land is poor and work is slack during the long winter, so that although there is no abject poverty in the sense in which it is known to cities, there is also little time or inclination for the mere prettinesses of life.

An element of the picturesque is supplied by an Indian camp. . . . [where they] speak their own language, and follow the peaceful trades of basket-weaving, moccasin-making, and the building of birchbark canoes. Their little dwellings – some of them tents, some of them shanties covered with tar-paper and strips of bark – are scattered about, and in the shadow of one of them sits a lady of enormous girth, who calls herself their queen, and who wears, perhaps as a badge of sovereignty, a huge fur cap even in the hottest weather. She is not less industrious than other 'regular royal' queens, for she sells baskets, and tells fortunes even more flattering than the fabled tale of Hope. Some of the young men are fine, swarthy, taciturn creatures, who look as though they knew how to put a knife to other uses than whittling the frame of a canoe....

The whole encampment is pungent with the acrid smoke of green wood, and many children—round, good natured balls of fat in all shades of yellow and brown—roll about in close friendship with [odd] little dogs. . . . It is curious to see in the characteristic work of these people the survival of [an] instinctive taste. . . . The designs cut on the bark of their canoes, the cunningly blended colors in their basket-work, are thoroughly good in their way; but contact with [another] civilization seems to have affected them as it has the Japanese, turning their attention chiefly to making napkin-rings and collar-boxes, and to a hideous delight in tawdry finery . . . modeled on current American fashions. [15]

With the formal establishment of the seasonal Indian village by Ledgelawn Avenue, Indian encampments along the north shore of town were now officially banned, as evidenced in this excerpt from the deed for a piece of property on the corner of West and Bridge streets:

All rights, privileges and benefits derived under and all rights whether in law or equity to enforce certain restrictions upon other lands, which restrictions are so imposed for the benefit of the land herein described as conveyed, in and by a certain warranty deed thereof from Sylvanus Jordan to Charles F. Mayer, which deed is dated July 11th, 1893, and recorded July 12th, 1893, in the Hancock County, Maine, Registry of Deeds, Book 271, Page 403. This conveyance of said parcel is made subject to the restriction on said parcel (not a condition subsequent) that no fish houses nor fish stands nor stable, except such private stable as may be appurtenant to a residence thereon, shall ever be erected or operated on said parcel, *nor shall any Indians or vagrants ever be allowed to occupy or encamp thereof.* [16]

Unsanitary and Threatening Conditions

In 1892 a new branch of the Village Improvement Association known as the "Sanitary Committee" worried that the Ledgelawn encampment—often referred to as "Squaw Hollow"—was fraught with unsanitary conditions that could breed disease. Thus, at the end of that summer season the *Bar Harbor Record* printed this announcement:

The Board of Managers be advised by the [Sanitary] Committee [of the Bar Harbor Village Improvement Association] to communicate to the Board of Health our opinion of the unsanitary and threatening condition of 'Squaw Hollow.' In the present possibility of a visitation of cholera to this country next summer, it is of the gravest importance to every community that any unhealthy spot should be thoroughly cleansed, and your Committee believes the only safe way of dealing with 'Squaw Hollow' is to empty it of its inhabitants and have its whole neighborhood disinfected. [17]

Some may argue the Improvement Association's actions were more motivated by patronizing or even racist discrimination than by than honest concerns about the health of the encampment's inhabitants. However true such charges may be in some measure, health issues were a legitimate public responsibility. Indeed, as the Bar Harbor encampment grew during the 1870s and '80s, becoming increasingly crowded and lacking decent sanitation and regular access to safe drinking water, reports of illness became quite common. In fact, the same year the Improvement Association called for an emptying and disinfecting of the encampment, the state's Indian agent for the Penobscot Tribe reported that "measles, brought home [to Old Town] from Bar Harbor, gained a temporary foothold [in the Indian Island community]." Moreover, he added, "two entire families returned from Moosehead lake [another popular tourist resort with an Indian encampment on its shores] seriously ill with typhoid fever." [18]

During the late 19th and early 20th centuries, Wabanakis relied increasingly on non-Indian medical assistance, although they also turned to specialists from their own reservations, who continued to practice in significant numbers. According to Dr. Frank Speck, writing about Wabanaki medicinal practices in the early 1900s, "an almost inexhaustible fund of knowledge exists on the subject" in the region's tribal communities. While some Native healers employed the old-time herbal remedies (sometimes with a dose of traditional shamanism), others mixed Wabanaki medicinal treatments with those of American mainstream society. Among the most respected Penobscot doctors of the period was Sabattis Mitchell, trained in conventional Euramerican medical methods of the day as well as in traditional Wabanaki herbal practices. He also spent time on Mount Desert Island, and one of his visits earned this mention in the *Mount Desert Herald* in September 1886: "Dr. Mitchell, the only Indian college graduate in New England is stopping for a few days at the Indian encampment. Dr. Mitchell graduated from the Portland medical school two years ago, and has practiced in Portland since that time." [19]

In the course of the 1890s and early 1900s, the Village Improvement Association initiated a range of changes, including running a sewer through the Indian encampment to keep it "clean and healthy." [20] In 1901, responding to fears that "typhoid fever might occur among the Indians living in Squaw Hollow because they were compelled to drink the water of Cromwells Harbor brook which contains much sewage," members of the Sanitary Committee solicited the water company to install a pipe and faucet providing safe drinking water. [21] Meanwhile, other white folks in town focused on what they saw as the purification of souls. As one Bar Harbor resident speaking of this era recalled: "The Indian village was where the ball field is today. We used to go from tent to tent buying sweet-smelling baskets and admiring the children and babies. Lovely young Alice Shepard (later Morris) went every week to give the children a Sunday school lesson. [22]

From Tents to Automobiles

By the 1920s, Bar Harbor's white citizens had lost interest in hosting a summer Indian encampment on what was now valuable property near the center of "their" town. One novel proposition for the Ledgelawn site came from the creators of Mount Desert Island's new national park, who sought to capitalize on this "empty lot" by turning it into an income-generating public campground. That happened around 1922, when the site was converted into a short-lived auto camp for visitors to the island's recently established national park.[23]

Although Bar Harbor's big annual Indian encampment ceased to exist, some Indian families continued to return to the Mount Desert area for their seasonal sales, while others sought new locations. Most adjusted their designs to meet society's shifting aesthetics and avoided shoulder-to-shoulder competition by setting up individual roadside camps and stalls at coastal and lakeside places. As one local newspaper reported in 1924:

Early auto campers in Lafayette National Park (renamed Acadia in 1929), ca. 1924. Around 1922, the site of the Ledgelawn Indian encampment site was converted into a short-lived auto camp for visitors to the recently created park. At the wheel here is Roshanara (Olive Craddock) (1894–1926), an Oriental dancer of British origin, born in Calcutta, India, where she studied local dance styles. At age sixteen she began performing ethnic dances across Europe and in 1913 moved to the United States, where she continued to perform until her early death at age 34.

> Whatever may be the truth of western Indians, those of Maine are a thrifty class of people. They know how to coax dollars from the pockets of the tourists who come their way. It is only in winter that you will find them all back on the home reservation and hugging the home fires. At other seasons of the year, those times when the summer visitor from Massachusetts and other States are coming that way, they are scattered many miles from home engaged in the occupation of helping tourists enjoy their vacation by bringing them a chance to spend their money. All along the roadside one sees them camping. [24]

After the stock market crash of 1929, the demand for fancy baskets shrank as the Great Depression set in and Victorian tastes became old-fashioned. Many Indian families turned to new seasonal work opportunities: harvesting blueberries in Washington County during August and picking potatoes in Aroostook County in September. The latter job called for harvesting containers, and Wabanakis proved ready to provide sturdy woodsplint "potato baskets" by the thousands. Still, ties to Mount Desert Island continued, with some Wabanakis living in rental properties on the island seasonally or year-round, making baskets and doing various menial jobs, from gardening to quarrying, housecleaning, waiting tables, bell-hopping, or working in fish factories.

Among the many who remained attached to Mount Desert Island was Hattie Loring Gordius (born in 1892), daughter of J. Mitchell Loring and granddaughter of Big Thunder. Her non-Indian mother, Phoebe Manchester of Tremont, was descended from a family that was shipwrecked on Ship Harbor. She had met Mitchell during one of his summer sojourns on Mount Desert Island. After marrying, Phoebe and Mitchell raised their children primarily at the Loring family home on Olamon Island, part of the Penobscot reservation, about fourteen miles upriver from Indian Island. But they kept up ties to Mount Desert Island and their children developed ties of their own to the place. In 1907 Hattie began the first of 75 years of seasonal work at William Underwood's fish factory in Bass Harbor, canning sardines, clams, shrimp, etc. The following excerpt is from a newspaper profile of Hattie published toward the end of her long life:

> Hattie reached the sixth grade in the one-room Olamon school. . . . An early memory is of a pot of simmering sweetgrass, harvested along the coast that could then be braided for basketmaking. The braid sold for two to three cents per yard. "My father used to come down and give swimming lessons to the summer people at Bar Harbor, and take them out in canoe rides. I was only 14 when my father died [in 1906]. . . . [and] I was only about 16 when I got married. . . . My husband was 28. . . ." Her husband was Nelson Gordius, whose father, a Frenchman, arrived as a stowaway from his native country. [The couple lived on Mount Desert Island. After fathering nine children, Nelson died at an early age. Then,] for years, widowed and bringing up nine children, Hattie walked from her Bass Harbor job to work another shift at Addison's cannery [originally Wass Cannery, later Stinson's] in Southwest Harbor. "I always raised hens, had a garden," Hattie said. "If you have nine children, you have to do something. . . . There's fish in the ocean, the clam on the shore, and the potato in the field. . . . My boy, when he was young, worked for the CCC [Civilian Conservation Corps] camp on [Mount Desert Island]. They put some good roads in." Hattie's daughter Frances recalled that the family would "go up to Indian Island in the fall, when the factory was finished." At the time, she said, tribal members had to return every five years to remain on the census. [25]

Hattie was not the only Wabanaki who settled at Mount Desert Island. Quite a few other Penobscots, as well as Passamaquoddies, found permanent work on the island and rented rooms there or bought their own houses. Moreover, the automobile revolution not only transformed American society at large, but also the tribal reservation communities—particularly after the grip of the Great Depression loosened. Instead of traveling by canoe, train, or steamboat, growing numbers of Wabanakis also traveled by private car. Becoming even more mobile

than before, individuals now made the journey faster than ever before, and at their own schedule. And so it was that some Wabanakis now made a quick car trip, either alone or with a few relatives or friends, to Mount Desert Island, delivered a load of handmade Indian baskets and other traditional arts and crafts to local shop owners, then left again. But these developments also meant that the traditional inter-tribal rendezvous at the seacoast had become a thing of the past—a perfect shame, indeed.

Bar Harbor, Mt. Desert Island, 1886. The Indian encampment is not indicated on this map, but it was located at the foot of Holland Ave., near Hamor's wharf.

Key (provided by authors):

1=Eddy Brook outlet

2=Hamor's wharf

3=Indian encampment site

4=Rodicks wharf

5=Bathing Club

6=Steamboat wharf & Maine Central Railroad Ferry

7=Roberts wharf

8=West End Hotel

9=Rodick Hotel

10=Rockaway Hotel

11=Newport Hotel

12=Albert Meadow

13=Bar Island.

(Boston: Geo. H. Walker & Co. Lithographers. Authors' collection. Numbers added by authors.)

Epilogue: The Art of Survival

Where did the red man come from?" This is the question we intend to answer! We intend also, to remove the fear, that the life of the red man will pass away unwritten, and this is written because there is an abundance of evidence showing that there is a general desire among the people that some one ought to write it now if ever. (Joseph Nicolar, Preface. Life and Traditions of the Red Man, 1893)

When Penobscot Joseph Nicolar of Indian Island wrote these words, the myth of the "vanishing Indian" was popular, not only in the United States, but also abroad. Many American Indians themselves also believed that their peoples, if not their cultures, were destined for extinction within a few generations. Epidemics and warfare had wiped out millions of their relatives and ancestors and nearly all their land had been taken from them. Moreover, they confronted a powerful new ideology of progress, which defined them as savages in the lowest order of human evolution, primitive remnants from a prehistoric wilderness. Representing his Penobscot Tribe in the Maine State Legislature for many years in the late 19th century, Nicolar was painfully familiar with the political consequences of this dominant worldview. The same is true for his Passamaquoddy colleague Louis Mitchell of Pleasant Point. About twenty years younger than Nicolar, he, too, was repeatedly reelected to represent his own tribe in the legislature. Since their terms in Maine's capital city overlapped in the 1880s, they must have known each other well. Both recognized the importance of history in defending the traditional rights of their tribal communities. And both worked hard to preserve the rich cultural heritage of the Wabanaki. Nicolar did this through public lectures and by writing a book that he published himself in 1893, just a year before his death. Mitchell did so by sharing his knowledge, orally and in writing, with well-connected outsiders such as Leland, Prince, Gatschet, and Eckstorm—scholars who shared this information with a much wider public.

Over the generations, many other Wabanakis have been inspired to share knowledge about their cultural history. Some penned, others dictated. Beyond words, they have helped to preserve cultural traditions by retelling old stories, singing songs, performing dances, or making artful crafts, some of which became parts of collections held by individuals and museums. The Abbe Museum in Bar Harbor has probably the largest and most representative collection of pre-historic, historic, and contemporary Wabanaki arts and crafts objects—in particular basketry.

Indicative of the many major positive changes since Nicolar and Mitchell did so much to preserve a collective memory of Wabanaki cultural traditions, the Penobscot and Passamaquoddy now have small tribal museums on their reservations. Moreover, the Abbe Museum of Stone-Age Antiquities has greatly improved its mission in recognizing that Wabanaki Indians *did not vanish* and that their ancestral traditions are more than relics of the past; they endure and are kept alive by dedicated individuals all across Maine and beyond.

One of the organizations committed to the continuance of traditional Native crafts in the region is the Maine Indian Basketmakers Alliance. Founded in the early 1990s, it began holding (in cooperation with the Abbe Museum) a yearly festival in Bar Harbor. Another notable aid in the survival of Maine Indian culture is the Wabanaki Educational Curriculum, the ever-evolving education program spawned by 2001 state legislation requiring the teaching of Maine Native American history and culture in Maine schools. (Notably, this legislation was introduced by Frank "Big Thunder" Loring's great great granddaughter, Donna Loring, when she served as Penobscot tribal representative to the state legislature, along with Passamaquoddy representative Donald Soctomah.) Also of note is the National Park Service's decision to fund our extensive historical study of Wabanaki peoples, titled *Asticou's Island Domain: Wabanaki Peoples at Mount Desert Island, 1500-2000*, digitally published in 2008 and freely available on the Internet.

Telling the stories of so many Wabanakis who seasonally encamped at Mount Desert Island, frequently on or near sites also periodically inhabited by their ancestors since time out of mind, the book in hand heralds the "art of survival" epitomized by the island's summertime Indian encampments in the 19th and early 20th centuries. It represents an effort to make a long-lasting contribution to the cultural historical legacy of a beautiful seacoast island where we can still experience nature in peace and quiet, thanks to all those people, Native and non-Native, who have done so much to preserve and protect it—and to honor its original inhabitants.

Acknowledgments

Where to start? Our gratitude and debts are deep and manifold. So many have helped in so many ways. The book in hand, covering about one hundred years, sprang from a chapter in a two-volume study we wrote for the National Park Service—*Asticou's Island Domain: Wabanaki Peoples at Mount Desert Island 1500-2000*. The catalyst for that research project was Wabanaki Indian dismay that Acadia National Park (ANP) signage and literature barely mentioned the fact that their indigenous ancestors had seasonally inhabited this coastal region for thousands of years. Park officials took this complaint to heart, as did Dr. Chuck Smythe, Ethnography Program Manager for Northeast Region National Park Service. Dr. Smythe secured funding for the study, and park staff members Rebecca Cole-Will, David Manski, and Lee Terzis joined us in collaborating with Wabanaki advisors Bernard Jerome (Mi'kmaq), Bonnie Newsome (Penobscot), Fred "Sonny" Tomah (Maliseet) and Donald Soctomah (Passamaquoddy). All of them fueled our effort with enthusiasm, networking, information gathering, and insightful critique. Two additional Penobscot advisors—James Francis and Donna Loring—stepped forward when we began working on this book and its three-dimensional incarnation: an exhibition at the Abbe Museum in Bar Harbor, 2010–2011. The help we have received from these individuals has been invaluable, as has assistance from Abbe Museum staff members past and present—most notably Julia Clark, Raney Bench, Diane Kopec, and Betts Swanton. Special thanks to Charlotte Singleton, director of the Mount Desert Island Historical Society, for helping us sort out the early lodging options offered by the Somes family.

The visual richness of this book is thanks to folks who partnered with us in tracking down the wide array of images that reveal so much of the story we have tried to tell: Deborah Dyer (Bar Harbor Historical Society), Dr. William Haviland (University of Vermont, emeritus), Nancy Howland (Jesup Library), Darith James (Clark Point Gallery), John McDade (Acadia National Park Archives), Charlotte Morrill and Meredith Hutchins (Southwest Harbor Public Library Collection of Photographs), Robert Pyle (Northeast Harbor Library), and Raymond Strout (Ahlblad's Frame Shop). We're particularly indebted to fellow photophiles Earle Shettleworth (Maine Historic Preservation Commission), Donald Soctomah (Passamaquoddy historian and tribal representative to the state legislature), and Lydia Vandenbergh. Unfortunately, in a book printed in black-and-white, their names can't appear in the neon red they deserve.

Friends with boats are especially appreciated when writing about a coastal area and looking for the mariner's point of view. Special thanks to our "captains," Bill Haviland, Bruce Jacobson (NPS), Dale Mitchell (Passmaquoddy), and storyteller par-excellence Jan Willem van de Wetering, who we wish had lived for at least another chapter.

Oral history played an important part in our research, and for that we extend special thanks to those who shared personal and familial reminiscences woven into this story: Margaret Apt (Passamaquoddy), David Francis (Passamaquoddy), Susan Snow Holmes (Passamaquoddy), Lois Crabtree Johnson (Hancock Historical Society), Donna Loring (Penobscot), John Bear Mitchell (Penobscot), the late Theodore Norris Mitchell (Penobscot), Ralph Stanley (Southwest Harbor resident/historian), John Stevens (Passamaquoddy) and Dr. Edmund Carpenter (Frank Speck's student and assistant in the 1940's).

Finally, heartfelt thanks to Carole Binette of the Penobscot Nation and Sheldon Goldthwaite of Bar Harbor for genealogical data that helped us link individuals in the historic record to present-day Wabanakis.

Bunny McBride & Harald E.L. Prins
Flint Hills, Summer 2009

End Notes

CHAPTER 1

[1] Somes, Abraham.

CHAPTER 2

[1] Somes-Sanderson, p.70. This is an unusually early date for Wabanaki splint basketry.

[2] According to historian Samuel Eliot Morison (1960, p.77), "When the people of this part of Mount Desert petitioned the General Court for a separate township in 1796 they asked to be named Adams after Governor Samuel Adams. But there was already an Adams township in Berkshire County, and when the bill went to the Governor, in February, 1796, the new town was named Eden, evidently for the Garden of. Alexander Baring, after sailing to Mount Desert that very summer of 1796, states in the long letter he wrote about it, in December 1796, 'that part of Mount Desert is incorporated into a town by the name of Eden, which the inhabitants gave it in consequence of its fertility.'"

[3] Bancel de Confoulens in Morison, 1960, p.29.

[4] Personal communication, Charlotte Singleton, Mount Desert Island Historical Society. See also Thornton, p. 243; Nichols, p.339. Since 1888, perhaps earlier, it has been known as Mount Desert House.

[5] Thornton, p.243. See also Pugh et al, in Hansen, p.46.

[6] A. Joy 13:1-2. See also Somes-Sanderson, p.71, Thornton pp.254-56. (Note: It is likely that Mrs. "Glassene" was Sarah Classian (born ca. 1815), whose son Sabatis was two years older than Dell.)

[7] "Editor's Easy Chair," *Harper's Magazine,* October 1863, p711.

[8] A.Joy, 13:2-3 and 14:2.

[9] A. Joy 14:1-2. This section of the reminiscence is attributed to Eunice Deering.

[10] Somes-Sanderson, p.69. See also Pugh et al, p.42.

[11] Wilmerding, p.28.

[12] Cole, January 1836.

[13] Morison, 1960, p.45. Although Morgan never built a cottage on the island, he anchored his yacht there and spent time at the cottage of his daughter, Mrs. Herbert Satterlee. J. P. Morgan was a patron to Edward S. Curtis, providing this now famous photographer $75,000 in 1906 for a series on American Indians. Curtis eventually published a classic, 20-volume work entitled "The North American Indian."

[14] Helfrich and O'Neil, p13.

[15] Helfrich and O'Neil, p13.

[16] *Eastport Sentinel,* 7/10/1872; *MDH,* 10/28/87. Cf.Sweetzer, 1888, p.71.

[17] *The Bay State Excursion of 1871.* Martin, 1874, also mentions the "annual encampment" at Bar Harbor.

[18] Hobart (Passamaquoddy Indian Agent), 1875.

[19] Indian Agent Report (Penobscot) for 1880, p.14.

[20] Indian Agent Report (Penobscot) for 1882, p.9.

[21] Indian Agent Report (Passamaquoddy) for 1883, p.5.

[22] Indian Agent Report (Penobscot) for 1887, p.7.

[23] Indian Agent Report (Penobscot) for 1888, p.6.

[24] Smith letter to Admiral Du Pont's widow, 2 September 1877, in Torchia, p.5.

CHAPTER 3

[1] Personal communication from Donald Soctomah, May 2005.

[2] William.Haviland, p.c.10/26/05. Noting that Eggemoggin Reach can be difficult to paddle "when the wind blows out of the northwest or south," Dr. Haviland describes an alternate route to a straight shot through the reach – from Punch Bowl southeast between Little Deer Isle and Deer Isle, continuing south along the west flank of northern Deer Isle into Northwest Harbor, carrying over into Long Cove, which gave access to several options for reaching Blue Hill Bay.

[3] By 1885 direct steamship service between Bangor and Bar Harbor was available. (Ryan. See also Richardson, Short & Sears, Albion et al.) By 1882, the steamship *Admiral* offered direct service from Eastport to Bar Harbor. (See *Eastport Sentinel* 9/9/1882.)

[4] According to Short and Sears (p.121), the steamer *T.F. Secor,* "was built at New York in 1846 by the T.F. Secor Company for the Belfast, Ellsworth, and Bar Harbor, Maine, route, connecting with the Boston Boat at Belfast." However, we have yet to find any corroborating information that a steamer stopped at Bar Harbor before 1857.

[5] *Mount Desert Herald* 8/20/1881, p.3.

[6] *Eastport Sentinel* 7/10/1872. See also *MDH,* 8/20/1881, p.3, re. Eastern Railroad Co. purchasing several acres of land in 1866 for building a wharf at Bar Harbor to accommodate steamships.

[7] *MDH,* 7/17/1881, p.3.

[8] *MDH,* 8/6/1881, p.3.

[9] *MDH,* 8/22/1884.

[10] Thoreau, p.593.

[11] Albion et al, p.212.

[12] *The* [Bangor] *Industrial Journal,* 7/21/1893.

[13] *MDH* 9/11/1885, p.2.

[14] Stevens, interview by McBride. John Stevens' maternal grandparents, Eleanor and Wallace Louis/Lewey, appear on the 1910 Federal census for Peter Dana Point as 22 and 41 years old, respectively. Wallace is identified as a guide and their daughter Maria is listed as a one-year-old.

[15] Stevens, interview by McBride.

[16] Hunter, Joyce. "Robert Fifield – a man who did more than he thought he could do." *Island Ad-vantages,* 9/1/2005, p.10. Courtesy of Wm. Haviland. See also Haviland, "Indians, porpoises and Crockett's Cove," *Island Ad-vantages*, 12/22&29/2005, p.5.

[17] For example, see MIA I:29, VII: no.49, no.751; Johnson, pp.66-67.

[18] Nichols, p.338.

[19] McBride, 1999, pp.73-94. Notably, a porcupine weave ash basket Molly gave to fur trader Manly Hardy as a wedding gift in 1862 became part of the Abbe Museum's Mary Cabot Wheelwright Collection, no doubt by way of the long friendship between Wheelwright and Manly's daughter Fannie Hardy Eckstorm.

[20] See Eckstorm, 1945, p.16. Green Lake was then known as Reed's Pond.

CHAPTER 4

[1] *Eastport Sentinel* 7/10/1872.

[2] Street, p.335.

[3] Nichols, p.327.

[4] Street, p.331.

[5] Nichols, p.325.

[6] Nichols, pp.328-29.

[7] Nichols, pp. 331, 336.

[8] Warner, pp. 417-18.

[9] Crawford, p.284.

[10] Warner, p.420.

[11] Street, 1905, p337.

[12] *Mount Desert Herald* 7/24/1885.

[13] E.B. Chase, p.183.

[14] Warner, p. 418.

[15] "Beautiful Bar Harbor Days," *New York Times*, 27 August 1883.

[16] Warner, p.422. In fact, it is nearly 500' lower than Cadillac Mountain's summit.

[17] *Bar Harbor Blue Book*, pp. i, 7.

[18] *Mount Desert Herald*, 7/31/-9/3/1881.

[19] Among numerous sources that give this figure is Hubbard, 1883, p.19.

[20] *Bangor Daily Whig & Commercial*, 1/28/1898, p. 4. See also *Daily Kennebec Journal*, 7/6/04; *Oldtown Enterprise*, 11/10/88. On federal censuses in the latter 19th and early 20th centuries it is not at all uncommon to see "guide" or "hunter" noted in the occupation column alongside the names of Wabanaki men.

[21] *Mount Desert Herald*, 8/23/1883.

[22] Underwood, 1927. See also Lyons, pp.15-18, for more on Joe Mell & Wm. Underwood. Lyons' book is the source for the small portrait of Joe Mell that appears on the previous page.

[23] *MDH*, 8/16/1883. The Indian participants were all Passamaquoddies, appearing in the 1900 Federal census for Pleasant Point as: Mitchel Francis (basketmaker, born 1865), Joseph Lola (basketmaker, c1830), Lola T. Lola (basketmaker, 1864), Sebatis Lola (hunter, 1861), Johnny Maggie (hunter, 1854), Charles Mitchell (basketmaker, 1867), Sopiel Mitchell (hunter, 1855), Frank Stanley (hunter, 1867).

[24] "From Bar Harbor," in the *Daily KennebecJournal*, p.1.

[25] E.B. Chase, p.186.

[26] Warner, p. 423.

[27] Warner, p.424.

[28] *Bangor Daily Whig & Courier*, 19 August 1886.

[29] *Bangor Daily Whig & Courier*, 24 July 1891.

[30] *Bangor Daily Whig & Courier*, 17 August 1893.

[31] Crawford, p.271

[32] *Mount Desert Island Centinniel Souvernir*, published by *Mount Desert Herald*, p.20, July 1896.

[33] *Bangor Daily Whig & Courier*, 15 August 1893.

[34] Personal communication, David Rockefeller to B. McBride, Dec. 2006, Aug. 2007.

[35] Street, 1905, p.341.

[36] *Bar Harbor Record*, 8/20/1897. See also *Bangor Daily Whig & Courier*, 8/21/1897. The cover of the sheet music for Dr. Sweet's song "Sweetheart Good-Bye" (published by Oliver Ditson & Co. in Boston), identifies him as the composer of operas "Our College Boys" and "The Professor's Daughter," along with "popular songs, 'I Am the Ruler of the Sea', 'The Bold Rover', and 'Sweet Little May', etc. etc."

[37] *Mount Desert Herald*, 8/27/81.

[38] Coe, Harrie B. (ed.) 1928. Vol. 2, pp.771-74. (emphasis added)

[39] *Litchman*, pp. 4, 251.

[40] *MDH*, 11/23/1888.

[41] Portland Tribune 3/30/1844, p.407.

42 http://millhill.co.nz/Madan.htm

[43] Harrison, pp.86-87.

[44] "Celebration...."

[45] *Eastport Sentinel*, 17 Sept. 1890.

CHAPTER 5

[1] Parker, p.40.

[2] Thornton, pp.167.

[3] Today the map and basket are in a private collection.

[4] Interview by McBride, Jan. 2004. Closson is related to the late Hattie Gordius of Bass Harbor & SWH. Born in 1892, Hattie was granddaughter to Frank "Big Thunder" Loring (c1827-1906).

[5] Interview by McBride, Jan. 2004.

[6] Ted Mitchell, interview by McBride, June 2004. [Note: Sabattis Joe Mitchell (b.1829) appears on 1868 Penobscot census with wife Elizabeth (b.1830) and children John (Bear, b.1855), Mary A. (b.1858), Mitchell (b.1860), Margaret (b.1863) and Thomas (b.1866).]

[7] John Bear Mitchell, interview by McBride, Jan. 2004.

[8] Interview by McBride, Jan. 2004.

[9] Dwelley, pp.11-12. See also Irene Bartlett quoted in Locke & Montgomery, p.28.

[10] Demolished in 1938, Newport House stood just south of present-day Agamont Park. Higgins' list of Bar Harbor Indian encampment sites does not mention the one behind Ells Store on Eden Street by the Eddy Brook outlet – unless "Uncle Jake's Creek" refers to Eddy Brook. Also, because no other sources mention a site "on Eden street, near Duck Brook," it's possible he mistakenly referred to "Duck Brook" instead of "Eddy Brook."

[11] Drake, 1891, pp.306-313.

[12] Innes MacPike, interviewed by Ellen Lerner Nov. 1985. F.W Lewey appears with his second wife Delphine (born 1871) on the 1910 Federal census for Eden (Bar Harbor), living on Upper School St. She is listed on the town's 1900 census as Delphine Laumiere, boarding at the Indian encampment with her aunt, Christine Laumiere.

[13] Interview by McBride. Jan. 2004.

[14] Interview by McBride, Jan. 2005. The area described by Johnson is now owned by Lawrence and Marion Alley. Johnson added that "Crabtree Neck is the old part of Hancock, originally affiliated with Sullivan. The northern part of Hancock was always more connected to Ellsworth."

[15] Smith in Hansen, p.53. This association may well have preceded Josephine Gray's childhood since Pretty Marsh Harbor and Squid Cove were entry points to Mount Desert Island for Wabanakis paddling to the island from Blue Hill or from Union River/Ellsworth. From Pretty Marsh and Squid Cove, Wabanakis could follow a well-established canoe & carry route to Somesville and Somes Sound.

[16] DeCosta, pp.96-97.

[17] *Bar Harbor Blue Book & Mount Desert Guide 1881*, p.7.

[18] *MDH*, 1/1/1887.

[19] *Bar Harbor Record*, 6/10/1896.

[20] "One of the Attractions of Bar Harbor." *Frank Leslie's Illustrated Newspaper*, 8/23/1884, p.6.

[21] DeCosta 1871, pp.172, 2.

[22] Leighton, p.411.

[23] Mrs. Fred Sylvester's scrapbook, c1898-99 – p.c. Wm. Haviland. See also McLane & McLane, p.304.

[24] The men are listed on the census as: Joseph Dana (born 1852, Tribe Governor) m to Ester (1862, "ration Indian"); Lola D. Dana (1878, hunter); Sabatis Lola (1861, hunter); Swassin Lola (1869, picture-framer); Thomah Loring (1879, basketmaker); Thomas Polis (1852); Dan Sacobie (=Daniel Secovy, 1882, basketmaker); Joseph Sockabasin (1866, Tribe Sheriff) m to Susan (1875, "ration Indian").

[25] Graham, Frank, Jr. *Gulls*. Citation provided by Wm. Haviland, p.c.

[26] Conkling, p159-60. Citation provided by Wm. Haviland, p.c.

[27] *Eastport Sentinel*, 9/20/1899. In Soctomah 2002 p.63.

[28] *Eastport Sentinel*, 11/29/1899. In Soctomah 2002 p.65.

[29] Gooden Grant (born 1876), interview by Lynn Franklin. See Bunting, 2000, p.70; cf n.l on p.358: "Grant was also quoted as saying that Indians from 'East Quoddy' [Pleasant Point] as well as Old Town visited Isle au Haut." Anthropologist Dr. William Haviland, who

knew Grant, noted (p.c. 1/16/05) that Grant "lived at Head Harbor, on the [south] seaward end of Isle au Haut … where [apparently] these Indians camped. This makes sense for gull hunting, as Head Harbor, with its good beach for hauling out canoes, is the most convenient spot to set off for Great and Little Spoon Islands, which are major bird nesting islands. There are also a number of good seal haulouts on that side of Isle au Haut." Noting another Indian encampment at the north end of Isle au Haut where the summer cottage colony began in 1880, Haviland said Indians there "seem to have been less interested in bird hunting than in selling baskets and craft items."

[30] *Eastport Sentinel,* 2/20/1901. In Soctomah 2002, p.76.

[31] Enk, p.327. Dr. William Haviland, p.c. 11/15/05 noted, "Lighthouse Cove . . was the best access point for going to nearby Hardhead Island, where gulls (not to mention guillemots & cormorants) nest in large numbers. Maybe this was one of the draws to Eagle Island? Also, the Quinns ran a summer boarding house on Eagle, and on neighboring Butter Island in 1896 a summer resort opened (see McLane & McLane); both would have afforded opportunity for sale of baskets and other crafts."

[32] *Oldtown Enterprise,* 6/1/1889. John B. Mitchell (born 1851) is listed on the 1880 Federal census for Indian Island, married to Penobscot Maria Newell (1858) with one child, Martha (1878). On the 1900 census he appears with 4 children in addition to Martha – Elizabeth (1889), Theodore (1890), Clara (1892) and Sabattis (1897). By this time, his first wife was gone and he had married a woman named Mary (born 1873).

[33] Leighton, p. 416.

CHAPTER 6

[1] See Adney & Chapelle, p.73.

[2] E.B. Chase, 1884, p.191.

[3] *MDH*, 8/8/1884, p.3. Peter J. Gabriel, born in 1841, appears on the 1900 Federal census for Perry/Pleasant Point as a basketmaker married to Sarah (born 1864) who was listed as a "ration Indian."

[4] Recurring ad in *MDH*, 8/8-9/19/1884, p.2 or 3.

[5] *MDH*, 7/31/85, p.3.

[6] *MDH*, 8/14/85, p.3.

[7] This pipe-smoking woman appeared in *Frank Leslie's Illustrated Newspaper* (8/23/1884 p.5) collage of the encampment (reproduced in Chapter 4) with a brief article identifying her as Passamaquoddy. Describing her as "the largest Indian we ever saw," the writer said she "must have weighed 300 pounds [and that] she wore a man's hat and shoes, carried a stout staff, and sat on a bench complacently smoking a T.D. pipe. Later we saw this big [woman] promenading up Mount Desert Street … hat, pipe and all. . . ." In all likelihood, she is "Lola, the queen," either Josephine Lola (born1843), a widow and mother of 4, or Hannah Lola (born1837), married to Nicolas Lola (born 1825).

[8] Harrison, pp.85-97. Notably, Harrison wrote this description as if it were from the vantage point of a dog visiting the encampment with its owner. "Lola, the queen" was no doubt related to Joe Lola, profiled in Chapter 8. However, it was probably not his wife, for she was not a woman of "generous proportions."

[9] *Frank Leslie's Illustrated Newspaper,* 8/23/1884, p.6.

[10] "One of the Attractions of Bar Harbor." *Frank Leslie's Illustrated Newspaper,* 8/23/1884, p.6.

[11] Speck, 1940, pp. 95, 46.

[12] Eckstorm 1932, pp. 24-25; Speck 1940, pp.137-38; Whitehead &

McGee, pp.30-31.

[13] "Colors the World."

[14] Mabel Bell, letter to Mrs. Alexander Melville Bell (Eliza Grace Symonds Bell), 20 August 1882. Alexander Graham Bell Family Papers, posted on website http://memory.loc.gov/)

[15] Lash, 1971, pp.53-55. Eleanor's father was Theodore Roosevelt's brother. An alcoholic and a widower, he died shortly after writing his daughter at Mt. Desert Island, leaving her orphaned.

[16] United Features Syndicate, in *The Kansas City Star,* 10 February 1943. For more details on this event, see McBride, 2001, p.154.

[17] Sprague, pp.3-9.

[18] Personal communication, Margaret "Dolly" Apt, Pleasant Point, 9/23/04. Geneologist Sheldon Goldthwait places Margaret's birth at 8/12/1896. Both of her parents were Passamaquoddy: Frances (Frank) Basset (b.1872) and Francis (Fannie Lolar) Basset (b.1877).

[19] Indian Agent Report (Penobscot) for 1891, pp.8-9.

CHAPTER 7

[1] Edwin Tappan Adney and Howard I Chapelle, *The Bark canoes and Skin Boats of North America.* Washington DC: Smithsonian Instition, 1964, Pp . 58, 74.

[2] *Bar Harbor Blue Book & Mount Desert Guide 1881,* p.43.

[3] *Calais Advertiser,* Feb. 18, 1880

[4] Recurring ad in *MDH,* 7/31-9/3/1881, p.3.

[5] This appeared in a recurring ad for renting canoes (and Indian guides) in Bar Harbor, *MDH,* 7/31-9/3/1881, p.3. A profile of Mitchell appears in Chapter 9.

[6] Sweetser, 1888, p.61.

[7] Verrill, 1932, p.109 and 1954, p.97.

[8] Leighton, p.410.

[9] Gooden Grant, interview by Franklin. See Bunting, 2000, p.70.

[10] Sweetser 1888, pp.20-21. For more information on canoe services, see the profile on Frank "Big Thunder" Loring in the "Notable Wabanakis" section of this chapter.

[11] *BHR, Centennial Souvenir Edition 1796-1896.* July 1896, p.22.

[12] Briggs, pp. 355, 278, 279, 398. For additional passages about Big Thunder and Mitchell, see pp. 228, 261, 276, 343, 353, 397, 399.]

[13] Adney and Chapelle 1964, pp. 14-17, 27-35, 79-89.

[14] *MDH,* 9/3/1881.

[15] *The [Bangor] Industrial Journal,* 5/15/85. This article also describes scarcity of suitable white birch trees and method of building canoe and making paddles.

[16] *Wulegessis* is the piece of bark fitted over the fold of the gunwales, which formed the flaps below the outwales on each side, and often was decorated with the personal mark of the owner identifying the owner's habits, activities, or simply his personal likings.

[17] Adney & Chapelle, pp.71, 76-77.

[18] *The [Bangor] Industrial Journal,* 7/21/1893.

[19] Helfrich & O'Neil, p.111; Sweetser 1888, pp.20-21.

[20] Hale, pp.172.

[21] Cole, pp.60-62, 67, 90, 95-97.

[22] *Bangor Daily Whig & Courier,* 15 August 1893.

[23] *Bar Harbor Record,* 7/4/96, p.1; Francis Dana may be Frank Dana, listed in *Penobscot County Directory* for 1893-94 as based on "Mattanaqcook Island, opp. Lincoln." J.M. Loring might be Penobscot Joseph M. Lolar (born 1871), listed in 1900 Federal census for Indian Island as married to Mary J. (1870), father of Joseph M. jr. (1899), Hannah (n.a.) and Alice (1883).

CHAPTER 8

[1] This run with Barnum is mentioned, among other places, on a placard announcing Loring's Indian Exhibition in Wiscasset, ca. 1870. See www.mainememory.net

[2] For a scholarly discussion of the new concept of indigeneity, see *Social Anthropology* (2006), 14, 1, 17–32.

[3] See Prins 1998 for the most complete telling to date of Loring's life.

[4] Johnson 1861, p.41.

[5] Johnson 1861, p.43.

[6] Johnson 1861, p.44.

[7] Eunice Deering in A. Joy,

[8] See Johnson 1861, p.41.

[9] See A. Joy,

[10] *MDH*, 8/27/81, cited in Abbe Museum permanent hall exhibit, summer 2003.

[11] Loring's first wife, Mary/Molly Lola Socoby (born 1832) was from the Passamaquoddy reservation. They had at least 7 children together, including those on the placard: Susie (1872), Peter (1876), (Joseph) Mitchell (1863). We did not find Alzoma on censuses – that may have been a nickname or stage name. Mitchell is the great grandfather of Donna Loring (1948), Penobscot representative. to the state legislature 1997-2004, 2006-2008. He married Phoebe Manchester of Tremont and his son George M. and grandson George M. jr. (Donna's father) were born in Bar Harbor in 1888 and 1914.

[12] Briggs, pp. 355, 278, 279, 398. For additional passages about Big Thunder and Mitchell, see pp. 228, 261, 276, 343, 353, 397, 399.

[13] Cartwright. 1982. "'When the Lord's ready for me, I'll go' Penobscot woman packed sardines 75 years,'" *Wabanaki Alliance*, July.

[14] July 1896, p.22.

[15] Gooden Grant (born 1876), interview by Lynn Franklin. See Bunting, 2000, p.70; cf n.l on p.358: "Grant was also quoted as saying that Indians from 'East Quoddy' as well as Old Town visited Isle au Haut." William Haviland, who knew Grant, noted (p.c. 1/16/05) that Grant "lived at Head Harbor, on the [south] seaward end of Isle au Haut … where [apparently] these Indians camped. This makes sense for gull hunting, as Head Harbor, with its good beach for hauling out canoes, is the most convenient spot to set off for Great and Little Spoon Islands, which are major bird nesting islands. There are also a number of good seal haulouts on that side of Isle au Haut." Noting another Indian encampment at the north end of Isle au Haut where the summer cottage colony began in 1880, Dr. Haviland said Indians there "seem to have been less interested in bird hunting than in selling baskets and craft items."

[16] Enk, p.327.

[17] McBride 1995, p.46. See also Prins 1998 re. Loring's controversial reputation.

18 Chamberlain, pp.2-3.

[19] This excerpt comes from a 1907 booklet titled *Historic Maine and Indian Mythology* appears a short profile on Loring, including a story he told to the author-writer—identified as West in his drawing of Loring. A year later, Loring told the same story to the *New York World* (see *Sandusky Daily Star*, 9/3/1900).

[20] 6/6-11/1905, quoted in Prins 1998, p.152. Note: The author of this article erroneously identified Penobscots as "Tarratines."

[21] In Prins, 1998, p.152.

[22] *Frank Leslie's Illustrated Newspaper*, 8/23/1884, pp.5-6.

[23] *MDH*, 7/26/1883, p.3.

[24] *MDH*, 8/16/89 p3, 8/9/1889, p.3.

[25] Born in 1835, the Penobscot Elizabeth was just four years older than Elizabeth Francis of Pleasant Point. She was married to fellow Penobscot Thomas Francis and some individuals at the Old Town reservation referred to her as his "queen," adding to the confusion between the two women.

[26] *MDH*, 9/20/1889, p.3.

[27] *MDH*, 9/27/1889, p.3.

[28] *BHR* 6/24/96, p.1.

[29] For more on this, see anthropologist profiles in Chapter 9.

[30] *MDH*, 7/31-9/3/1881, p.3.

[31] Sweetzer 1888, pp.20-21.

[32] *Eastport Sentinel*, 9/7/1898.

[33] Prince, J.D. 1897, p.481. The records Mitchell gave Prince came through oral tradition from the *po-too-us-win* (wampum keeper) Sopiel Selmo (also spelled Selma or Selmore), one of the Passamaquoddy's last delegates to the Great Council Fire in Caughnawaga in 1870. See Raymond; Speck, 1915, pp.492-508. The preface to Prince's 1921 publication, *Passamaquoddy Texts* (featuring the Wampum Records, and several legends) notes, "These documents…came into my possession some years ago, but were all destroyed by fire in 1911, since which time Mr. Mitchell industriously reproduced them at my request from memory."

[34] Mitchell, 17 May 1930, Letter to Eckstorm.

[35] *MDH*, 1/6/1888

[36] *Eastport Sentinel*, 4/29/1891. In Soctomah 2002, p.44.

[37] *Eastport Sentinel*, 2/20/1901. In Soctomah 2002, p.76.

[38] *Eastport Sentinel*, 12/17/1902. In Soctomah 2002, p.81.

[39] *Eastport Sentinel*, 6/23/1920.

[40] *Eastport Sentinel*, 12/25/1901. In Soctomah, 2002, p.78. Joseph Dana is listed in 1900 Federal census for Pleasant Point as "Tribal Governor."

[41] *Eastport Sentinel*. In *MDH* 6/8/1888, p.3.

[42] *Eastport Sentinel*, 2/26/1902. In Soctomah, 2002, p.79.

[43] *MDH*, recurring ad, 7/3-8/28/1885, p.4.

[44] The Journal, 12/27/1889, p.3.

[45] *Eastport Sentinel*, 1/11/1893, In Soctomah, Donald 2002 p.29.

[46] It appears that he was the son of Lewis Snow, listed as Lewy Snow, head of a household of three, on the Indian agent's Passamaquoddy census taken Nov. 1876. Lewis served as tribal representative to the state legislature in 1874 and possibly 1876 as well. A description of Lewis by Wilbur Day (1864-1924) appears in *Wilbur Day: Hunter, Guide, and Poacher*: "The first hunt that ever I had with an Indian, I was quite a young boy, and the Indian's name was Lewis Snow. … He lived at Pleasant Point near Eastport. That man was a prince, six-feet-six-inches tall in his stocking feet and weighed two hundred and sisty pounds. He had not once ounce of useless flesh. . . . I was allowed to go [on a hunt with him]. … Mr. Snow got two or three deer and canoe bark. He built himself a big hand sled and put on his load and started to drag it to Pleasant point…." (For the full story of Day's hunt with Lewis Snow, see Ives, pp.64-65.)

[47] Figures in the two censuses are contradictory, but it is clear that Mary Ann was older than John (by 9-16 years) and that previously she was married to John M. Francis (born 1843-98, son of Mary Socktomah Lola & Joseph Mitchell Francis). Of the seven children Mary Ann gave birth to, only one survived and is not listed as living with the couple on the 1900 or 1910 censuses. (The surviving child must have been Alice (Tellis) Francis, listed in the Penobscot Nation genealogical records as born ca.1873 on Olamon Island to Mary Ann Fransway and her first husband John M. Francis. After

growing up, Alice had three husbands before her death in 1953: Anselm Sapiel, Newell B. Miles, & Joseph M. Swassian.)

48 All Susan Snow Holmes quotes in this brief profile come from her 2004 interview with McBride.

49 Locke.

50 Information in this paragraph comes from Erin Damon, "The Search for John Snow: An Intern's Quest for a Local Icon." Abbe Museum exhibit. 2003.

51 Dana.

52 Date of this letter mislaid.

53 Coatsworth.

CHAPTER 9

1 Much of this profile on Nicolar comes from McBride 2001.

2 *Old Town Enterprise*, 1/1/1910, 12/11/1924.

3 It has been republished twice since then, most recently in 2007 by Duke University Press, edited by Dr. Annette Kolodny and with a Foreword by Nicolar's grandson Charles N. Shay of Indian Island.

4 Leland, in Leland and Prince 1902, p.18.

5 E.R. Pennell 1906 [1970], vol.1, pp.256-57.

6 Leland 1892, pp. 252-53, 14.

7 4/18/1881, to Walter Besant. In Pennell, vol 2, p.101.

8 Pennell, vol 1, p.21.

9 *MDH*, 1/17/1884. The statement "Peter Gabriel [and] his son," appears to be a misquote by the newspaper, since in the front pages of his *Algonquin Legends* book Leland credits "John Gabriel, and his son Peter J. Gabriel." (It was Peter Gabriel who was responsible for bringing electric lighting to the Indian encampment—the same year this article appeared.) Leland's summer field assistant Abby L. Alger of Boston found the work of collecting these legends "so delightful" that she continued gathering on her own and in 1897 published her book, *In Indian Tents: As Told By: Penobscot, Passamaquoddy and Micmac Indians.* "The supply of legends and tales," she wrote, "seems to be endless, one supplementing and completing another, so that there may be a dozen versions of one tale, each containing something new."

10 Leland, 1884, p.65.

11 Psesuk is probably Pesuk, also spelled P'ais-unk, a variation of Ah-bays'auk, meaning "clambake place." It refers to Mt Desert Island, especially Bar Harbor (see Eckstorm 1978, p.207).

12 The two name deletions in this excerpt are Leland's.

13 Leland 1884, pp.342-43.

14 Brinton had authored several other early publications on American Indian folklore and linguistics, in including *The Lenâpé and their Legends: With the Complete Text and Symbols of the Walam Olum* (1885).

15 David Macritche to Leland, 1888, cited in Pennell vol.2, p. 192.

16 Leland, in Leland and Prince 1902, p.16, 17.

17 Letter to Mary A. Owen, 8/13/1902. In Pennell vol. 2, p.420.

18 Chamberlain, pp.2-3.

19 Pennell, vol. 2, pp.425-26,

20 Lewy Soctomah appears on 1900 Federal census for Pleasant Pt. as Lewy Soctomah, b1823, living with son Solomon (b1851) and daughter Hannah (also b1851).

21 *Eastport Sentinel*, 3/31/1897: entire article in Soctomah 2002, pp.49-50.

22 Lesourd, p.446.

23 Gatschet (1858, p.299) in Lesourd, p.446.

24 Her grandfather began his furtrade career at Castine in the early 1830s, harvesting mink, etc., from the Penobscot valley and eastward as far east as MDI, Frenchman Bay and Machias. See Krohn, p.4.

25 Ring, p.51.

26 Ring, p.51.

27 Eckstorm 1960.

28 See details on these comments in the profile on John Snow, several pages ahead in this section.

29 In 1930, financed by Mary Wheelwright, Eckstorm traveled to the Passamaquoddy reservations and purchased several pieces. See Eckstorm 2003 (reprint of Eckstorm 1932, preface by Rebecca Cole-Will).

30 *MDH* 10/28/87.

31 It appears that Prince's Dutch ancestors came to the U.S. some time in the 19th century and originally spelled their name "Prins."

32 Prince 1897, p.481.

33 Prince 1888, p.316.

34 Nine years earlier, in Calais, Maine, Jesse Walter Fewkes of the Bureau of American Ethnology had made the first sound recordings of any Native American language – using the newly available phonograph to record Passamaquoddy songs, texts and vocabulary. Prince lived in New Jersey, near the lab of Thomas Edison, who invented this recording device.

35 Prince 1900, p.181.

36 Lesourd, pp.441-42. Cf. Prince 1888, p.311, 1901, p.381; Leland & Prince 1902, p.21; Fewkes 1890; Brady et al. 1984, p.3. [Note: Newell S. Francis is on the 1900 Federal Census for Eden (Bar Harbor) as a basketmaker (b1840) married to Sarah (b1836) with 4 children: Hannah (b1886), Thomas (b1879), Joseph (b1877), and Benett (b1874), plus daughter-in-law Adeline (b1874) and granddaughter Mary (b1897). He and Sarah also appear with their children on the 1900 Federal census for Pleasant Point/Perry, apparently with incorrect birthdates.]

37 Prince 1902, pp.18, 29.

38 1940, p.2.

39 Email to Harald Prins, 2 June 2004.

40 Speck 1917b, p.11, n.4. Notably, Speck dedicated *Penobscot Man* to his former professor, Dyneley Prince, for whom Bar Harbor had been a key research location. Speck's comment that he spent the summers of 1907-1912 with Penobscots "at home *and in their summer camps*" (emphasis added) places him at their seasonal camps during years that overlap with Prince's sojourns to the summer Indian encampment in Bar Harbor.

41 In McBride 1995, p.56.

42 Fenton 1990: 97-8; Prince and Speck 1903a: 347.

43 Prince and Speck 1903b, p.196.

44 McBride 1995, p.61.

45 Street, 1905, pp.338-39.

46 Unless otherwise indicated, the quotes and information about pioneer landscape architect Charles Eliot, Jr., come from *American Landscape Architecture: Designers and Places,* edited by William H. Tishler for the National Trust for Historic Preservation and American Society of Landscape Architects.

47 Dorr, pp.13-15.

48 Baker.

49 Dorr, pp.50-55, 70-74.

CHAPTER 10

1 *MDH*, 7/14/1881 & 17/1881.

2 Higgins, 1934.

3 *MDH*, 6/16/1882. See also *Souvenir of Bar Harbor.* A bird's-eye illustration of Bar Harbor published in this booklet situates the

Indian encampment c1882 sprawled on the shore between Bar/ Bridge Street and Holland Ave., indicating a slight westward movement from the center of town toward the newly built Hamor's Wharf. Although Hamor's wharf is excluded from this illustration, it appears on a map of the town in the same booklet. (See maps in the encampment inventory featured in Chapter 20.)

4 *MDH*, 7/18/1882.

5 *MDH*, 7/25/1882.

6 Harrison 1887, pp.85-97.

7 *MDH*, 6/2/1887. See also Sweetser 1888.

8 "Plan of Bar Harbor" pub. by Colby & Stuart. June 1887. Copy in Library of Congress. The 1880 federal census for Bar Harbor lists Arthur W. Ells as a carpenter and his wife Julia as a housekeeper, so it appears they established their store after 1880. Since the 1890 Federal census was destroyed, we have no census record of this couple at the time they had the store with the Indian encampment situated behind and extending down the slope to the sea. In the 1900 census, Julia appears as a widow with four sons – Edward (age 24), Leroy (19), Daniel (?) (14) and Johnnie (11). She working as a laundress and Leroy is listed as a salesman.

9 Sweetser 1888.

10 *MDH* 6/26/1889, p.3.

11 *MDH* 8/2/1889, p.3.

12 *MDH* 8/9/1889, p.2.

13 Drake, 1891. (Note: Published in 1891, this passage probably refers to the scene as it was in 1890, suggesting the relocation of the Indian camp took place that year.)

14 *MDH*, 10/2/1890.

15 Crawford, 1896, p.272.

16 Excerpt from 7/11/93 deed re. shore property on NW corner of West and Bridge streets. Emphasis added.

17 Third Annual Report of the Village Improvement Association. 1892, pp.17-18.

18 *Report of Agent [George Hunt] of the Penobscot Tribe of Indians*, 1892, p.7

19 *MDH*, 9/10/1886, p.3; also in *The Daily Herald* 9/3/86, p.3. [Note: This is *not* Sabbatis Mitchell, born in 1824 and identified as "Dr" in the 1868 Penobscot census. Rather it is Passamaquoddy Joseph Mitchell, profiled a year earlier as follows: "A Pleasant Point Indian, named Joseph Mitchell, is practicing medicine in Portland, Maine. He graduated recently from the Lewiston Eclectic Medical College. This is the first instance of a member of the Passamaquoddy Tribe entering one of the learned professions" (*Eastport Sentinel* 2/19/1885).

20 Fifth Annual Report of the Bar Harbor Village Improvement Association, 1894, p.7.

21 Thirteenth Annual Report of the Bar Harbor Village Improvement Association. 1902, p.13.

22 Peabody.

23 Foulds. In his 1996 *Cultural Landscape Report* for Acadia National Park, Fould's wrote, "One abandoned [Indian] encampment between Park Street and Ledgelawn Avenue was put into service by the town as a public campground. This site, owned by the Town of Bar Harbor, is today a public park, featuring a large playing field." This comment appeared in the caption for a "c1922" photo of cars and four tents at the site.

24 "Indian Camps Lure Tourists in Maine." *Eastport Sentinel*, 8/24/1924.

25 Gordius, in Cartwright, July 1982, pp.1, 8.

Bibliography

Adney, Edwin Tappan and Howard I. Chapelle. 1964. *The Bark Canoes & Skin Boats of North America.* Washington, D.C.: Smithsonian Institution Bulletin 230.

Albion, Robert G. *et al.* 1972. *New England and the Sea.* Middletown, CT: Wesleyan U Press.

Alger, Abby L. 1897. *In Indian Tents: Stories Told by Penobscot, Passamaquoddy and Micmac Indians.* Boston: Roberts Brothers.

Baker, William J. 2008. "Investing in Acadia: The Invisible Hand of John Stewart Kennedy." *Friends of Acadia Journal.* Spring 2008, pp.12–13.

Bangor Daily Whig & Courier. 1800s. Various notices and articles.

Bangor Weekly Commercial. 1800s–1900s. Various notices and articles.

Bar Harbor Blue Book and Mount Desert Guide 1881. Perhaps published by MDI/Boston storekeeper Albert Bee.

Bar Harbor Record. 1800s. Various notices and articles. Of particular note is the Centennial Souvenir Edition 1796–1896, July 1896.

Bar Harbor Village Improvement Association Annual Reports 1890–1939. Bar Harbor: Mount Desert Publishing Co.

The Bay State Excursion of 1871, A Record and Souvenir of Eight Days' Pleasure on the Eastern Coast. Boston: Published by the Excursionists.

Bell, Mabel Gardiner Hubbard. 1881. Letter to Mrs. Alexander Melville Bell. (In Alexander Graham Bell Family Papers, posted on website *http://memory.loc.gov/*)

Briggs, Caroline C. 1897. *Reminiscences and Letters of Caroline C. Briggs.* Edited by George S. Merriam. Boston & New York: Houghton, Mifflin and Co.

Bunting, William H. 2000. *A Sampler of Maine Photographs 1860–1920. Part II.* Gardiner: Tilbury House Publishers.

Burnham, Horace M. 1918. "Pharmacy of the Red Man." *Sprague's Journal of Maine History*, vol.6 (Aug/Sep/Oct) No. 2, pp. 69–71.

Cartwright, Steve. 1979–82. *Wabanaki Alliance.* Various issues of this intertribal newspaper, edited and largely written by Cartwright.

"Celebration at Holy Redeemer by Papal Delegate Attending Marked Tercetenary of First Island Colony." No author. In *Holy Redeemer Parish 100th Anniversary 1883–1993*, pp. 9–10.

Chamberlain, Montague. 1898. "The Penobscot Indians: A Brief Account of Their Present Condition." *The Cambridge Tribune.* 8 Feb. Reprint, Augusta: Maine State Library.

Champlain, Samuel de. 1902. *The Voyages and Explorations of Samuel de Champlain, 1604–1616, Narrated by himself.* Edited with introduction and notes by Edward G. Bourne. 2 vols. New York: Allerton Book Co.

—. 1907. *The Voyages and Explorations of Samuel de Champlain, 1604–1618.* Edited by Grant, W.L. and J. Franklin Jameson. New York: Charles Scribner's Sons.

—. 1922–36. *The Works of Samuel de Champlain.* Edited by H.P. Biggar. (6 vols). Toronto: The Champlain Society.

Chase, Eliza Brown. 1884 *Over the Border: Acadia, the Home of 'Evangeline.'* Boston: J. Osgood.

Coatsworth, Elizabeth. 1968. *Maine Memories.* Brattleboro, VT: Stephen Green Press.

Coe, Harrie B., ed. 1928. *Maine: Resources, Attractions and its People. A History.* NY: The Lewis Historical Publishing Co.

Cole, John. N.d. *Summer Hotel: The Claremont Story 1884–94.* Augusta: Printed by JS McCarthy, Co.

Cole, Nan. 1970, "Natives of Old Bar Harbor," *Down East Magazine.* Sept., pp. 60–62, 67, 90, 95–97.

Cole, Thomas. 1836. Essay on American Scenery, *American Monthly Magazine,* January.

Colors the World: Wonderful Business Built up by a Maine Dyer. 28 January 1893. *Lewiston Jounral.*

Conkling, Phillip W. 1981. *Islands in Time: A Natural and Human History of the Islands of Maine.* Camden: Down East Books.

Cook, David S. 2007. *Above the Gravel Bar: The Native Canoe Routes of Maine* (3rd ed). Solon, Maine: Polar Bear & Co. Crawford, Marion F. 1894. *Love in Idleness, a Tale of Bar Harbor.*

—. 1896. "American Summer Resorts III." Bar Harbor. *Scribner's Magazine* vol.16(3) pp. 268–85. NY: Charles Scriber's Sons.

Daily Herald, The. 1886. Various notices and articles.

DeCosta, Benjamin Franklin. 1871. *Rambles in Mount Desert.* New York: Randolph & Co. 1871.

—. 1880. *The Handbook of Mount Desert, Coast of Maine.* Boston: A. Williams & Co.

Dorr, George B. 1997. *The Story of Acadia National Park.* Bar Harbor: Acadia Publishing Co.

Drake, Samuel Adams. 1891. *The Pine-Tree Coast* [illustrated] Boston: Estes & Lauriat.

Dwelley, Hugh L. 1990. *A History of Little Cranberry Island, Maine.* Islesford Historical Society. Pages 10–12 re. Indians—includes Francis Fernald's recollection of Indians coming by canoe to Little Cranberry in 1930s.

Eastport Sentinel. 1800s. Various notices and articles.

Eckstorm, Fannie Hardy. Personal Papers. UMO/Fogler Special Colls. Various boxes. For details on contents of this collection see Jeanne Patten Whitten's *Fannie Hardy Eckstorm: A Descriptive Bibliography of Her Writings, Published and Unpublished.* Northeast Folklore XVI. Orono: University of Maine Press. 1975/76.

—. 2003 (1932). *Handicrafts of the Modern Indians of Maine.* Bar Harbor: Abbe Museum. This reprint of the 1932 edition features a new preface by Rebecca Cole-Will and color photographs of the objects described.

—. 1945. *Old John Neptune and Other Maine Indian Shamans.* Portland, ME: The Southworth-Anthoensen Press.

—. 1960. Ballads Old and new. *Bulletin of the Folksong Society of the Northeast* (p9–16). Philadelphia: American Folklore Society.

Eliot, Samuel A. 1870. "The Romance of Mount Desert." *Atlantic Monthly,* vol. 25(151.) May.

Enk, John C. 1973. *A Family Island in Penobscot Bay: The Story of Eagle Island.* Rockland: The Courier-Gazette, Inc.

Fairfax, Mildred. 1893. *At Mount Desert: A Summer's Sowing.* Congregational Sunday-School and Publishing Society. A novel.

Fewkes, Jesse Walter. 1890. "A Contribution to Passamaquoddy Folk-Lore." *Journal of American Folklore III,* pp. 257–80.

Foulds, H. Eliot. 1996. *Cultural Landscape Report for Blackwoods and Seawall Campgrounds, Acadia National Park: History,* *Existing Conditions, Analysis & Treatment Recommendations.* Boston: National Park Service.

Frank Leslie's Illustrated Newspaper. 1800s. Various articles and images.

Graham, Frank. 1975. *Gulls: A Social History.* New York: Random House.

Hale, Jr., Richard W. 1949. *The Story of Bar Harbor.* New York: Ives Washburn, Inc.

Hansen, Gunnar, ed. 1989. *Mount Desert An Informal History.* Published by the Town of Mount Desert, Maine.

Harrison, Mrs. Burton. 1887. *Bar Harbor Days.* NY: Harper & Brothers.

Haviland, William A. 2004. *Safe Passage to the Sea: An Ancient Canoe Route at Deer Isle, Maine.*

—. 2005. "Indians, Porpoises, and Crockett's Cove." *Island Ad-vantages,* 12/22&29, p.5.

Helfrich, G.W. and O'Neil, Gladys. 1982. *Lost Bar Harbor.* Camden: Down East Books.

Higgins, A. L. 1934. "Good Old Days." *Bar Harbor Times* June 20.

Hornsby, Stephen J. 1993. "The Gilded Age and the Making of Bar Harbor." *American Geographical Review.*

Indian Agent Reports. 1800s–1900s. Nearly annual report written by Passamaquoddy and Penobscot Indian agents, held at the Maine State Archives.

Industrial Journal, The. [Bangor]. 1800s. Various notices and articles.

Johnson, John. 1861.

Ives, Sanford. 1986. *Wilbur Day, 1864–1924: Hunter, Guide, and Poacher: An Autobiography.* Northeast Folklore, Vol 26.

Jack, Edward. 1895. "Maliseet Legends ('Glooscap')." *The Journal of American Folklore, 8* (30), pp193–208.

Jellison, Connie. 1990. *Hancock County A Rockbound Paradise: A Bicentennial Pictoral.* Norfolk: Downing Co. Pubs.

Johnson, John W. 1861. *Life of John W. Johnson Who was Stolen by Indians.* Biddeford.

Joy, Adelma ["Dell"] Somes. Ca. 1915. *Reminiscences of Somesville.* (NEHL)

Joy, Barbara Ellen. 1966. *Historical Notes on Mount Desert Island. Part I, vol. 1.* Unpublished. (SWH Library.)

—. 1974 *Historical Notes on Mount Desert Island, Part II, vol. I.* Unpublished. (SWHL, MS Library)

—. 1975. *Historical Notes on Mt. Desert Island, vol. III.* Unpublished. (SWHL)

Lapham, William B. 1808. *Commissioners' Proceedings at Mount Desert, 1808.* Collections of MaHS, Series 2, vol. 2, pp. 439–48.

—. 1888. *Bar Harbor & Mount Desert Island.* Augusta: Maine Farmer Job Print. Third edition.

Lash, Joseph P. 1971. *Eleanor & Franklin: The Story of Their Relationship based on Eleanor Roosevelt's Private Papers.* NY: W.W. Norton & Co.

Leighton, Alexander H. 1937. "The Twilight of the Indian Porpoise Hunters." *Natural History,* June, pp. 410–416, 458.

Leland, Charles G. 1884. *The Algonquin Legnds of New England.* Boston: Houghton, Mifflin and Co. (Reprint. 1992 as

Algonquin Legends, NY: Dover Publications, Inc.).

Leland, Charles G. and Prince, John Dyneley. 1902. *Kulóskap the Master*. New York: Funk & Wagalls.

Lerner, Ellen. 1985. *Memories and Stories about the Native American People of Mount Desert Island and the Surrounding Area*. Unpublished oral histories (tapes and written summary at Abbe Museum.)

Lesourd, Philip. 2000. "The Passamaquoddy 'Witchcraft Tales' of Newell Francis." *Anthropological Linguistics,* vol.42 No.4. Winter, pp.441–98.

Lester, Joan. "'We Didn't Make Fancy Baskets Until We Were Discovered' Fancy-Basket Making in Maine." In *A Key into the Language of Woodsplint Baskets*. Edited by Ann McMullen and Russell G. Handsman. Washington, CT: American Indian Archaeological Institute, 1987, pp.38–59.

Litchman, Charles H., ed. 1893. *Official History of the Improved Order of Red Men*. Boston: The Fraternity Publishing Co.

Locke, Marie, and Montgomery, Nancy. 1998. Memories of a Maine Island: Turn-of-the Century Tales and Photographs. *Northeast Folklore, vol. 33*. Orono: Maine Folklife Center.

MacDougall, Pauleena. 1998. "Native American Industry: Basket Weaving among the Wabanaki." In Morrison, Dane, ed. *American Indian Studies: An Interdisciplinary Approach to Contemporary Issues* ((167–92). NY: Peter Lang.

McBride, Bunny. 1995. *Molly Spotted Elk: A Penobscot in Paris*. Norman: University of Oklahoma Press.

—. 1999. *Women of the Dawn*. Lincoln: University of Nebraska Press.

—. 2001. "Lucy Nicolar: The Artful Activism of a Penobscot Performer." In *Sifters: Native American Women's* Lives (pp.141–159.). Edited by Theda Perdue. Oxford University Press.

—. 2003-2004. Interviews. For Prins & McBride. 2007. *Acadia National Park Ethnographic Survey 1600–2004*. Transcripts in Acadia National Park Archives.

Closson, Larry, Mount Desert Island, Jan. 2004

Dana, Dolly (Passamaquoddy), Pleasant Point, Sept. 2004

Francis, David (Passamaquoddy), Pleasant Point, July 2003

Holmes, Susan Snow (Passamaquoddy), Old Town, Jan. 2004

Loring, Donna (Penobscot), Richmond, Me., Jan. 2004

Johnson, Lois Crabtree, Hancock, Jan. 2005

Mitchell, John Bear (Penobscot), Indian Island and UMO, Jan. 2004

Mitchell, Theodore Norris (Penobscot), Indian Island, June and Sept. 2004

Soctomah, Donald (Passamaquoddy), Princeton, Jan. 2004

Stanley, Ralph (Bar Harbor resident), Bar Harbor, Jan. 2004

Stevens, John (Passamaquoddy), Princeton, Jan. 2004

McLane, Charles B. and McLane, Carol Evarts. 1997. *Islands of the Mid-Maine Coast Volume I: Penobscot Bay*. Gardiner: Tilbury House, Publishers. & Rockland, Me: The Island Institute.

McMullen, Ann and Russell G. Handsman. 1987. *A Key into the Language of Woodsplint Baskets*. Washington, Ct: American Indian Archaeological Institute.

McMullen, Ann and Diane Kopec, eds. 1989. *An Island in Time:*

Three Thousand Years of Cultural Exchange on Mount Desert Island—Essays by David Sanger & Harald E.L. Prins. Bar Harbor: The Robert Abbe Museum.

Machias Observer. 1800s, Various notices and articles.

Martin, Clara. 1866. *Mount Desert on the Coast of Maine*. Portland: B. Thurston and Co., Printers. (WL)

Mechling, W.H. 1913. "Malecite Tales." *Journal of American Folklore 26*, pp.219–58.

—. 1914 *Malecite Tales*. Canadian Dept. of Mines, Geological Survey, Anthropological Series, No. 4, Memoir 49.

—. 1959. The Malecite Indians with Notes on the Micmacs. *Anthropologica* 8:239–263.

Mitchell, David J. *The Jesuits, a History*. New York: F.Watts, 1981.

Mitchell, Lewis. 1887. "Address." Maine State House of Representatives, 63rd Legislature, Augusta, Maine, No.251.

Morison, Samuel Eliot. 1960. *The Story of Mount Desert Island*. Boston: Atlantic Monthly Press of Little, Brown, and Co.

"Mount Desert." *Harpers New Monthly Magazine,* vol, 45 (267). Aug 1872.

Mount Desert Herald. 1881–88. Various notices and articles.

Nichols, George Ward. 1872. "Mount Desert." *Harpers New Monthly Magazine,* vol. 45, issue 267 (August). New York: Harper's Brothers.

Nicolar, Joseph. 1893. *Life and Traditions of the Red Man*. Bangor: C.H. Glass. Reprinted with introduction by James D. Wherry. 1979. Fredericton: Saint Annes Point Press.. Reprinted with introduction by Annette Kolodny, 2007. Duke University Press.

Old Town Enterprise. 1800s. Various notices and articles.

Parker, Jesse L. 1955. *Recollections of Southwest Harbor, Maine 1885–1894*. (SWHL)

Peabody, Marion. 1969. "Old Bar Harbor Days." *Down East Magazine*.

Pennell, Elizabeth Robins. *Charles Godfrey Leland: A Biography*. Boston: Houghton, Mifflin & Co. 1906. 2-vol.

Phippen, Sanford, dir. 1986. *A Century of Summers: The Impact of a Summer Colony on a Small Maine Coastal Town 1886–1986*. The Hancock Historical Society.

Prince, John Dyneley. 1888. "Notes on the Language of Eastern Algonkin Tribes." *American Jounral of Philogogy*, vol. 9(3), pp. 310–316.

—. 1897. "The Passamaquoddy Wampum Records." *Proceedings of the American Philosophical Society 36:156*, pp. 479–95.

—. 1900. "Some Passamaquoddy Witchcraft Tales." *American Philosophical Society Proceedings*, vol.38 (160), pp. 181–89.

—. 1901. "Notes on Passamaquoddy Literature." *Annals of the New York Academy of Sciences, 13*(4): 381.

—. 1921. "Passamaquoddy Texts." *Publications of the American Ethnological Society*, vol. 10. Edited by Franz Boas, ed. Pp. 1–85. New York: G.E. Strechert & Co.

Prince, John Dyneley, and Speck, Frank G. 1903. "The Modern Pequots and Their Language." *American Anthropologist 5*, pp. 193–212.

Prins, Harald E.L. 1989. "Natives and Newcomers: Mount Desert Island in the Age of Exploration." (pp.21–41) *An Island in*

Time: Three Thousand Years of Cultural Exchange on Mount Desert Island. Robert Abbe Museum Bulletin XII. Bar Harbor: Robert Abbe Museum. (Reprinted 1994).

—. 1994a. "Maliseet." In *Native America in the Twentieth Century: An Encyclopedia*. M. Davis, ed. P. 328. New York: Garland Publishing.

—. 1994b. "Micmac." In *Native America in the Twentieth Century: An Encyclopedia*. M. Davis, ed. Pp. 339–340. New York: Garland Publishing.

—. 1994c. "Passamaquoddy." In *Native America in the Twentieth Century: An Encyclopedia*. M. Davis, ed. Pp. 435–436. New York: Garland Publishing.

—. 1994d. "Penobscot." In *Native America in the Twentieth Century: An Encyclopedia*. M. Davis, ed. Pp. 441–442. New York: Garland Publishing.

—. 1994e. "Children of Gluskap: Wabanaki Indians on the Eve of the European Invasion." *In American Beginnings: Exploration, Culture and Cartography in the Land of Norumbega*, Emerson W.Baker, et.al., eds. Pp. 165-211. Lincoln: U. Nebraska Press.

—. 1995. "Turmoil on the Wabanaki Frontier 1524-1678." *In Maine: The Pine Tree State from Prehistory to Present*. Pp. 97-119. R. Judd, et.al.., eds. Orono: U Press of Maine.

—. 1996. *The Mi'kmaq: Resistance, Accommodation and Cultural Survival*. Ft. Worth: Harcourt Brace.

—. 1998. "Chief Big Thunder (1827–1906) The Life History of a Penobscot Trickster." (pp.140-158) *Maine History, vol.37*, No.3 (Winter).

Prins, Harald E.L., and McBride, Bunny. 1992. "A Social History of Maine Indian Basketry." *The Kennebec Proprietor* 6 (2), pp. 18–21.

—. 2007. *Asticou's Island Domain: Wabanaki Peoples at Mount Desert Island 1500–2000*. Washington, DC: National Park Service.

Rand, Edward L. and Redfield, John H. 1894. *Flora of Mount Desert Island, Maine: A Preliminary Catalogue of the Plants Growing on Mount Desert and the Adjacent Islands*. Cambridge, MA: John Wilson & Son.

Richardson, John M. *Steamboat Lore of the Penobscot*.

Ring, Elizabeth. 1953. "Fannie Hardy Eckstorm: Maine Woods Historian." *Northeast Quarterly*, vol.26 pp.45–64.

Ryan, Allie. 1972. *Penobscot Bay Mount Desert and Eastport Steamboat Album*. Camden: Down East.

Sawtelle, William Otis. 1923. "The Island of Mount Desert." *Sprague's Journal of Maine History*, vol. 11(d).

Sherman, W.H. 1890. *Sherman's Bar Harbor Guide, Business Directory and Reference Book*. Printed by Bar Harbor Press Co.

Short, Vincent and Edwin Sears. 1955. *Sail & Steam*. Portland: Bond Wheelwright Co.

Soctomah, Donald, ed. 2002. *Passamaquoddy at the Turn of the Century 1890–1920: Tribal Life and Times in Maine and New Brunswick*. (Available at the Abbe Museum)

Somes, Abraham. 1816. Letter to Eben Parsons, Esq. 20 April, accompanied by statement. (BPL, Barton Ticknor Collection, listed under Abraham Somes).

Somes-Sanderson, Virginia. 1982. *The Living Past: Being the Story of Somesville, Mount Desert, Maine, and its Relationship with Other Areas of the Island*. Mt. Desert: Beech Hill Publishing.

Souvenir of Bar Harbor. Ca. 1882. No author, but may have been put together by MDI & Boston store owner Albert Bee (Authors' coll.).

Speck, Frank G. 1915. "Penobscot Tales." *Journal of American Folklore* 28, pp. 52–58.

—. 1917. "Medicine Practices of the Northeastern Algonquians," pp. 301–21, *Proceedings of the 19th International Congress of Americanists*. W.F. Hodge, ed. Washington.

—. 1940. *Penobscot Man, the Life History of a Forest Tribe in Maine*. Philadelphia: University of Pennsylvania Press.

Sprague, John Francis. 1916. "The Indians of Maine." In *Sprague's Journal of Maine History*, vol. 4(1), (June).

Street, George A. 1905. *Mount Desert, a History*, edited by Samuel A. Eliot. Boston & NY: Houghton Miflin.

Sweetser, Moses Foster. 1873. *New England, a Handbook for Travellers: A Guide to the Chief Cities and Popular Resorts of New England, and to its Scenery and Historical Attractions, with the West and North Borders from New York to Quebec*. Boston: JR Osgood.

—. 1879 & 1880. *Picturesque Maine*. Portland: Chisholm Bros.

—. 1883. *Summer Days Downeast*. Portland: Chisholm Bros.

—. 1888. *Chisholm's Mount Desert Guide-Book*. Portland: Chisholm Bros.

Thornton, Mrs. Seth S [Nellie]. 1938. *Traditions and Records, Southwest Harbor and Somesville, Mount Desert Island, Maine*. Privately printed, Auburn, ME.: Merrill & Webber Co.

Thoreau, Henry David. *The Maine Woods*. New York: Norton, 1950.

Verrill, A. Hyatt. 1933. *Romantic and Historic Maine*. New York: Dodd, Mead & Co.

—. 1954. *The Real Americans*. New York.

Ward, Charles. 1880. "Porpoise-Shooting." *Scribner's Monthly*, vol. 20(6), (Oct.), pp. 801–811.

Warner, Charles Dudley. 1886. "Their Pilgrimage." *Harper's New Monthly Magazine*, vol. 73 (435), (Aug.), pp. 416–426.

Whitehead, Ruth, and McGee, Harold. 1985. *The Mi'kmaq*. Halifax: Nimbus.

Wilmerding, John. 1994. *The Artist's Mount Desert*. Princeton, NY: Princeton University Press.

Index